EC Data Protection Directive

David Bainbridge BSC LLB PhD CEng MICE MBCS, Barrister
Lecturer in Law
Aston University

with a contribution by
Nick Platten

Butterworths
London, Dublin, Edinburgh
1996

United Kingdom	Butterworths a Division of Reed Elsevier (UK) Ltd, Halsbury House, 35 Chancery Lane, LONDON WC2A 1EL and 4 Hill Street, EDINBURGH EH2 3JZ
Australia	Butterworths, SYDNEY, MELBOURNE, BRISBANE, ADELAIDE, PERTH, CANBERRA and HOBART
Canada	Butterworth Canada Ltd, TORONTO and VANCOUVER
Ireland	Butterworth (Ireland) Ltd, DUBLIN
Malaysia	Malayan Law Journal Sdn Bhd, KUALA LUMPUR
New Zealand	Butterworths of New Zealand Ltd, WELLINGTON and AUCKLAND
Singapore	Reed Elsevier (Singapore) Pte Ltd, SINGAPORE
South Africa	Butterworth Publishers (Pty) Ltd, DURBAN
USA	MICHIE, Charlottesville, Virginia

Publications and Information Manager
Sandra Dutczak, LL.B.

Senior Publications Editor
Alan Grierson, D.B.P.P.

Printed in Great Britain by Antony Rowe, Chippenham, Wiltshire

With the momentum of change within the Community gathering pace it is hard to keep abreast of developments and obtain expert opinion and analysis together with original texts of legislation or cases as and when such events occur.

The *Current EC Legal Developments Series* is designed to provide the lawyer, consultant, researcher etc with commentary and source materials of relevant practical interest on fundamental changes in Community law.

Each title in the series has a similar format presenting the full text of proposed or enacted legislation or judicial decisions under review and provides analysis and comment written by leading practitioners in the subject area under consideration.

The views expressed by the author are personal and are not intended to be applied to particular situations.

Any queries as to the nature or content of the *Current EC Legal Developments Series* should be directed to the Publications Manager, Butterworths European Information Services Department, Halsbury House, 35 Chancery Lane, LONDON WC2A 1EL.

Butterworths

Current EC Legal Developments Series

Consultant Editor for the Series
DAVID VAUGHAN, QC

Titles already published in this Series :

Since the passing of the Data Protection Act 1984 the pace of change in information processing and the development of new and imaginative uses of data have been little short of phenomenal. The Act as it stands is no longer able to provide effectively for the protection of individuals in respect of personal data relating to them whilst providing a fair and equitable environment for the processing of data.

As in many other areas, the stimulus for change has come from Europe and the Commission of the European Communities first produced a proposal for a data protection Directive in 1990. A later proposal in 1992 drew impressive and hostile opposition especially in the United Kingdom, largely on account of the perceived costs of compliance with its provisions. This criticism came from commerce, industry and government. It was against this backdrop that a study was undertaken on behalf of the European Commission by Aston University and the University of Leiden with a brief to determine objectively the true costs of compliance. Needless to say, the results were significantly less than an earlier study carried out by the CBI for the Home Office. Eventually, following further changes, the Directive was adopted on 25 October 1995.

The primary objectives of this book are to describe and analyse the Directive as it is likely to be implemented in the United Kingdom and to examine how it will impact on those involved with processing personal data. A number of case studies, looking at various types of data controllers in the public and private sector, are intended to show the Directive in a practical context and to introduce and discuss some of the issues for those concerned with data protection compliance in those sectors

Chapter 2 of the book has been contributed by Nick Platten who has worked in DGXV of the European Commission since 1993. The views he expresses are his own personal views and can in no way be attributed to either the European Commission or the Data Protection Registrar, for whom he worked previously. It should also be clearly understood that my own views regarding the Directive are not necessarily shared by Mr Platten, the European Commission or the Data Protection Registrar.

Chapter 3 contains a legal analysis of the Directive and is followed by chapters looking at the Directive from various viewpoints such as the controller and the data subject. The case studies are intended to provide an insight into some of the issues. Of course, it has not been possible to deal with each type of organisation in full detail - this would take a substantial book for each. Rather, some of the most important issues and impacts have been dealt with. It is inevitable that someone's data protection "hobby horse" has not been addressed and I apologise in advance for that.

Writing this book has proved to be very enjoyable. I have been very fortunate in being helped and supported by a number of people. In particular, I wish to extend my thanks to Graham Pearce who was the manager of the Aston University research team and played a major role in the formulation of the idea of writing this book and has contributed to many fruitful discussions about the Directive since. Nick Platten has my thanks for writing an excellent scene setting chapter which will equip the reader with a much deeper understanding of the Directive. Sandra Dutczak and Alan Grierson of Butterworths have been most helpful, encouraging and patient. Lorraine Keenan has worked hard on the diagrams and tables. Finally, I would like to thank my wife, Sylvia, for her continuing support, encouragement and patience.

David Bainbridge
14 November 1996

Table of Contents

CASES

Part I : Introduction and Background

Chapter 1 : Introduction

In the post-industrial world we are moving towards, information is the most important asset that many organisations, commercial or otherwise, possess. Information is power and this is even more so when that information concerns living individuals. The storage and use of personal information poses numerous dangers. For example, the information may be of a particularly sensitive nature, it may be excessive, going beyond that required by the person using it for his or her legitimate needs, or it may be inaccurate. A man of good character without any criminal convictions was arrested and charged with driving whilst disqualified because incorrect information was stored against his name on the police national computer. The information had been entered against his name by mistake. As a consequence of this, he lost his job and had his car impounded. It took him four months to trace the man to whom the conviction related and who had a very similar name before he could clear his name[1].

There are real and significant dangers related to processing personal data. Apart from being adversely affected by inaccurate data, there are other issues such as the impact on individuals' privacy. On the other hand, there is a very real need to facilitate the use of personal data by all manner of organisations. Personal data is of considerable commercial value to many organisations whilst for others, they need to hold and process personal data to perform their activities and obligations effectively. Retailers wish to target their advertising at persons likely to be interested in their products, employers need to keep information about their employees in order to be able to carry out employee administration, pay salaries, and fulfil their legal obligations as employers. Health care providers have to keep data about their patients or clients so that they can deliver appropriate and effective treatment and general health care. Some organisations, particularly those providing financial services wish to disclose and share personal data to reduce the possibility of fraud and to minimise the number of bad debts. Even the humble High Street newsagent keeps personal data so

---

1   The Times, 8 May 1990 p4.

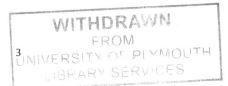

that he can organise deliveries of newspapers and magazines and keep track of payments.

Every organisation both in the private sector and the public sector uses personal information. A large number of sole traders and self employed persons also make use of personal data. There are millions of organisations and individual persons who have a need to or are required to process personal data. Data protection law is of vital interest to them all.

Each and every one of us has information about ourselves which is stored and used by others. We all have a substantial interest to see that the nature of the information stored and the manner in which it is used is controlled within acceptable limits. The task for law in the area of data protection is to provide a framework which is capable of reconciling the needs and interests of those who make use of personal data with those of persons to whom those data relate. This is no easy matter. Too little control and the opportunities for abuse, prejudicing the rights and freedoms of individuals, are manifold. Too much control and the operation of organisations, whether in the public or private sector, will be seriously hampered by the excessive bureaucracy and interference by bodies administering this important area of law.

No law is perfect, but it seemed as if a reasonable balance had been struck in the United Kingdom by the Data Protection Act 1984. The experience of the operation of this legislation and the work of the Office of the Data Protection Registrar and the Data Protection Tribunal generally, in spite of some criticism from both sides of the line, has been good[1]. The worst abuses have been controlled or suppressed whilst the burdens on those who use personal data have been relatively light. The Data Protection Act 1984 was directed exclusively at the automatic processing of personal data because, given the advent of computers and the increasing power of data processing, this was perceived to be most in need of legislative control[2].

However, rights and freedoms are funny things. They are often taken for granted in the United Kingdom with its long and stable traditions. The lack of a written constitution provides ample support for this view. The same cannot be said for some other parts of Europe and the

---

1   However, the Parliamentary Ombudsman was highly critical of the Office of the Data Protection Registrar in a case where a man was refused a credit card on the basis of a conviction which had been quashed. He had to wait 15 months for a response; Moules, J "Ombudsman slams DPR for unacceptable delay", *Computing*, 15 February 1996, p3.
2   Although "manual processing" is not within the scope of the Act, other areas of law could have some impact such as the law of breach of confidence, copyright law and the law of defamation.

experience of the last century explains, perhaps, a general desire there to take positive action to protect the rights and privacy of individuals. To some extent, this may account for the general tone of the Data Protection Directive or, to give it its full name, Directive 95/46/EC of the European Parliament and the Council of 24 October 1995 on the protection of individuals with regard to the processing of personal data and on the free movement of such data.

Data users and data subjects

The identity of two types of person are central to data protection law. The organisations or persons who store and use personal data are the data users (known as controllers in the Directive). The persons to whom personal data relates are known as data subjects. We are all data subjects and many of us also are data users.

According to the latest figures, there are some 188,584 registered data users[1]. There are probably at least as many more who should be registered but have failed to register, in spite of such failure being a criminal offence of strict liability. The number of data users, or controllers in the language of the Directive, is set to increase many times when the Directive is implemented.

Data users, being persons "holding" personal data, increasingly are likely to make use of the personal data in ways other than those directly associated with their traditional and conventional business activities, legal obligations or public duties. Many data users now see personal data as a commodity in its own right, something which has commercial value and which can be traded. For example, a retail company may sell copies of its customer database to other retailers which offer other goods or services. The *Innovations* mail order company, which was subject to an adverse decision at the Data Protection Tribunal[2], made around one-third of its profit from selling customer lists to other traders; an activity known as "list trading". The fact that the turnover attributable to such list trading was only 20% of *Innovations'* total turnover at the time of the case gives an indication of the commercial significance of list trading.

Data processing is becoming more sophisticated. New, and potentially sinister uses are being made of personal data. One example is "data warehousing" where massive amounts of personal data are collected and stored. Information relating to a particular individual may come

---

1   Data Protection Registrar, *Twelfth Annual Report of the Data Protection Registrar,* HMSO, 1996 p21.
2   *Innovations (Mail Order) Ltd v Data Protection Registrar,* 29 September 1993, Data Protection Tribunal.

from a number of sources and may be combined, a process known as data matching[1].

One organisation, *Makro*, matches information from electronic point of sale systems against personal records of its three million clubcard customers. By doing this, response to promotions have improved by 2% per annum because they are better targeted[2].

Sophisticated and powerful tools are being used to "dig for gold" in customer data warehouses. These involve the use of the following techniques[3]:

— neural networks which ask questions like "which of my products will this sort of customer be likely to buy?" and "who is most likely to respond to our new direct mailing programme?";

— clustering, which determines which groups of customers have similar buying patterns;

— genetic algorithms, used to find the characteristics of the kinds of customer likely to spend above a certain amount of money over a given period of time;

— other techniques including expert systems, data visualisation, case based reasoning and fuzzy logic.

Clearly, there is a need to control such powerful uses of personal data requiring that, where they are permitted, the interests of private individuals are not eroded altogether. This is especially so when quotes like the following are being uttered from within the computer industry: "We don't care about the quality of data before it is in the warehouse. If you try to clean it up you could wind up with nothing. We think it's about 90% clean anyway"[4].

The value of personal data is exemplified by the lengths some data users seem prepared to go to get their hands on it. We are all familiar with the "tick box" approach which is designed to keep to a minimum the numbers of customers or clients objecting to the subsequent use of their data for marketing. Some commercial organisations require objection to be signified by sending a request to a particular address, usually not the one the customer returns his or her order to. Having to

---

1   Data warehouses are described as a "goldmine of information", Anon, "Treasure Trove", *Computing*, 10 October 1996, p42.
2   Ibid p42.
3   Ibid p47.
4   Attributed to an employee of an important computer company in Anon, "Support Act", *Computing*, 10 October 1996 p44.

take such positive steps must discourage many individuals from objecting. The author suspects that even where individuals do object, this fact is not always recorded[1].

Other techniques involve the obtaining of data relating to a spouse or partner. One major company in the brewing and restaurant business invited persons to apply for a "gold card" to collect points which would entitle the card holder to a discount. The information asked for included personal data relating to a spouse with no requirement that the spouse knew of this or had given permission for the disclosure[2]. Some might think this an excessive intrusion into privacy especially as the information included date of birth.

Another technique is to flatter the data subject in order to obtain personal data. One example is the publication of a "Who's Who" book. Individuals are sent information about the book together with a lengthy form to be completed designed to elicit a considerable amount of personal data. Individuals appear to have been specially chosen for inclusion in the book and will appear alongside such notable persons like Jacques Chirac, Desmond Tutu, Boris Yeltsin, Václav Havel and Gérard Depardieu. The catch is that there is no obligation on the "publisher" to include the individual's details in the book. A further complication is that the form is to be posted direct to an address in the United States[3]. The information asked for may include details of spouse, children, political affiliation and activities, military service and career details[4].

Another recent example of a possible abuse of personal data is the unsolicited sending of letters from Albanian students, asking the target individual to contribute to the poor student's education. Usually, there is a hand written letter from the student together with a photograph. Of course, this practice may be totally unconnected with disclosures of personal data but it is likely that the letters are sent to persons targeted as being most likely to contribute on the basis of personal data indicating lifestyle or a prior record of charitable donations[5].

---

1   This suspicion is based on the recent experience of friends and acquaintances.
2   It is probable that this practice contravenes existing data protection law in that such data relating to a spouse and disclosed without his or her knowledge is not fairly obtained; a breach of the first data protection principle.
3   I am grateful to Sandra Dutczak for letting me see material she received from a "Who's Who" publisher.
4   Even details of prior marriages and the children of such marriages were asked for.
5   Charities are not exempt from data protection law. The case of *Data Protection Registrar v Amnesty International (British Section)*, 8 November 1994, Queen's Bench Division, demonstrates that, as much as any other data user, charities may be in breach of data protection law. The charity had recklessly disclosed data in contravention of its register entry.

Of course, data users make substantial use of personal data in the context of their traditional and more conventional interests but it is important to appreciate how the use and disclosure of personal data is changing and how much more powerful, and potentially damaging and threatening, new uses of personal data can be. This accounts in part for the need to introduce additional checks and balances in relation to the use of personal data.

The Present Law

The Data Protection Act 1984 owes its origins to the Council of Europe's Convention on Data Protection which was signed by the United Kingdom in 1981[1]. Postponed from the previous year because of a general election, the timing of the Act was impeccable in Orwellian terms. The Act came into force in a number of stages, the last of which concerned individuals' rights of access and came into effect on 11 November 1987.

Data users who hold personal data and computer bureaux providing services to such data users must register under the Act unless exempt. The acid test for registration is whether the data protection principles, deriving from the Council of Europe Convention, will be breached by the declared processing. Once registered, the data user is relatively unhindered in the processing of personal data, providing that processing is within the scope of the registration. Applying for registration is seen by many data users as a necessary chore. It can be time consuming, especially for large organisations with considerable processing activities. However, initial registration lasts for up to three years and subsequent renewals are easier to deal with.

According to the Data Protection Registrar, registration serves five functions:

1   providing a public declaration of the purpose of processing carried out by the data user;

2   allowing the Registrar to refuse an application if satisfied that the applicant is likely to contravene any of the data protection principles;

3   facilitating subject access by making information about processing available to data subjects;

---

1   There had been earlier concerns and from 1961 there have been Parliamentary Bills, Reports and White Papers concerning privacy and data protection. See especially, *The Lindop Report* (Report of the Committee on Data Protection, Cmnd. 7341, HMSO, 1978).

4   it provides for the direct application of the criminal law to certain acts of a registered data user, his servants and agents and unauthorised third parties; and

5   enabling the Registrar to ensure compliance with the data protection principles by enforcement and, where necessary, de-registration[1].

Data subjects are given specific rights of access to personal data relating to them and rights to have inaccurate data rectified or erased and rights to compensation in respect of inaccurate data or because of loss or unauthorised disclosure of their data. There are a number of exemptions from the subject access rights. In many cases, data subjects prefer to complain to the Registrar rather than take individual action.

It is reasonable to consider that a fundamental principle underlying data protection law is that data subjects should be able to find out, relatively easily, who holds their personal data and what uses may be made of them. Whilst this is true of some categories of data users, such as employers and organisations in a past or present direct relationship with the data user[2], it is not always so. Indeed, the effectiveness of the Data Protection Act 1984 can be questioned because the principle of transparency of processing is not guaranteed under the present law. It does not provide an effective way for individuals to discover all the various data users that hold their personal data[3]. There remain many concerns about the use of personal data by organisations in the private sector (for example, banking, credit reference, insurance) and in the public sector (for example, the police, health care providers and the child support agency)[4]. Levels of subject access are generally low although the Registrar does receive several thousand complaints from individuals each year[5].

---

1   Data Protection Registrar, *Twelfth Report of the Data Protection Registrar,* HMSO, 1996 p20.
2   For example, organisations in a contractual relationship with the data subject and bodies like the Inland Revenue, National Health Service, local authorities and the DSS.
3   A welcome step has been the recent placing of the data protection register on the Internet. The address for the register is http://data.protection.register.gov and the Data Protection Registrar's home page address is http://www.open.gov.uk/dpr/dpr home.htm.
4   A watershed report was the Tenth Report of the Registrar, the last one with Eric Howe as Registrar. Chapter 3 of that report discusses numerous issues and concerns in the United Kingdom concerning data protection law; Data Protection Registrar, *Tenth Report of the Data Protection Registrar,* HMSO, 1994. The current Registrar, Elizabeth France, has continued the debate, see Data Protection Registrar, *Twelfth Annual Report of the Data Protection Registrar,* HMSO, 1996.
5   The practice of many data users to have multiple registrations increases the difficulty and expense of subject access.

It is clear that, given the pace of change in information technology and the power of processing techniques that the current legislation would need modifying and strengthening to address the dangers associated with the information society, even in the absence of the Directive[1].

Philosophy underlying the Directive

The Directive has twin aims. By guaranteeing the rights and freedoms of individuals as regards personal data relating to them by means of safeguards provided by the Directive, this will allow the "free movement of personal data within the Community". In complying with the Directive, Member States will not be able to prevent or restrict personal data flows.

Rights and freedoms associated with personal data are best protected by making data processing transparent. Data subjects should be aware of all the organisations (controllers) which process their personal data and should be able to object to processing where their rights and freedoms are likely to be prejudiced and, in other cases, data users should only be able to process personal data with the data subject's express consent. Apart from these checks and balances, the Directive imposes obligations as regards security of processing and targets particular forms of processing that pose particular dangers for data subjects. Examples are automated decision-making, marketing by mail and the processing of sensitive data.

Formal registration is not as central to data protection law under the Directive as it is under current law as Member States may adopt widespread exemptions from or simplification of the notification requirements. In many respects, registration will no longer play such a key role as the data subject will be far better informed as to the processing of his or her personal data. However, controllers exempt from notification are required to make information about their processing available to any person on request, thus maintaining the principle of transparency of processing.

The new law will apply to manual processing of personal data files in addition to automatic processing. This is a major step which is accounted for, in part, a desire not to distinguish between manual and automatic processing[2]. Otherwise, the use of information technology might be prejudiced, particularly if it resulted in a heavier administrative

---

1   Harry Cohen MP has been calling for changes to the present law for some time. He sponsored a private member's bill to implement the Directive during 1996; *Data Protection and Privacy Bill,* 20 June 1996.
2   The Directive (EC) 96/9 harmonising the legal protection of databases, adopted on 11 March 1996, OJ L77 27.3.96 p20 also applies to computer and paper databases.

and bureaucratic burden than manual processing. Thus, organisations like the Economic League which kept details of individuals' membership of, *inter alia*, trade unions and details of political affiliation on paper cards will no longer be able to escape the provisions of data protection law.

Concerns about the Directive already expressed by data users have concentrated on the extension of data protection law to manual processing, presently outside data protection law, and the burdens associated with informing data subjects. Then there are concerns which affect particular sectors. For example, the financial sector is worried about whether the new law will compromise the fight against and detection of fraud and the "junk mail" industry is concerned as to whether it will be seriously prejudiced by the Directive.

Summary

There are no general laws of privacy recognised by English law. Implementing the Data Protection Directive will go some way to affording a limited right of privacy in respect of personal data[1]. However, it is interesting to note that current concerns in the United Kingdom about invasions of privacy by journalists are not dealt with effectively in the Directive. There are specific exemptions or derogations from the main provisions of the Directive, which are not optional, for personal data processing carried out for journalistic purposes[2]. Perhaps the rest of Europe sees a real need to protect the freedom of the press whilst, in the United Kingdom, the concept of free speech is so secure and deeply ingrained into the culture of the nation that concerns are directed at a desire to curb the worst excesses of the press. There are historical reasons for this divergence.

The Directive will affect everybody processing personal data whether by computer or manual methods. Data users (controllers) ignore the consequences of the Directive at their peril. The implications of the Directive for persons and organisations processing personal data are very significant. Controllers must address the substantial changes to data protection law that lie ahead immediately. Leaving things to the last moment is likely to prove very costly and disruptive. The main provisions of the Directive must be implemented by 24 October 1998 and the opportunity should be taken to analyse the Directive and evaluate its impacts in order to develop cost effective and timely strategies for compliance.

---

1   There is a right to privacy in certain commissioned photographs and films under section 85 of the Copyright, Designs and Patents Act 1988.
2   Article 9. Also excepted is processing for the purpose of literary or artistic expression if necessary to reconcile the right to privacy with freedom of expression.

After looking at the background and history of the Directive, the remainder of this book is intended to assist those processing personal data, whether controllers, processors, recipients and others, and data subjects to understand the Directive, how it is likely to be implemented in the United Kingdom and the implications of compliance with its provisions. In addition to dealing with the background to and analysis of the Directive, its effects on the various players in the data protection game are discussed. The book also contains a number of case studies in which some of the implications for various categories of organisations in both the public and private sectors are examined.

Finally, it must be stressed that the scope of the Directive is breathtaking. Of course, it does not apply to processing for activities outside the scope of Community law and there are other exemptions, for example, in relation to processing by natural persons purely for personal or household activities. Nevertheless, the Directive is of much wider application than the present law, not only in terms of the number of controllers which will be increased dramatically by the extension of data protection law to manual processing, but in the reach of its provisions. For example, recital 14 makes it clear that the Directive will apply to the capture of sound or image data, affecting video surveillance[1]. The definition of processing is much wider than the equivalent definition in the Data Protection Act 1984. Data subjects are given a right to object to processing and, in some circumstances, their positive consent may be required for processing to be lawful. The Directive contains provision for prior checking of processing posing specific risks to rights and freedoms and imposes restrictions on the transfer of personal data to countries outside the European Community which fail to provide adequate levels of protection for personal data. It is a very significant piece of legislation.

---

1   Except where carried out on grounds of public security and the like; recital 16.

Chapter 2 : Background to and History of the Directive
By Nick Platten[1]

The Problem

Data protection is best understood as the legal response to a real but often elusive problem: the threat posed to the privacy and identity of all of us as individuals by the mass processing of information.

Of course the issue is not a new one. It has been a favourite subject with philosophers and writers throughout the twentieth century. Indeed for a number of the classic novels of this period, the idea that information has the power to dominate and subjugate the individual is a central theme. In terms of its impact on the public consciousness the most notable of these works is undoubtedly George Orwell's "1984" with its all-seeing, all-knowing "Big Brother", published in 1949. But perhaps even more chilling is Franz Kafka's "The Trial" (1926) in which the unfortunate Josef K battles unsuccessfully to retain his identity in the face of a bureaucracy before whom he is only a number, and whose data files can never be challenged.

For years after they were written, however, such novels (one could probably add Huxley's "Brave New World" to the list) still belonged firmly to the realm of fiction. Although their success was perhaps indicative of an underlying public unease about the potential risks to privacy in a modern society, the reality of these risks, in the Western world at least, was not apparent.

This all changed with the onset of computerisation in the sixties and seventies. The power of the early big mainframe computers was by today's standards unimpressive, but for civil libertarians the echoes of Big Brother were all too obvious - the Orwellian nightmare was underway. And as the enormous potential of the digital revolution became ever more apparent, so the calls for specific measures to protect individuals became louder.

---

1   The views expressed in this Chapter reflect the personal opinions of the author and can in no way be attributed to either the European Commission or the Data Protection Registrar.

The Early Response at International Level

The first international organisation to address this emerging problem was the Council of Europe. Formed after the 1939-45 war with the aim of seeking greater unity between like-minded governments of European countries, human rights issues had traditionally been the focus of its activities. Indeed by virtue of the landmark Council of Europe Convention on Human Rights and Fundamental Freedoms (1949) a basic right to privacy had been created across Europe[1]. This was particularly significant because the Human Rights Convention, unlike all subsequent conventions drawn up by the Council of Europe, established a legal mechanism to ensure that its rules were observed. The Strasbourg-based European Commission of Human Rights and European Court of Human Rights were and still are solely concerned with cases brought under this Convention.

But the new data processing power of computer technology clearly raised problems which could not be adequately dealt with by a general right to privacy. In 1968 therefore the Council of Europe's Committee of Ministers decided to undertake an examination of the extent to which existing law among its Member States offered adequate protection of personal privacy bearing in mind the modern state of science and technology. By 1974 the Committee of Ministers had adopted two resolutions seeking to establish minimum standards to protect individuals with respect to information held in data banks.

Early National Responses

An actual data protection law had meanwhile been adopted in 1970 in the German federal state of Hesse. The growing opportunities to manipulate individual behaviour through sophisticated processing of personal data were cited as the justification for the law, which was the first of its kind anywhere in the world. The use (or rather abuse) of national population registers under the Third Reich probably explain the particular sensibility of Germans to data protection issues, but while Germany was in the vanguard of data protection law development, others were not far behind. By the end of the seventies a total of seven Council of Europe Member States (Austria, Denmark, France, Germany, Luxembourg, Norway and Sweden) had enacted general data protection laws, while two others (Portugal and Spain) had included the protection of privacy as a fundamental right under constitutional provisions.

---

1   Council of Europe Convention on Human Rights and Fundamental Freedoms, Article 8(1) reads: "Everyone has the right to respect for his private and family life, his home and his correspondence".

Not Just a National Problem

By the beginning of the 1980s it was becoming apparent that personal data processing was not confined to isolated mainframe computers, but was becoming increasingly based around networks. While some such networks were entirely located within one country, others were international in nature. Indeed the networks in the financial services sector dealing with bank transfers and credit card payments and those in the transport sector concerned with aircraft passenger seat reservations were evolving into enormous worldwide operations involving the continuous transfer of information about individuals across national borders and even between continents.

Such transborder flows of personal data presented a fresh challenge to national regulators seeking to secure a measure of protection for their citizens. How could compliance with a national law be ensured when only a small part of a much bigger global network was located on home territory and when those companies or organisations responsible for the running of the network were based abroad? Furthermore, what was to prevent home operators wishing to circumvent the law from simply relocating their data processing activities abroad in countries without data protection laws, and then importing the data, if necessary, at a later date?

To deal with this problem of "data havens", most countries that enacted data protection laws had included provisions aimed at regulating flows of data abroad. But with international data flows becoming increasingly necessary for the very functioning of world trade, the problem was quickly becoming too big to be solved in this way. To prohibit transborder data flows to countries without data protection laws in any kind of systematic way would have enormous economic and therefore political consequences. For the most part, therefore, such action was in practice unfeasible, even for those European countries such as France and Germany, that attached the greatest importance to data protection matters.

By the early 1980s it had therefore become clear that an international solution to the question was required.

The OECD Guidelines Governing the Protection of Privacy and Transborder Flows of Personal Data (1980)

The first attempt to make progress at international level on the question was made by the Paris-based Organisation for Economic Co-operation and Development (OECD), which in September 1980 adopted a recommendation urging its Member countries to take into account a set of guideline principles on the protection of privacy.

The OECD's main concern with data protection and privacy laws was the potential they had to disrupt flows of personal information and thereby international trade. The answer seemed simple: agree a common set of data protection principles to which all Member countries could adhere, and combine this with a basic rule that personal data transfers between these countries should then be unrestricted.

The policy is a sound one, appealing both to the civil libertarians anxious to ensure that national data protection laws are not circumvented and indeed are recognised on a wider international scale, and to the business lobby eager to discourage the newly created data protection authorities in a number of European countries from interfering in the international flow of personal data.

The guidelines in themselves do a good job in setting out a central core of data protection rules, setting limits on the collection, use and disclosure of personal data, and requiring basic standards of data quality, security and openness. They also lay down clearly a basic right of access to data for all individuals, together with a right to challenge the content of the data and if necessary have it corrected.

But despite the good quality of the drafting, the OECD response was ultimately unsuccessful. The main problem was the nature of the OECD as essentially a cooperative organisation. Although it is does have the ability to draft instruments which are binding on its members, in the data protection field it did not feel sufficiently confident to do so. It therefore issued a simple recommendation to its Member countries to follow the guidelines. If this were not enough, the guidelines themselves were carefully worded so as to preserve a Member country's freedom to prohibit transfers where another Member country does not provide equivalent protection[1]. Equally the guidelines left considerable room for manoeuvre in terms of how they are implemented. Member countries are free to adopt "legal, administrative or other procedures or institutions for the protection of privacy" but need only "*endeavour* to adopt *appropriate* domestic legislation" [author's italics]. The OECD was unable to bring about real equivalence in levels of protection, and without this its Member countries were unwilling to agree to complete free flow of data between them.

---

1   *OECD guidelines governing the protection of privacy and transborder flows of personal data* (1980), Part Three, paragraph 17.

Council of Europe Convention 108

In Strasbourg, however, a more significant attempt to address data protection on the international level was being made by the Member States of the Council of Europe. The prospects for success here were better from the outset for two reasons. First the Member States of the Council of Europe were culturally and historically less diverse than those of the OECD. The likelihood of finding agreement on a more detailed set of rules was therefore greater. Secondly the Council of Europe had the power to do more than adopt recommendations and guidelines; it could draw up conventions that constituted binding instruments of international law. Thus it had the means to produce an instrument that more effectively guaranteed equivalent levels of protection.

As it transpired the result of the negotiations in Strasbourg was just such an instrument: the Convention for the Protection of Individuals with regard to Automatic Processing of Personal Data (Convention 108), which was opened for signature on 28 January 1981.

There is little doubt that this was a significant achievement, setting out for the first time the basic tenets of data protection in an international legal text. Indeed the mixture of obligations on those responsible for the processing of data ("data controllers") and rights for individuals ("data subjects") constitutes what is still considered the blueprint for a minimum standard of protection in national law. Convention 108 also introduced the idea that certain special categories of data (racial origin, political opinions, religious or other beliefs, data related to health or sexual life, criminal convictions) should not be processed at all unless appropriate safeguards are provided in law[1].

But in spite of these achievements, Convention 108 still has its weaknesses. A fundamental problem concerns the enforceability of the Convention itself. In theory parties to the Convention are required to "take the necessary measures in (their) domestic law to give effect to the basic principles of data protection"[2]. In general this obligation is met in practice, but there is no overriding supranational legal structure to ensure that this is always the case. It cannot therefore be automatically assumed that the parties to the Convention share a common minimal level of data protection. For instance Spain ratified the Convention in January 1984 but did not bring into force any domestic legislation until 1993. Similarly Greece ratified the Convention in August 1995 yet at

---

1   Council of Europe Convention for the Protection of Individuals with regard to Automatic Processing of Personal Data, Article 6.
2   *Ibid*, Article 4(1).

the time of writing has no data protection law on the statute book. Even for those parties to the Convention who adopted legislation prior to ratification (the vast majority), there are some difficult questions to answer. The United Kingdom, for example, has never provided any specific safeguards for the special categories of data listed in Article 6 of Convention 108, although any orthodox interpretation of the text would see this as a requirement.

The Problems of Regulating International Data Processing

Other criticisms of the Convention centre on what is omitted from the text, rather than what is included. The introduction to the explanatory report identifies in paragraph 10 the difficult problem of determining which national law applies to cross-frontier processing:

> When automatic processing of personal data involves parties in different countries (for example, a data bank in one country linked to terminals in other countries) it may not always be easy to determine which State has jurisdiction and which national law applies.

However, having outlined the problem the Convention does not then seek to propose a solution, satisfying itself with a partial system of mutual assistance between national authorities to help individuals exercise their rights when processing takes place in the territory of another party to the Convention.

Another, perhaps more serious problem concerns the way the Convention regulates transborder flows of personal data. Article 12 establishes, albeit subject to some exemptions, a principle of free movement of data between parties to the Convention. This is logical in that the Convention seeks to establish an equivalent minimum level of protection between all contracting parties. However, the question of data transfers to non-contracting states is not covered by Convention 108. Parties to the Convention are free to do as they wish in this regard. Although this preserves a maximum degree of flexibility for contracting states, it inevitably means that their confidence in one another as "safe" destinations for personal data flows is undermined. If country A transfers data to country B, the fact that both are parties to the Convention does not help if country B is free to allow a further transfer to country C which has no data protection law. Indeed the failure to address the problem of transfers to non-contracting parties led to a watering down of the very principle of free movement of data between contracting parties, by the introduction of an exemption in Article 12 (3)(b):

"(Nevertheless, each party shall be entitled to derogate from the provisions of paragraph 2 (free movement)) when the transfer is made from its territory to the territory of a non-Contracting State through the intermediary of the territory of another Party, in order to avoid such transfers resulting in circumvention of the legislation of the Party referred to at the beginning of this paragraph."

Other Limitations in the Approach of Convention 108

By the time the Convention was opened for signature a significant number of national data protection laws were already in place among Council of Europe Member States. These laws differed but they all had in common the fact that they not only outlined a set of data protection principles but also included extensive provisions on the supervision and enforcement of these principles. The most common approach was to establish some sort of independent authority or commission with supervisory powers together with a system of registration or even licensing for those organisations wishing to process personal data.

Surprisingly, however, the Convention does not include much in the way of specific procedural provisions. Parties to the Convention must give effect to the data protection principles in domestic law and must establish appropriate sanctions and remedies for violations of these legal provisions. But a supervisory authority or ombudsman is not required and neither is a public registry of data processing operations.

Finally, the Convention, like the OECD Convention before it, only applies to automatic processing of data. Paper or manual files are excluded. This reflects in many ways the belief that the real threat to individuals lies with digitised information processed by computers, rather than the traditional dusty filing cabinet. However, by the early 1980s increasing numbers of experts were beginning to question this assumption. After all, for the individual data subject it matters little how information about him/her is held, but rather how it is used. This issue was to become one of the central battle themes during the negotiations on the EU directive some 14 years later.

The Data Protection Act (1984)

In the United Kingdom pressure for legislation to protect individuals from the dangers of computerised data had been mounting throughout the 1970s. The Younger Report of 1972, although coming out on balance against legislation, had set out a series of ten information handling principles. In 1976 the government of the day established a committee under the chairmanship of Sir Norman Lindop to advise both on the permanent control machinery needed to secure the protection of personal data and to consider the objectives to be incorporated into legislation. The report of the committee, presented to Parliament in December 1978, was to a great extent a blueprint for a future data protection law. The opening of the Council of Europe Convention for signature in 1981 led the government to also see a data protection law as increasingly necessary to ensure the smooth operation of international trade, which was now becoming heavily dependent on transborder data flows. It was also believed that the nascent British data processing industry would benefit from the consumer confidence that legislation would bring.

And so it was that on 12 July in the wonderfully appropriate year of 1984 the Data Protection Act gained Royal assent and passed into law. The UK subsequently ratified the Convention on 26 August 1987.

It is not the intention here to make a substantial analysis of the 1984 Act, but it is nevertheless interesting to take note of the broad approach taken by the Government, in seeking to give effect in national law to the very general principles set down in Convention 108.

Particularly striking is that the basic set of substantive rights and obligations laid down in the Convention is restated in the 1984 Act without any significant attempt to define their precise meaning when applied in practice[1]. The Act instead leaves interpretation of the "data protection principles" to a supervisory authority "the Data Protection Registrar", under the judicial control of a specialist data protection tribunal. This has meant that the meaning of general principles such as "fair obtaining of data"[2] has only gradually emerged with the caselaw of the intervening years.

The 1984 Act does, however, include a number of procedural, institutional and enforcement-related elements which do not feature explicitly in the Convention. Indeed the centre-piece of the legislation is a national register of those who hold information about individuals on computer. The register is central to the system of the Act. There are very few exemptions from the duty to register, and the main criminal sanctions created by the Act relate to registration. Meanwhile the Registrar can only take enforcement action for a breach of the data protection principles against organisations that have already registered.

---

1   Some of the principles do benefit from a "statutory interpretation" in Part II of Schedule 1 of the Act, but this interpretation remains very general in nature.
2   Data Protection Act 1984, the first data protection principle reads: "The information to be contained in personal data shall be obtained, and personal data shall be processed, fairly and lawfully".

With hindsight this emphasis on registration may have been a mistake. A data protection register is a means to an end. It allows the public to know which companies and other bodies process personal data, and for what purposes, and it is as an instrument which a supervisory authority can use for the purposes of enforcing the data protection principles, compliance with which is, after all, the real objective. In the UK, however, registration has tended to become an end in itself. As the number of organisations using computers to process personal data has risen exponentially, so the Registrar has been obliged to devote considerable resources to dealing with the deluge of registration applications. Despite this, the sheer number of such applications has tended to make an in-depth assessment of the registered particulars all but impossible. Registration therefore becomes simply a form-filling exercise serving, in data protection terms, very limited purposes.

Data Protection in France and Germany

During the 1970s and 1980s other European countries, particularly Germany and France, were developing their own distinctive approaches to data protection matters.

The pioneering 1970 law in the "Land" of Hesse was followed by legislation in the rest of the German "Länder" as well as a Federal Law in 1977 (revised in 1990) dealing with personal data held by the federal administration. A distinguishing feature of German data protection has been the adoption of different rules for the public and private sectors. Generally separate supervisory authorities are also created. As a result while data processing in the public sector has been tightly controlled, the monitoring of the protection in the private sector has been less rigorous. Another interesting feature is the importance attached to ensuring that all processing of personal data has a legal basis. Traces of this "legal positivist" approach are still to be found in Article 7 of the EU Directive.

An important legacy of German data protection has been the concept of "informational self-determination", which originates from a landmark judgment of the German constitutional court on the question of the use of census data[1]. This principle essentially stipulates that all processing of personal data is an intrusion of privacy and therefore needs specific justification. It therefore follows that personal data should be obtained only for a specific purpose and that all further uses are prohibited without the consent of the individual. A unique decentralised system of data protection supervision is another German invention. Betriebliche Datenschutzbeauftragte are independent officials employed by

---

1   The Census judgement is reported in NJW 1984, 419.

companies to ensure their compliance with data protection law. Such officials have an independent status (eg they are protected from dismissal) and have privileged contacts with the data protection supervisory authority. (Such officials are specifically envisaged by Article 18(2) of the Directive).

A general data protection law was adopted in France in 1978[1]. Although of broad application, covering manual and automatically-processed data, it includes some particularly interesting elements in sections 2 and 3 regarding the automatic "profiling" of individuals. Such concerns about the possible adverse consequences for individuals of such profiling techniques were ultimately reflected in Article 15 of the EU Directive. The French law also includes in section 26 an individual right of opposition to data processing, and a possibility in section 17 for simplified registration of data processing which complies with certain pre-established norms. Both these ideas were later incorporated into the directive (Articles 14 and 18(2) respectively).

The main distinctive feature of the French data protection tradition, however, has been the creation of an extremely powerful central supervisory authority, the Commission Nationale de l'Informatique et des Libertés (or CNIL). The CNIL has a number of regulatory powers and there is also an obligation for it to be consulted regarding new legislative proposals impacting upon data protection. Although the UK's Data Protection Registrar's Office and other such authorities around Europe also enjoy significant formal powers, the CNIL is endowed with an additional moral and political authority, and its opinions are rarely ignored inside France. It also has the power to conduct prior checks on certain proposed data processing operations mainly in the public sector. If its opinion on the proposed processing is unfavourable, this can only be overturned by the Conseil d'Etat. Considerable importance was attached to this procedural power by the French delegation during negotiations on the directive.

Calls for Action at European Community Level

Within the European Community institutions there was an awareness of this legislative activity in the Member States and a certain disquiet that the approaches being adopted were very different from one another. Indeed the European Parliament adopted resolutions in 1976, 1979, and 1982 calling on the Commission to propose a directive to harmonise data protection laws. The Commission's response was limited initially to a recommendation that Member States ratify the Council of Europe Convention before the end of 1982, although it did

---

1   Loi N°78-17 relative à l'informatique, aux fichiers et aux libertés.

reserve the right to propose a Community measure if ratification of the Convention on the part of the Member States was not forthcoming within a reasonable timeframe.

However as the 1980s progressed two things became clear: first Member States were not rushing to ratify the Convention (by 1990 only seven community countries had data protection legislation), and second, among those that had ratified, significant differences in the level of protection were evident. In short the Commission saw that the Council of Europe Convention was not an effective means of producing a level playing field of data protection law.

During this time it was becoming clearer that data protection - a human rights issue - also raised questions linked intimately to trade and the functioning of the international economy. Economic activity was becoming ever more dependent on the processing of personal data, whether about customers, clients or employees, and free flow of such data across national frontiers was becoming an essential element of economic integration. This point was not lost on the Commission, which was in the full throes of creating a regulatory framework to ensure the proper functioning of the Internal Market by 1992. The basic freedoms established by the EC Treaty - free movement of goods, services, persons and capital - could be inhibited if one Member State were to block the transfer of personal data to another on the grounds that the recipient State did not afford an equivalent level of protection. Furthermore, a Member State, would not be acting in breach of its Treaty obligations by acting in such a way. The diverse national data protection rules among the Member States therefore risked fragmentation of the European Community's grand project - the 1992 programme.

1990 and the First Commission Proposal

Emboldened by the general climate of enthusiasm for Internal Market harmonisation, and following a specific joint resolution of the Data Protection Commissioners of the European Community issued after their Berlin meeting in 1989, the European Commission at last adopted in September 1990 a package of proposed data protection measures[1], the centrepiece of which was a proposal for a general framework directive to harmonise the national legislation of the Member States.

It is fair to say that this came as something of a surprise. The proposal was issued with little advance warning - there had been no Green Paper and little advance consultation. There was also the perception that the

---

1   COM(90) 314 final - SYN 287 and 288.

European Community was an economic organisation, not entitled to deal with delicate human rights issues such as privacy and data protection. (This was despite the fact that a commitment to fundamental rights is included in the preamble to the Single European Act, and that the protection of such rights forms part of the general principles of law upheld by the European Court of Justice).

But the Commission was now confident that the link between personal data processing and economic activity was sufficiently strong to justify proposing a directive on the basis of Article 100a of the EC Treaty, in other words as a measure to ensure "the establishment and functioning of the Internal Market".

There is no doubt that the proposed directive was ambitious, and the Commission explained its reasoning very clearly in the explanatory memorandum accompanying the text. Firstly the approximation of national laws was to guarantee a high level of protection and not lead to any individual Member State lowering their existing level. Secondly, although the proposal takes up the basic principles of the Council of Europe Convention, it does not consider them sufficient to ensure a high level of equivalent protection. For the Commission equivalent protection meant harmonisation not only of the general rules but also of certain procedural aspects which ensure the application of those rules. Hence the proposal included a chapter on liabilities and sanctions and further provisions requiring the establishment of independent supervisory authorities in the Member States. Thirdly the Commission concluded that the proposal should cover all data processing which could pose risks to data subjects. The scope is therefore wide, covering manual and automated files, and data processing in both private and public sectors. And fourthly the proposal acknowledges the global nature of personal data flows and consequently includes provisions intended to regulate transfers outside of the Community on a systematic basis.

The 1990 proposal was destined to undergo radical changes before the directive was finally adopted nearly five years later, but these four key underlying principles, which result in a directive more complete and rigorous than any of the preceding international instruments, have always been retained.

Reaction to the 1990 Proposal

In the UK, reaction to the Commission's initiative was at best mixed. While the Data Protection Registrar and others were pleased to see the right to privacy explicitly recognised in Article 1 of the proposal, there was concern that in general the text was confusing in its structure. Although purportedly based on the principles of the Council of Europe Convention, these principles were hidden away in Article 16. Furthermore the proposal adopted the German approach of separate rules for the public and private sectors, an approach which, in the UK context of widespread privatisation, seemed curious if not ill-founded. Not surprisingly there was also concern about the consequences of applying data protection rules to manual files.

The overall impression was that the proposed directive signalled a major departure from the existing UK legislation, based too closely on the German model. This view is not strictly correct - there were aspects of the proposal that were new to the Germans too - but clearly the sudden arrival of the Commission initiative was met with a fair amount of suspicion.

A similar feeling was experienced in France, where the government and the CNIL were also caught off guard by the arrival of the proposal. Here there was a similar distaste for the public/private sector approach, and a difficulty in recognising any traces of the French data protection tradition in the substance of the text.

This widespread unease with the detail, although not the underlying principles, of the Commission's approach, was reflected in the first reading of the proposal before the European Parliament. Geoffrey Hoon MEP, who prepared the report of the Parliament's Legal Affairs and Citizens' Rights Committee, recommended approval of the proposal but subject to almost one hundred amendments. The Parliament broadly followed this line, voting with virtual unanimity.

The Amended Proposal of 1992

In its amended proposal issued in October 1992 the Commission not only responded to the numerous amendments submitted by the Parliament, but also took the opportunity to completely restructure the text. The distinction between public and private sectors was removed and the old-fashioned notion of "data file" was replaced by the more technology-neutral notion of "data processing". The fundamental principles taken from Article 5 of Convention 108 were promoted to centre stage as Article 6 of the amended proposal, and the German influence was supplemented by ideas drawing on French, Dutch and, it was argued, British data protection traditions.

The French influence is apparent in the introduction of a right of opposition and an article on automatic profiling, as well as the "avis préalable" (prior opinion) of the supervisory authority for data processing posing specific risks, and a notification system including the French notion of simplified norms. The Dutch tradition was recognised by the introduction of two articles on codes of conduct, an enforcement tool well used in the Netherlands. Codes of conduct and an extensive notification (or registration system) were familiar features of the existing UK law.

Throughout the Community the revised proposal was received as a significant improvement. Most Member States that had laws were able to recognise at least traces of their national systems in the amended proposal. The Commission was able to achieve this while at the same time avoiding the obvious danger of a "hotch-potch" of incoherent and contradictory national features. The amended proposal laid down a coherent and logical framework of rules, the main contents and structure of which, despite the three years of intensive negotiations and lobbying which were to follow, remain more or less intact in the final text of the directive.

The Early Negotiations in Council

The Council of Ministers is the most powerful decision-making institution among the institutions of the European Community. Whereas the Commission has the exclusive right to propose measures, it is the Council, made of representatives from each of the Member State governments that decides (along with the Parliament where it is a question covered by the co-decision procedures established in the Maastricht Treaty) the fate of the Commission's proposals. For internal market proposals such as the data protection directive, the Council decides by qualified majority[1], which means that no single Member State is able to block progress.

Soon after the Commission had transmitted its amended proposal to the Council in October 1992, a Council Working Group which had been considering the initial Commission proposal since 1990, began a detailed examination of the new text. During the last few months of the UK presidency and the full term of the subsequent Danish presidency[2] (up until June 1993) the group completed a first reading of all 37 articles, during which each delegation signalled its degree of support for the proposed directive, and outlined the particular areas of the text which created difficulties.

---

1   Each Member State is given a number of votes weighted according to its size, and roughly two thirds of the total votes are required for adoption of a decision.
2   Each Member State takes it in turn to hold the presidency of the Council for a period of six months.

It quickly became clear that neither the UK or Irish governments were particularly keen on the amended proposal, believing that simple ratification of the Council of Europe Convention by all Member States would be a sufficient step. The Danish delegation had similar sympathies. By contrast the Benelux and Mediterranean countries (including France) were broadly happy with the main thrust of the amended proposal, and were keen to see it adopted quickly so that free movement of data within the internal market could be assured, and distortions of competition between Member States with different levels of protection could be avoided.

The position of the German delegation was somewhere in between the two camps. On the one hand Germany is a country which takes data protection very seriously, applying, in the public sector at least, its long-standing domestic rules with a rigour rarely seen elsewhere in Europe. The idea of an EU Directive establishing a high level of protection across the 12 (now 15) Member States was therefore an attractive one in principle, for it would ensure that German industry would not be disadvantaged by rules which did not exist elsewhere in the Community. However, the German delegation felt unsure about the amended proposal, preferring the Commission's initial text which reflected German data protection traditions more closely. It was particularly nervous about the application of a seamless data protection system to both public and private sectors. Furthermore the Germans had a number of quite specific problems with the text, particularly the provisions on notification and sensitive data, which they considered too inflexible, and with the requirement for an independent supervisory authority, which in respect of private sector supervision they feared would run counter to the German constitution.

The arithmetic of qualified majority voting meant that the German position became absolutely critical for the directive's future. With Germany on their side, the UK, Ireland and Denmark could effectively block further progress. If, on the other hand, Germany could be persuaded to support the directive, an agreement[1] would be close at hand.

Opposition from Industry

Throughout 1993 and 1994 a number of industries were lobbying both the Member States and the Commission hard. The most aggressive opposition to the directive came from the banking sector, where there was concern that the way banks use personal data would be overly

---

1   At this stage the adoption of a Council "common position" was the goal. The text would then be able to begin its second reading in the Parliament.

restricted and that the costs of compliance would be high. The UK and Dutch delegations in Council began to echo this latter concern particularly. In the UK the cost question was seen primarily to result from the retrospective inclusion of manual records, something which the UK government fought hard against, though ultimately without success.

Other sectors also raised concerns. The direct marketing industry, which depends on a trade in personal data for its very existence, was broadly happy with the principle of an EU-wide "opt-out" for customers who do not wish to receive unsolicited mail, but was concerned about the obligations on data controllers to provide information to individuals even where the data in question was publicly available (electoral lists, for example).

Meanwhile medical researchers, particularly those involved in epidemiological studies, feared that the directive could render access to data originally collected for administrative purposes, but now of interest to their research, nigh on impossible. The Danish delegation was particularly susceptible to the concerns being aired by the researchers, and was ultimately successful in obtaining a number of significant changes to the text which, for the most part, resolved the problem.

A Blocking Minority in Council

Meanwhile in Council the successive Belgian and Greek presidencies (July-December 1993 and January-June 1994 respectively) made strenuous efforts to achieve a common position - the equivalent of a political agreement on "first reading" in the Council - working closely with the Commission to produce revised compromise texts for almost every article. Some progress was undoubtedly made, (for example, agreement was reached on deleting Article 10 of the proposal, reformulating its contents and combining it with Article 21 on the publicity of proposing), but overall things moved forward at a slow pace, and many problems remained to be resolved.

Given the sheer complexity and wide scope of the text (it had an impact on the activities of almost every industry, and on large parts of the public sector), it was inevitable that the Council would have a difficult task. At one stage the number of specific problems raised by the different delegations numbered more than 100. Negotiations were always therefore likely to take some time.

However the momentum towards a common position appeared to have been eroded when in late 1993 a paper of proposed amendments to the text was tabled jointly by the UK, Irish, Danish and, critically, German delegations. The proposals, which essentially sought to weaken the harmonising effect of the directive by giving more flexibility to Member States, were for the most part unacceptable to the Commission and the other Member States, who were unwilling to agree to the free flow of personal data between EC countries if the directive could not ensure the proper approximation of national laws. The work in the Council working group was effectively deadlocked.

The Window of Political Opportunity That Broke the Log-jam

For proponents of the directive, however, some unforeseen help was on its way. For although progress at the technical level of the Council working group was proving difficult, giant strides forward were being made in the wider political debate.

The successful Clinton-Gore campaign for the US presidency in 1992 had trumpeted the arrival of the "information superhighway", making the development of such a technological infrastructure a key part of its programme. The success of this idea was not lost on Jaques Delors who, following the difficulties caused by the Danish referendum vote against the Maastricht Treaty, was looking for a package of new ideas to renew and revitalise the recession-stricken European Union. Delors' efforts were presented in the Commission's White Paper on "Growth, Competitiveness and Employment - the Challenges and Ways Forward into the 21st Century"[1] published in June 1993. One of the key ideas of the White Paper was the promotion and development of an "information society", where new technology and distributed networks transform the world in which we live and do business. The White Paper proposed that the EU become a "common information area" in which the new technology-based services could develop. As part of this policy a legal environment was needed which among other things addressed the issue of the protection of data and privacy[2]. Furthermore, to study these "information society" issues in more detail, the White Paper suggested the creation of a high level group of government and industry representatives, mandated by and reporting to the European Council[3].

This suggestion was duly taken up and a group was formed under the chairmanship of Martin Bangemann, the high profile German member of the European Commission. The group submitted its report "Europe and the Global Information Society" to the European Council meeting at

1   Bulletin of the European Communities, Supplement 6/93.
2   *Ibid*, specifically chapter 5, pages 92-98.
3   The European Council is the meeting of heads of government which takes place every six months, generally towards the end of each Council presidency.

Corfu in June 1994. It included a specific section on privacy, culminating with the following conclusion:

> The Group believes that without the legal security of a Union-wide approach, lack of consumer confidence will certainly undermine the rapid development of the information society. Given the importance and sensitivity of the privacy issue, a fast decision from Member States is required on the Commission's proposed Directive setting out general principles of data protection.

The report was well received by the heads of government in Corfu. The Presidency conclusions from the summit included a full page about the information society including some fairly clear instructions to the Council:

> At the level of the Community, the necessary regulatory framework has to be established as soon as possible. The European Council invites the Council and the European Parliament to adopt before the end of the year measures in the areas already covered by existing proposals.

These conclusions, together with the clear line taken by the Bangemann report, completely changed the political climate of the negotiations on the data protection directive. Suddenly it was a priority issue on which the EU heads of government wanted to see swift and decisive progress.

The Happy Coincidence of a German Presidency

There was one further factor which helped unblock the negotiations. In July 1994 the Council presidency passed into the hands of the Germans, the very delegation whose position was the key to achieving qualified majority support for the proposal. This was important for two reasons. First it meant that the German delegation began working, as all presidencies tend to do, with the Commission's services. This dialogue helped calm the German unease with the proposal which had previously led them to form their blocking alliance with the UK, Ireland and Denmark. Secondly there was the factor that all presidencies like to be seen to achieve results. After Corfu the data protection directive was a prime candidate for a common position, but this would require some movement in the German position. The mantle of the presidency therefore encouraged the Germans to make some sacrifices so that the negotiations could move forward.

The second six months of 1994 therefore saw a major effort on the part of the presidency and the Commission to achieve agreement.

During this period important changes were made to the text. A series of amendments were introduced to deal with the medical research question. An extended 12 year transition period for manual records was introduced. Qualms about the costs for industry of the directive were addressed, at least in part, by a Commission-sponsored study which found that for most organisations such costs would not be significant.

As a result of these efforts both the Irish and Danish delegations were able to drop their opposition. Thus at the Internal Market Council meeting on 8 December 1994 Ministers came to a political agreement on the text. For technical reasons (the text was not available in advance in all community languages) this was not a formal common position, but effectively the deal had been struck. Only the UK dissented from the agreement.

The Common Position

So thanks to the hard work and sacrifices of their neighbours from across the Rhine, the French presidency was able to take the glory of achieving the common position. It was formally adopted without further discussion at the General Affairs Council on 20 February 1995.

From the beginning of 1995 the Community had welcomed three additional Member States - Austria, Sweden and Finland. All had been involved as observers in the negotiations of the previous six months, and indeed the Swedish delegation had been active in securing an additional recital concerning the relationship of the text with national rules concerning access to official public documents. By the time of their accession, all three countries were broadly happy with the text. The enlargement of the Community therefore only served to reinforce support for the Directive.

Nevertheless throughout those first few weeks of 1995 the UK government had made strenuous efforts to convince their European partners to go back on the agreement reached on 8 December. These efforts were unsuccessful and the actual text of the directive was not discussed further.

However, even for issues which are decided by qualified majority, the Council usually does its utmost to reach a consensus. At the CoRePer[1] meetings in January and February 1995 there was therefore a great

---

1   The committee of permanent representatives, comprised of Member States ambassadors or deputy ambassadors. It is the committee which comes between the working group and the actual Council where ministers are represented.

willingness to make concessions if this could help the British lift their opposition to the directive. Unfortunately for the UK there was by now no question of such concessions involving the substance of the text. In the end the UK agreed to abstain on the final vote, while making a number of statements of interpretation in the Council minutes.

Delegations which acted earlier, before the deal had effectively been struck - the Danes being a good example - left the negotiating table a great deal happier.

Second Reading and Final Adoption

After nearly two and a half years of tough negotiation in Council, the second reading before the European Parliament went by in the blink of an eye. Although some 60 amendments were submitted, the rapporteur for the Citizens Rights and Legal Affairs Committee, Mr Medina Ortega, recommended retention of only a handful of minor changes to the text. These amendments were acceptable both to the Commission and the Council. Directive 95/46/EC was officially adopted when signed by the Presidents of the Parliament and the Council on 24 October 1995. Five years after the Commission's original proposal, a community framework for data protection legislation was at last in place.

Part II : The Directive

Chapter 3 : Legal Analysis of the Directive

Introduction

The Directive contains a number of provisions that are new to data protection law in the United Kingdom. Data subjects will be more informed about personal data concerning them and given greater control over what happens to that data. Obligations are placed on data users to inform data subjects about the collection, recording or disclosure of personal data. In some circumstances, data users can object to processing of their personal data and their consent is required. Particular provisions are aimed at automated decisions affecting data subjects and marketing by mail. Manual processing, excluded from the ambit of the Data Protection Act 1984, will fall within the scope of data protection law. All of these new controls and obligations appear to place heavy burdens on data users with little in return, apart from the possibility of exemption from registration. Subsequent chapters will demonstrate that this is not necessarily so and, although the Directive is very much data subject driven, practical measures can be taken by data users to significantly reduce or eliminate the costs of compliance with the Directive. In some cases, there will be positive benefits for data users. Indeed, the Directive should encourage good or improved data processing practices to be established and developed.

The legal analysis of the Directive, with comparison with present United Kingdom law where appropriate, lays the foundation for the more practical approach taken in subsequent chapters. A thorough understanding of the legal effects produced by the Directive is essential to the development of efficacious and economical strategies and policies ensuring the new law on data protection is fully complied with. This will strengthen the fair use of personal data in the context of an ever-expanding information society in which it is vital that individuals' freedoms and privacy are not unduly compromised.

This chapter commences with a look at the basic mechanisms of data protection law under the present United Kingdom law and as proposed in the Directive. The detailed analysis of the legal effects of the Directive follows, commencing with the aims of the Directive, the definitions contained in it and dealing with particular aspects of the Directive's provisions.

Present UK law

The Data Protection Act 1984 is based on an admirably simple set of rights and obligations as shown in Figure 3.1. Indeed, the main thrust of the Act, the long title of which is "An Act to regulate the use of automatically processed information relating to individuals and the provision of services in respect of such information", is the principle of transparency of processing. This is achieved, in large part, by a system of registration by data users and computer bureaux. Data users, being those who hold personal data, and computer bureaux providing data processing services for data users (whether by processing personal data for them or by providing facilities for such processing) must register under the Act with the Office of the Data Protection Registrar.

Registration, by section 4 of the 1984 Act requires, *inter alia*, the submission of details concerning the nature of the personal data, the purposes for which the data are held or used, a description of the sources of the data, a description of persons to whom the data will be disclosed and details of any countries or territories outside the UK to which the data may be transferred[1]. The Data Protection Registrar may refuse an application if the details given are insufficient or if he considers that the applicant is likely to break the Data Protection Principles; section 7(2).

The focus of the 1984 Act is on registration as a means of controlling the processing of personal data and this is borne out by practical experience of enforcement. Failure to register is a criminal offence[2] and in the year ending 31 March 1996, out of a total of 39 charges for criminal offences under the Act, 25 were for the offence of holding personal data without being registered[3]. Apart from prosecuting offenders under the Act, the Registrar has powers of enforcement and the Registrar may serve notices on data users or computer bureaux requiring compliance with the Act or prohibiting the transfer of data or giving notice of de-registration.

---

1   The name and address of the data user must also be given and an address for subject access requests. For computer bureaux, the entry is much simpler comprising name and address only.
2   Section 5(1).
3   Data Protection Registrar, *Twelfth Report of the Data Protection Registrar*, HMSO, 1996, p39.

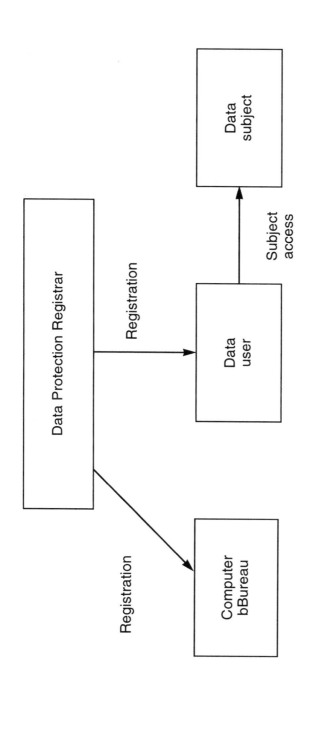

Figure 3.1 Mechanism under the Data Protection Act 1984

Other means of controlling the use of personal data are effected by the exercise of data subjects' rights including their right of access and right to have inaccurate or incomplete data corrected or erased. Additionally, anyone may complain to the Data Protection Registrar who may take appropriate action following an investigation of the complaint. In most cases, the data subject has to take a proactive role in relation to the processing of his data and much of the case law on data protection has arisen because an individual has complained about the use or disclosure of his personal data. In the year to 31 March 1996, a total of 2,950 complaints were received by the Office of the Data Protection Registrar[1].

The Mechanism of the Data Protection Directive

The apparent complexity of the Directive is highlighted by the numerous rights and obligations contained therein as Figure 3.2 clearly shows. In particular, the controller[2] is taxed with duties to notify or inform the data subject about the processing of personal data. The data subject is given more rights to control the processing by controllers of personal data relating to him.

On first inspection, the legal constraints over processing look daunting. But this is just the beginning. The number of persons and organisations having to comply with data protection law will be increased significantly because the rules applying to processing personal data will apply to paper files as well as computer files. The Data Protection Act 1984 was solely concerned at the control of automatic processing but the Directive applies to all processing of personal data, whether automatic or manual.

Obligations are imposed on controllers (data users are referred to as "controllers" in the Directive) to:

1   inform data subjects:

    (a)   on collection of their personal data;

    (b)   (to notify) on recording or disclosure of their data;

    (c)   before disclosure for the purposes of marketing by mail;

---

1   Data Protection Registrar, *Twelfth Report of the Data Protection Registrar*, HMSO, 1996, p42.
2   The term "controller" is used in the Directive and should be taken as synonymous with "data users", the term used in the Data Protection Act 1984. The terms are used interchangeably as appropriate in this chapter.

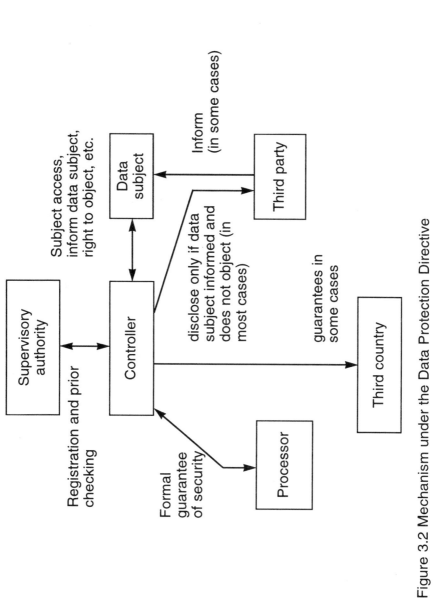

Figure 3.2 Mechanism under the Data Protection Directive

2   to obtain data subjects' consent to processing;

3   to block personal data at the request of data subjects.

These are new to data protection law in the United Kingdom, except in as much as the law has been developed by precedent, for example, requiring controllers to inform data subjects of non-obvious uses to which data are to be put[1]. It should be noted, however, that there are a number of exceptions to these obligations contained within the Directive so that they are not quite as alarming as they might seem at first sight. Controllers will not be required to maintain a barrage of correspondence with data subjects keeping them informed as to what is happening to their personal data. Nor will controllers have to continually seek the approval of data subjects to processing and disclosure of personal data. Even where the data subject has to be informed, by taking appropriate measures, controllers can ensure that this is done in such a way as to minimise the costs and administrative burdens, as will be discussed in following chapters.

At the present time it is probably true to say that the greatest burden for data users is the process of registration and renewal of registrations. This is largely an administrative task requiring the completion of an application form designed to provide the Registrar with sufficient information to assess whether the processing will comply with the Act. The fee payable is £75 for three years and, for most small and medium sized organisations, application for registration is not a particularly onerous task[2]. Under the Directive, exemptions from or simplification of registration (referred to in the Directive as "notification") are possible options for Member States. This should enable the United Kingdom to exempt from registration those organisations which only process non-sensitive data. At the present time, there are some 201,434 registrations in respect of some 188,584 data users under the 1984 Act[3]. The Data Protection Registrar has previously called for restrictions on the requirement of registration, exempting organisations carrying out non-sensitive processing[4] and such organisations will be afforded a small but welcome saving. Computer bureaux processing data for controllers will no longer be required to register but will be

---

1   *Innovations (Mail Order) Ltd v Data Protection Registrar* (unreported) 29 September 1993, Data Protection Tribunal.
2   Larger organisations, having considerable information processing operations, are likely to find the process of registration and renewal much more time consuming. Many such organisations have dedicated data protection officers.
3   As at March 1996, Data Protection Registrar, *Twelfth Report of the Data Protection Registrar*, HMSO, 1996 p21.
4   Data Protection Registrar, *Fifth Report of the Data Protection Registrar*, HMSO, 1989 Part B.

required to enter into binding obligations of confidence with controllers as to the security of personal data.

The processing of sensitive data is dealt with comprehensively in the Directive and, as might be expected, there are more constraints on such processing. The Registrar ("Supervisory Authority" in the Directive) is given the power to "prior-check" processing operations which are likely to pose specific risks to the rights and freedoms of individuals before the start of processing.

Subject access will be much as before though it should not be forgotten that this will apply also to paper files within the scope of the Directive. There are some differences in the amount and nature of information to be given to the data subject, being more extensive under the Directive. Individuals will continue to have a right to have incomplete or inaccurate data corrected or erased.

One of the aims of the Directive is the principle of the freedom of movement of personal data within the Community. By imposing a level playing field across the Community, transborder flows of personal data may be facilitated or even stimulated. Nevertheless, and bearing in mind the global nature of many processing operations, the Directive attempts, somewhat clumsily, to prohibit or restrict the transfer of personal data to third countries (that is, countries outside the Community) which do not afford adequate levels of security in respect of processing such data.

Before looking at specific aspects of the legal framework of processing personal data, it will be useful to consider first the aims of the Directive and then the definitions contained within it, noting differences where they exist with equivalent definitions in the Data Protection Act 1984.

Aims of the Directive

The primary aims of the Directive are twofold and are stated in Article 1 as being:

— the protection of the fundamental rights and freedoms of natural persons, and in particular their right to privacy with respect to the processing of personal data; and

— the prevention of barriers to the free flow of personal data across the Community by virtue of reasons connected with the above protection.

In other words, by harmonising data protection law across the Community, Member States are not allowed to restrict or prohibit the freedom of movement of personal data within the Community by arguing, for example, that another Member State does not provide an adequate level of protection for personal data. This mirrors the equivalent principles that apply to goods, services, persons and capital[1]. The recitals to the Directive stress and emphasise the twin aims and the desirability of harmonising data protection law so as to afford a high level of protection in terms of fundamental rights and freedoms, in particular, the right to privacy[2]. Recital 11 states that the protection of individuals' rights and freedoms contained in the Directive give substance to and amplify those contained in the Council of Europe Convention of 28 January 1981 for the Protection of Individuals with regard to Automatic Processing of Personal Data.

Throughout, the Directive strives to achieve a difficult balance between individuals and controllers. Although the interests of individuals and those processing personal data are apparently irreconcilable and contradictory, the Directive, in large measure, does achieve a fair balance. However, it is right to say that significantly more obligations are placed on controllers than is presently the case, but these are assuaged by a large number of exceptions, alternative and possible derogations contained in the Directive. In a number of places, the Directive states that a certain form of processing cannot be undertaken but this is quickly followed by a number of exceptions. One example is the processing of sensitive data which is prohibited by Article 8(1) but Articles 8(2) and (3) disapplies the prohibition in a number of situations and Member States are given the option of providing further limited exceptions by Articles 8(4) and (5).

Definitions

The basic definitions are contained in Article 2[3]. They are notable in their width compared to the equivalent definitions in the 1984 Act. For example, being in possession of personal data which has not been used for a long time but is locked away in a basement gathering dust could fall within the meaning of processing.

---

1   Article 7a of the EC Treaty.
2   Recognised in Article 8 of the European Convention for the Protection of Human Rights and Fundamental Freedoms. See recital 10.
3   The Data Protection Registrar recommends that the definitions should be set out with minimum amendment in the new legislation; Data Protection Registrar, *Consultation Paper on the EC Data Protection Directive: Response of the Data Protection Registrar,* 1996, para 4.1.

Personal data

> "... any information relating to an identified or identifiable natural person ('data subject'); an identifiable person is one who can be identified, directly or indirectly, in particular by reference to an identification number or to one or more factors specific to his physical, physiological, mental, economic, cultural or social identity."

The 1984 Act definition is expressed in terms of information relating to identifiable living individuals including expressions of opinion but not indications of the intention of the data user in respect of that individual. Data is personal data even if other information in the possession of the data user ("controller") is required to make the identification.

The Directive definition is wider and will extend to images and other non-textual information and recital 14 makes it clear that processing of sound and image data are to be covered by the Directive. This appears to be an extension of what can be classed as personal data at present because it is limited by the 1984 Act's definition of data being "information recorded in a form in which it can be processed by equipment operating automatically in response to instructions given for that purpose" which conjures up pictures of old fashioned data processing. However, given the advent of speech recognition software and image processing, it is at least arguable that the Data Protection Act 1984, as it now stands, would also apply to sound and image data.

A potential limiting factor in the Directive is that it particularises identifiers although it is difficult to think of an identifier that would not be included in those listed. Would a liking for football be considered to be a factor specific to cultural identity, social identity or neither? One might wonder why it was thought necessary to give any examples of types of identifiers. Surely, the basic requirement is that the data are in such a form that data relating to a given individual can be accessed with relative ease, as is borne out in a number of the recitals to the Directive[1].

There seems some doubt as to whether deceased persons are data subjects. It is unlikely, seeing as the definition of personal data refers to natural persons and dead persons[2] are no longer natural persons, if anything they are supernatural! However, there is a view in the Commission that it does extend to dead persons. This would beg the question - when required, from whom would the data be sought?

---

1   For example, recital 15 on the criteria for the control of manual filing systems.
2   House of Lords, *Protection of Personal Data*, HL Paper 75, HMSO, 1993 p86 per Mr Brühann, Head of Media and Data Protection Unit, European Commission.

Perhaps a medium would have to be engaged to contact the spirit of the deceased. This is not the first time the law has had to contemplate rights of deceased persons for, in *Cummins v Bond*[1], it was argued that one Cleophas who lived around the time of Christ, was the author of a literary work entitled "The Chronicles of Cleophas" when a medium at a seance who had contacted his spirit wrote down what he had to say. Also, authors of copyright works and directors of films have moral rights under copyright law which endure beyond their death. Notwithstanding all this the government does not intend to apply data protection law to deceased persons[2].

Processing of personal data

> "... any operation or set of operations which is performed upon personal data, whether or not by automatic means, such as collection, recording, organisation, storage, adaptation or alteration, retrieval, consultation, use, disclosure by transmission, dissemination or otherwise making available, alignment or combination, blocking, erasure or destruction."

This should be compared to the definition in the Data Protection Act 1984 which, for personal data, is amending, augmenting, deleting or re-arranging the data or extracting the information constituting the data by reference to the data subject. The definition in the Directive is considerably wider and, even then, non-exhaustive. In particular, it should be noted that it covers "storage" whatever that means. Presumably, the term should be "storing" or "having in store". If the latter, this will have serious consequences for organisations with large quantities of archived information. The recitals give no direct indication of whether the act of storing (that is, placing in a store) or the fact of being in possession or control of a store is intended. However, Article 32(2) suggests the latter. It allows derogation from the main impact of the Directive's provisions in relation to pre-existing manual filing systems for up to 12 years following national implementation but gives data subjects the right to have rectified, erased or blocked data which are, *inter alia*, "stored in a way incompatible with legitimate purposes of the controller".

---

1   [1927] 1 Ch 167. The argument failed as the judge felt his jurisdiction did not extend to extra-terrestrial beings. He decided the medium was the author of the work.
2   Home Office, *Consultation Paper on the EC Data Protection Directive*, HMSO 1996 p13.

Personal data filing system

This definition is relevant in terms of manual (that is, non-automatic) processing of personal data. A personal data filing system is any "structured set of personal data which are accessible according to specific criteria, whether centralised, decentralised or dispersed in a functional or geographical basis". There is no equivalent definition under the Data Protection Act 1984 which, of course, applies only to processing by automatic means.

From recital 15 it is clear that the primary objective to be achieved is that forms of manual processing that allow easy access to a specific individual's person data should be controlled. Thus, it is clear that a set of employee files, with each employee having his own discrete file with his name visible on the file, will be a personal data filing system. The same applies to a card index of employees, customers and the like arranged in alphabetical order. On the other hand, a general correspondence file with letters to numerous individuals arranged in date order will not be a personal data filing system. The determining factor is how easy it is to retrieve data relating to a particular person. It is likely that the type of criteria which may be within the definition, in line with the definition of personal data, will be widely construed and not simply limited to name or identification number. Thus, a card index system of identifiable persons classified by age, eye-colour, musical or literary tastes or academic qualification could all be personal data filing systems providing they permit easy access to the personal data in question. Of course, such classification systems will probably be hierarchical and within each major classification the individual cards could be arranged by name or national insurance number, for example.

The definition prevents circumvention of data protection law by splitting or dispersing the filing system in question.

The controller

The Directive uses the term "controller" instead of "data user", the equivalent under the 1984 Act. The controller is the person (natural, legal, public authority, agency or other body) which "alone or jointly with others determines the purposes and means of the processing of personal data; where the purposes and means of processing are determined by national or Community laws or regulations, the controller or the specific criteria for his nomination may be designated by national or Community law". The controller is, therefore, the person or persons who have the power or responsibility to decide what processing is carried out and how it is carried out. There is no requirement for the controller to be in actual possession of the data; rather it is the concept of control that is important.

Under the Data Protection Act 1984, a data user is a person who *holds* data. The data must form part of a collection of data processed or intended to be processed by or on behalf of that person and that person (either alone or jointly or in common with other persons) controls the contents and use of the data comprised in the collection. Although differently expressed, there is no significant distinction between a data user and a controller and the two terms can be treated interchangeably.

Recital 46 to the Directive suggests that, where a telecommunications or electronic mail service is used for the sole purpose of transmitting messages which contain personal data, the controller should be taken to be the person from whom the message originated, not the person providing the service who will be deemed to be controller only in respect of any additional personal data processed as necessary for the operation of the service.

The law applicable to controllers established in the territory of a Member State will be the national law of that Member State or, where a controller is established in a number of Member States, the relevant national law will apply to the controller's operation in each Member State; Article 4. Thus, if an English company, Nadir plc, has subsidiary companies in France, Nadir SA, and Germany, Nadir GmbH, then the parent and subsidiaries will be subject to United Kingdom, French and German national law respectively. Where a controller is not established in any Member State, the provisions of the national law of a Member State may apply by virtue of international public law. Controllers not established in any Member State will be subject to national provisions adopted in pursuance of the Directive if they make use of equipment (automated or otherwise) situated on the territory of a Member State[1]. In the latter case, the controller must designate a representative established in the territory of the appropriate Member State though this is without prejudice to any legal action taken against the controller personally.

Processor

A processor is a person (natural, legal, public authority, agency or other body) which "processes personal data on behalf of the

---

1   Unless the equipment is used for the purposes of transit through the territory of the Member State.

controller". The broad equivalent under the 1984 Act is a computer bureau and, certainly, many computer bureaux process data on behalf of the data user. But also within the definition of computer bureaux are those which supply the equipment so as to enable the data user to process the data. Both forms of bureaux have to register under the present Act but there is no requirement for processors to have to notify the supervisory authority under the Directive.

Third Party

A third party is simply anyone other than the data subject, controller, processor or other person, under the direct authority of either the controller or processor, who is authorised to process the data.

Recipient

The recipient is the person to whom data are disclosed, whether a third party or not. Authorities that may receive data in the framework of a general inquiry are not to be regarded as recipients. Apart from the exception for authorities (for example, disclosure to the DSS in accordance with its legal requirements) this should include any person to whom data are disclosed whether a third party, processor, a person in a third country, the data subject or the data subject's family, agents or servants. Whether persons handling data without inspection are deemed to be recipients is a moot point. Does, for example, a contractor engaged to destroy computer print-out have the data disclosed to him. It would seem not, although the presence of opportunity to inspect should be an important factor. Otherwise, an independent courier delivering computer disks in a sealed packet would be a recipient.

The importance of the meaning of recipient is that details of recipients or categories of recipients are amongst the information to be given to the data subject.

The data subject's consent

Where required, the data subject's consent must be "any freely given specific and informed indication of his wishes by which the data subject signifies his agreement to personal data relating to him being processed". There is no explicit requirement for the data subject's consent under the 1984 Act.

Supervisory Authority

The supervisory authority is, by Article 28, the public authority (or authorities) responsible for monitoring the application within its territory of the provisions adopted in pursuance of the Directive. The equivalent under the 1984 Act is the Office of the Data Protection Registrar.

Legal Analysis

Now that the basic definitions have been considered, an analysis of the main provisions of the Directive can be undertaken. The remainder of this chapter concentrates on an explanation of the legal framework postulated in the Directive. To this end, the following key aspects are examined individually:

— notification of processing;

— processing;

— security of processing;

— informing data subjects;

— data subjects' consent;

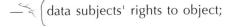
— data subjects' rights to object;

— automated individual decisions;

— transfer of data to third countries;

— manual processing;

— subject access;

— exemptions and derogations;

— supervisory authority.

Notification of Processing

Under the Data Protection Act 1984, all data users holding personal data and computer bureaux processing personal data for, or providing equipment to, such data users must register. Although the Registrar has argued for a reduction in the numbers of data users who should register, it has been held by the Divisional Court of the Queen's Bench

Division that even an accountant using a simple computer spreadsheet to prepare his client's accounts must register; *Data Protection Registrar v Griffin*[1]. However, the Directive is more liberal in this respect and, by Article 18(2), Member States may provide for simplification of or exemption from the notification requirements where the rights and freedoms of data subjects are unlikely to be affected adversely. Public registers, such as the electoral roll, may also be exempted from registration.

In the United Kingdom, the opportunity to allow full exemption from registration is likely to result in the equivalent of a "block exemption" for those data users engaging in the automatic processing of non-sensitive data. Some or all manual processing is also likely to be exempted from formal registration. Article 8 gives a clue as to the type of data in respect of which notification of processing will probably be required. Described as special categories of data, they are personal data revealing racial or ethnic origin, political opinions, religious and philosophical beliefs, trade union membership, and the processing of data concerning health or sex life. The Directive treats such data differently because they are "capable by their nature of infringing fundamental freedoms or privacy"[2]. Many organisations are likely to be exempt from registration, reducing the number of registrations to approximately one-third of its present size[3]. The types of organisations likely to benefit should include a large proportion of small retail shops, newsagents, small manufacturing businesses, small firms and self-employed persons.

Article 8(4) allows for further possibility for simplification of, or exemption from, notification in the case of the processing of sensitive data in the course of their legitimate activities, with appropriate guarantees, by foundations, associations and other non-profit-seeking bodies. A condition is that the processing must relate solely to the members of the body or persons having regular contact with it in connection with its purpose and that the data are not disclosed to third parties without the consent of the relevant data subjects. This should permit exemption from registration for charities and trade unions and would permit them to process personal data relating to, for example, workers for a charity, members of the trade union or subscribers to the body. If the body wished to disclose such data or process data relating to other persons, it will be outside any possible exemption or simplified registration procedure and should apply for registration in the normal manner, bearing in mind that the processing envisaged will have to be

---

1   (unreported) 22 February 1993.
2   Recital 33.
3   Data Protection Registrar, *Fifth Report of the Data Protection Registrar*, HMSO, 1989, Part B, p78.

within Article 8(2) which states the situations where sensitive data may be processed. The processing must also comply with Article 6 which states the "data quality principles" and Article 7 which gives the criteria for legitimate data processing.

Computer bureaux (not being controllers in their own right) are not within the notification requirements of the Directive and will not have to register. There are, however, provisions for contractual guarantees of security that will apply, *inter alia*, to such organisations.

The reduction in the number of registrations could, depending on what happens to the annual budget of the Office of the Data Protection Registrar, allow the Registrar to devote more resources to policing data protection law[1].

Those persons and organisations required to register will have to provide information similar to that required under the 1984 Act though there are some important differences. No longer is the source of the data to be notified (though this is balanced by requirements to notify the data subject when data that have not been collected from him are recorded or are about to be disclosed to a third party) but there is a requirement to give a description of the measures taken by the data user in respect of the security of data. This particular provision already has caused serious concern amongst existing data users who are fearful that their security measures would be compromised by giving such information. However, there has been a softening of the wording and Article 19 of the 1995 text requires "a general description allowing a preliminary assessment to be made of the appropriateness of the measures taken pursuant to Article 17 [Security of Processing] to ensure security of processing"[2]. This should permit a fairly general statement to be made confirming matters such as physical security of computer equipment and the adoption and monitoring of a security policy. This should include the use of audit trails, secure and regularly changed passwords and effective virus checking. The implementation of such a policy is no more than good information technology management practice and carries with it associated benefits. From the controller's point of view, the important point is that a detailed and explicit description of his security measures will not be required to be divulged to the Registrar.

---

1   The budget of the Office of the Data Protection Registrar is provided through the Home Office and is not inexorably linked to registration fee income.
2   This phrase represents a significant softening of approach compared to earlier versions of the Directive.

The Registrar is to keep a register open for public inspection containing all the above information with the exception of the description of security measures; Article 21(2). Thus, even though only a general description is required, the public will not have access to it.

Those persons and organisations exempt from registration will not find themselves free from *all* obligations associated with notification. Article 21(3) requires controllers that are exempt from notification to provide information equivalent to that provided to the Registrar to any person on request, with the exception of a description of security measures taken. The controller will be advised to prepare such a statement in advance though most are unlikely ever to be asked for a sight of it. However, in this way, the principle of openness of processing activity is maintained, theoretically at any rate.

An alternative route to simplification of, or exemption from notification is for the controller to appoint a personal data protection official who will be responsible for ensuring, in an independent manner, compliance with the national provisions implementing the Directive and keeping a register of processing operations such as that made available for public inspection by the Registrar. This provision could permit even more exemption from notification because it is by the appointment of such a person that rights and freedoms of data subjects are unlikely to be adversely affected; or so Article 18(2) suggests. In reality, this is unlikely to provide the necessary guarantees and it is artificial to consider a person who is being paid by the data user being able to operate in an independent manner. The alternative of appointing persons such as civil servants to fulfil such a role is unthinkable and unworkable. On balance, it is unlikely that the United Kingdom will adopt this approach except, perhaps, in the public sector

Whether or not data falls within the meaning of sensitive personal data as defined in Article 8, processing personal data can pose specific risks to the rights and freedoms of data subjects. For example, a person might be denied a job on the basis of his previous employment record, having been made redundant a number of times. By Article 20, Member States are to determine what processing operations are likely to present such risks and, before processing can take place, it must be examined by the controller or by the data protection official[1]. Such prior checking will be carried out following receipt of notification (from the data user or data protection official, if there is one). Checking of processing may also be required as regards specified forms of processing as a result of

---

1   In cases of doubt, the data protection official must consult the supervisory authority; article 20(2).

legislative action. For example, a statutory instrument may be made under the implementing legislation which requires checking of particular types of processing or the processing of particular types of data[1].

The Directive is silent on what should be done if prior checking causes concern. The supervisory authority will be given no explicit power to reject an application for notification on that basis alone and will not have a discretion in such a matter. The question of acceptance or rejection of an application for notification must be based on the relevant provisions such as those relating to data quality and the legitimacy of processing under the framework of data protection law under the Directive. Prior checking simply gives the supervisory authority an opportunity to gain a deeper insight into the proposed processing so that it is able to take a better informed decision as to whether it complies in all other respects. The way Article 20 is likely to be dealt with in the United Kingdom is to give the Home Secretary the power to make regulations in the future if certain forms of processing give rise for concern. The government has expressed concern about prior checking proving to be a hindrance to processing activities and it has stated that it intends to apply the requirement for prior checking only where there is a "clear and real risk". Furthermore, the role of the supervisory authority in respect of prior checking is likely to be limited to giving an opinion rather than the power to authorise such processing[2].

Possible areas where prior checking might be appropriate, notwithstanding that it is unlikely to be required in the United Kingdom in the near future on a significant scale, could be in terms of:

—   the disclosure of "white" data - that is, data showing that the data subject is a good credit risk;

—   incurred life databases, as might be used by insurance companies (information about diseases and illnesses that may make an individual a bad risk in terms of life assurance);

—   lifestyle databases, containing a profile of individuals buying, holiday, travel and other preferences, etc.

Processing

Constraints and restrictions on the processing of personal data are of fundamental importance to data users. Under the 1984 Act, the data protection principles are the touchstone for determining acceptable

---

1   A possible example might be the processing of personal data relating to AIDS or HIV.
2   Home Office, *Consultation Paper on the EC Data Protection Directive*, 1996 p36.

processing. Once registered, the data user will be unencumbered in his processing providing it is within the terms of the registration and does not contravene any of the principles. Enforcement is by way of criminal offences and notices served by the Registrar. Thus, from the data user's point of view, once registered, there is very little constraint in terms of processing providing he does not divert from his stated parameters.

The Directive contains data quality principles in Article 6 which, as far as they go, are broadly equivalent to those in the 1984 Act (Schedule 1), also being derived from the Council of Europe's Convention on Data Protection. Article 6 requires that personal data must be:

— processed fairly and lawfully;

— collected for specified, explicit and legitimate purposes and not further processed in a way incompatible with those purposes (however, further processing of data for historical, statistical or scientific purposes shall not be considered incompatible provided Member States provide appropriate safeguards);

— adequate, relevant and not excessive in relation to the purposes for which the data are collected and/or further processed;

— accurate and, where necessary, kept up to date; every reasonable step must be taken to ensure that data which are inaccurate or incomplete, having regard to the purposes for which they were collected or for which they are further processed, are erased or rectified;

— kept in a form which permits identification of data subjects for no longer than necessary for the purposes for which the data were collected or for which they are further processed. Member States shall lay down appropriate safeguards for personal data stored for longer periods for historical, statistical or scientific use.

The controller is charged with the responsibility of ensuring that the data quality principles are complied with. The remaining principles in the Data Protection Act 1984 find their equivalent in separate provisions in the Directive. So far so good. However, there are also a number of express provisions dealing with situations when data may or may not be processed and, if processing is to be allowed, the conditions that apply. Thus, at first sight, the Directive appears to contain a veritable minefield of restrictions which are themselves aggravated by the wider definition of "processing" as noted above.

Worried data users need look no further than Article 7 to realise their worst fears. It has the appearance of being very restrictive as to when processing of personal data can be carried out. Personal data may be processed only if:

(a)   the data subject has given his consent unambiguously;

(b)   processing is necessary for the performance of a contract to which the data subject is party or in order to take steps at the request of the data subject prior to entering into a contract;

(c)   processing is necessary for compliance with a legal obligation to which the controller is subject;

(d)   processing is necessary in order to protect the vital interests of the data subject;

(e)   processing is necessary for the performance of a task carried out in the public interest or in the exercise of official authority vested in the controller or in a third party to whom the data are disclosed; or

(f)   processing is necessary for the purposes of the legitimate interests pursued by the controller or by the third party or parties to whom the data are disclosed, except where such interests are overridden by the interests or fundamental rights and freedoms of the data subject which require protection under Article 1(1).

Appearances can be deceptive and it must be noted at once that the conditions in the above list are alternatives. For a particular processing operation, the controller has to comply with one only. In the vast majority of cases, controllers will be able to rely on (b) to (f) and will not require the consent of each and every data subject whose personal data are to be processed.

That Article 7 suggests that there may be circumstances in which the data subject's consent will be required is misleading and it is difficult to envisage situations where one of the conditions in (b) to (f) does not apply. However, all of these alternatives to seeking and obtaining the consent of data subjects are expressed as being "necessary". It is entirely reasonable to expect that the word "necessary" will not be interpreted in a strong sense and there is a helpful authority in favour of taking such a word in a weak sense which will benefit controllers. In

Amp Inc v Utilux Pty Ltd[1], a registered design case, the House of Lords took the view that the word "dictated" should not be interpreted in a strong sense otherwise the particular statutory provision would be reduced "almost to vanishing point". Thus, "necessary" should be taken to mean "reasonably necessary" despite the apparent contradiction of terms[2]. Any stronger meaning would be a nonsense and would result in the imposition of tremendous administrative and financial burdens on almost all controllers. Imagine the cost to banking or health services if all their data subjects had to be asked to consent to the processing of personal data relating to them, presumably periodically[3]. The Department of Health estimated that the cost of informing each member of the United Kingdom's population that their data are being processed and obtaining their written consent would be in excess of £1bn[4]!

Sensitive data

Subject to some exceptions, Article 8 of the Directive prohibits the processing of "sensitive data" which is described as data revealing racial or ethnic origin, political opinions, religious or philosophical beliefs, trade union membership or where the processing concerns health or sex life. The exceptions to the prohibition are given by Article 8(2) being where:

(a)   the data subject has given his explicit consent[5];

(b)   processing is necessary for employment law obligations and rights of the data user;

(c)   processing is necessary to protect the vital interests of the data subject or another where the data subject is physically or legally incapable of giving consent;

(d)   processing is carried out in the course of its legitimate activities with appropriate guarantees by a foundation, association or any other non-profit-seeking body with a political, philosophical,

---

1   [1972] RPC 103.
2   The same can be said for the use of the word in sections 50A to 50C of the Copyright, Designs and Patents Act 1988, concerning permitted acts in relation to computer programs, also the result of an EC Directive.
3   By Article 2(h), it would appear that nothing less than express and informed consent would do.
4   Department of Health, *Draft EC proposed Directive on Data Protection: Analysis of costs*, 1994.
5   Subject to national laws to the contrary.

religious or trade union aim[1] on condition that the processing relates solely to the members of the body or persons having regular contact in connection with its purposes and the data are not disclosed to a third party without the consent of the data subjects; or

(e)   the processing relates to data that are manifestly made public by the data subject or is necessary for the establishment, exercise or defence of legal claims.

An example of (b) is where an employer is required by law to make official returns, say specifying the number of disabled persons working for him. Exception (c) will be relevant in situations such as where the data subject is the unconscious victim of an accident in need of a blood transfusion or where he is a minor or insane. Whilst (d) and the first part of (e) are self-explanatory, the second limb of (e) could be important, primarily in the legal process of discovery. It would allow the disclosure of, for example, details of comparative earners to assist in quantifying damages for loss of earnings resulting from personal injury caused by an employer's negligence[2], and details of a data subject's past medical treatment where the data subject is suing the controller for personal injury. Data protection law should not be an instrument used to distort or interfere with the legal process.

Further exceptions allowing the processing of sensitive data are contained in the remainder of Article 8. Paragraph 3 allows processing for health purposes, being preventative medicine, medical diagnosis, the provision of care or treatment or the management of health care services. It is stated that an obligation equivalent to existing obligations of secrecy will apply to such processing, though it would anyway in the United Kingdom under the law of breach of confidence. By Article 8(4), Member States may lay down additional exemptions based on substantial public interest, subject to suitable safeguards. Recital 34 gives a clue as to what might be covered by this public interest exemption, being processing for purposes associated with public health and social protection, especially in order to ensure the quality and cost-effectiveness of the procedures used for settling claims for benefits and services in the health insurance system, scientific research and government statistics. The possibility of exemption for national

---

1   By recital 33, it would seem that the organisations intended are those whose purpose is to permit the exercise of the fundamental freedoms of data subjects. This may exclude some charities.

2   An argument that disclosure of such information was not permitted under the Data Protection Act 1984 failed in *Rowley v Liverpool City Council* (unreported) 26 October 1989, Court of Appeal.

insurance and DSS purposes seems to be a foregone conclusion. Whether an AIDS register would be seen as important for public health and social protection is another matter.

Article 8(5) permits processing of personal data relating to "offences, criminal convictions or security measures" only by or under the control of official authority, for example, the Home Office. The type of data included are not restricted to convictions and could include information about persons suspected of committing offences or persons cautioned for an offence. However, derogation is permitted subject to suitable safeguards and this possibility is most likely to be seized by the United Kingdom. Thus information about convictions can be kept by organisations concerned about detecting potential frauds such as banks and insurance companies (an insurance company would be pleased to know that a claimant for fire damage has previous convictions for arson, especially if the proposer failed to disclose this information). It should be noted, however, that a complete register of criminal convictions can only be kept under the control of official authority and there is no provision for derogation from this provision[1].

Article 8(6) allows Member States to require that data relating to administrative sanctions or civil judgments shall also be processed under the control of official authority[2]. It would appear that processing by others of such data will be allowed if otherwise complying with the provisions in the Directive. Thus, organisations giving loans or other forms of credit should be able to keep records of data concerning, for example, county court judgments against debtors. This should be deemed to be necessary to the legitimate interests of such organisations as, without such data, they would be very vulnerable to those who have a record of defaulting on loans[3].

Although the description of what can be sensitive data in Article 8(1) appears to be exhaustive, it cannot be so because of the later inclusion of data relating to offences, criminal convictions and civil judgments, etc. The acid test can be deduced from recital 33, being data that are capable by their nature of infringing fundamental freedoms or privacy of data subjects. This clearly can include criminal convictions and civil judgments although it should be noted that, in most cases, this information is publicly available anyway and may be published in newspapers. In only a small number of cases are there any restrictions

---

1   Note that this provision does not extend to offences or security measures.
2   The government does not intend to introduce any such requirement; Home Office, *Consultation Paper on the EC Data Protection Directive*, 1996 p28.
3   Credit giving organisations already share "black data" (concerning debtors who have defaulted for over three months) and "grey data" (debtors with defaults of up to three months).

upon reporting (for example, where a child under the age of 18 is being prosecuted for a criminal offence or in a rape case). The principle of open justice requires that fair use should be made of information relating to convictions and court judgments by organisations and persons likely to be affected by them in the ordinary course of their business[1].

Article 8(7) requires Member States to determine the conditions under which a national identification number or other identifier of general application may be processed. This would seem not to apply in relation to numbers presently in use in the United Kingdom that come close to being the equivalent of such an identifier, for example, NHS numbers, driving licence numbers, national insurance numbers, passport numbers. The reason is that these numbers are not of general application, they are used for specific purposes even though they may be used occasionally as a means of identification. If a national identification number is adopted in the United Kingdom, then there would have to be legislation laying down the conditions under which the number could be processed. It may be that processing would be restricted to authorities such as police forces, central and local government, hospitals, the armed forces, etc.

Security of processing

Security is dealt with by Article 17 of the Directive which requires the implementation of appropriate technical and organisational measures to protect personal data from accidental or unlawful destruction or accidental loss, alteration, unauthorised disclosure or access and all other forms of unlawful processing. The transmission of data over networks is singled out as a particular area of concern.

The controller must take measures commensurate with the risks represented by processing and the nature of the data having regard to the state of the art and the cost of implementation. Therefore, a balance is to be struck between the seriousness of the consequences of a failure in security and the costs involved. It is a shifting balance and higher standards of security will be expected as improvements in the appropriate technology are made. As manual processing of paper files containing personal data is within the scope of the Directive, security is not limited to physical security of computer equipment[2] and software

---

1   Notwithstanding the Rehabilitation of Offenders Act 1974.
2   Following a number of thefts of computers from doctors' surgeries the Data Protection Registrar warned general practitioners to review their security arrangements otherwise they could be in breach of the eighth principle under the current legislation; The Times, 2 December 1992 p3.

security techniques but will extend to effective physical security for paper files and to limiting access to such files to appropriate persons.

In most other respects the requirements under the Directive should equate to those in the eighth data protection principle which calls for "appropriate security measures". However, particular concern is shown over the relationship between the controller and the processor (being a person or an organisation processing data on behalf of the controller such as a computer bureau) requiring, by Article 17(2) that the controller chooses a processor that can "guarantee" security. "Processor" is widely defined and could include not only computer bureaux but also sub-contractors and agents. Even a sub-contractor engaged to destroy computer print-out is a processor. The same applies to organisations providing back up services (for example, keeping up to date copies of all the controller's software for disaster recovery).

The arrangement between the controller and the processor must be contractual in nature or governed by some other legal act; Article 17(3). The relevant parts of the contract or legal act dealing with security measures must be in writing or some other equivalent form; Article 17(4). It is not clear what the "other equivalent form" means - perhaps in software form. However, in the UK, the term "writing" is given a wide meaning; see, for example, the definition in Schedule 1 of the Interpretation Act 1978 - "'Writing' includes typing, printing, lithography, photography and other modes of representing or reproducing words in a visible form, and expressions referring to writing are construed accordingly". Lawyers drafting agreements between controllers and computer bureaux or other sub-contractors or agents must include an appropriate term and precedents should be modified accordingly.

The obligation to obtain security guarantees requires positive security measures to be taken by processors. Computer bureaux are at present subject to the eighth data protection principle and this should not make any significant difference for them. The controller should obtain an indemnity against any legal action arising through breaches in security. This is required by Article 17(3) which states that the security obligations shall be stipulated by the contract to be incumbent on the processor. The justification for such an approach is that computer bureaux will no longer be required to notify their activities to the Registrar. This may be particularly important where the processor is established in a different country to the controller. In the United Kingdom, the law of confidence would impose appropriate obligations on processors in most cases; the advantage of making the obligations explicit is that it brings them to the fore and encourages the parties to fully address security issues. It also reinforces the protection afforded by the law of confidence.

Informing data subjects

The Directive specifies two particular occasions when the controller must provide information to the data subject. This onerous duty is substantially ameliorated because in neither case need the information be given if the data subject is already in possession of it. The first situation where a data subject must be informed is on collection of personal data; Article 10. The data subject must be informed of:

(a)   the identity of the controller (and his representative, if any); and

(b)   the purpose or purposes of the processing for which the data are intended.

Further information must also be provided if necessary in the specific circumstances to guarantee fair processing in respect of the data subject. By Article 10(c) such further information includes:

—   the recipients or categories of recipients of the data;

—   whether replies to questions are obligatory or voluntary and the possible consequences of failure to reply; and

—   the existence of the data subject's right of access to and the right to rectify the data concerning him.

The second case where the data subject must be informed is where the data have not been obtained from the data subject. He must be informed, by Article 11, at the time the data are recorded or, if disclosure to a third party is envisaged, no later than the time when the data are first disclosed, as to:

(a)   the identity of the controller (and representative, if any);

(b)   the purpose or purposes of processing.

Also, if necessary having regard to the specific circumstances to guarantee fair processing in relation to the data subject, Article 11(1)(c) requires further information to be given such as:

—   the categories of data concerned;

— the recipients or categories of recipients; and

— the existence of the data subject's right of access to and the right to rectify the data concerning him.

By Article 11(2) there is an exception from the duty to inform the data subject on recording or disclosure, in particular for processing for statistical purposes or for historical or scientific research where the provision of the required information would prove impossible or would require a disproportionate effort or if the recording or disclosure is expressly provided for by law. Member States are required to provide appropriate safeguards. The exception is not restricted to statistical or research purposes but clearly should be fairly limited. Where the exception applies, recital 40 states that factors to be taken into account are the number of data subjects affected, the age of the data and any compensatory measures adopted. It is not clear how disproportionality of effort will be measured. Apart from the factors in recital 40, it could be based on difficulty or expense or both. An example might be where the data are not sensitive and some of the data subjects are difficult to trace having moved house or emigrated, although in such cases, there could be a breach of the data quality principles as the data are now, presumably, inaccurate.

It is important to note that Article 11 requires that the *identity* of the controller is made known to the data subject, not simply information as to categories of controllers. This would appear to require the provision of information specifically identifying the controller such as "... personal data relating to you is to be disclosed to the Mammoth Trading Company plc". Where data which have not been obtained from the data subject are recorded or to be disclosed to a third party and the new controller is a member of a group of companies or a department in a local authority, for example, giving information on original collection under Article 10 may suffice. In such cases, the inclusion of a statement such as "... personal data relating to you may be disclosed to other companies within the Acme group of companies [or other departments of Rutland County Council] and may be recorded and processed by such other companies [departments]".

In all other cases, unless the limited exception applies, controllers collecting data from subjects should identify subsequent controllers who will record the data or to whom the data are disclosed otherwise, this information must be provided under Article 11 and, in many circumstances, this may involve a separate mailing. It should also be noted that Article 11 applies when data that have been collected from the data subject directly by one controller are subsequently disclosed to another controller. This is made clear by recital 39. Controllers trading lists of data subjects will have to give careful thought as to how the provision of the relevant information under Article 11 can be made. For example, a controller selling a list of data subjects should have informed the data subjects accordingly and the controller buying the data should confirm that this is done and, perhaps, consider the insertion of an appropriate warranty or indemnity in the agreement under which the list trading takes place.

Consider a controller, X, who wishes to obtain personal data relating to data subjects A, B and C, perhaps for his own purposes but also with a view to giving or selling a copy of the data to controller Y who intends to use it for his own purposes which do not include disclosure to others or marketing by mail[1].

If controller X collects the data direct from A, B and C, he must inform them in accordance with Article 10. In the circumstances, the information should include a description of the recipient, controller Y without necessarily identifying him. Although the Directive does not state so expressly, this information should be given at the time of collection on the basis of the first data quality principle that the personal data must be obtained *fairly* and lawfully. When controller Y obtains the copy of the data, by Article 11, he will have to tell A, B and C that he is recording their personal data, unless the information given by data user X specifically mentions disclosure to Y and Y's purpose in processing that data. Where the purpose is marketing by mail, the situation is more complex and is described later.

These provisions apply only where the data subject does not already have the relevant information. Certainly, in many situations, it should be a simple matter to give the information as a note contained in or appended to a document used to regulate or formalise the arrangement between the data user and the data subject. For example, an appropriate note could be printed on the bottom of a form of contract, application form or order form. Fairly generalised statements should suffice as the Directive allows the information to describe categories of recipients and data rather than precise details. However, as noted above, it may be in the interests of recipients of the data that more precise information is given, otherwise they could find themselves having to furnish the data subjects with such information.

Article 13 contains a list of exemptions and restrictions (including national and public security, defence, in relation to criminal offences

---

1   Further controls apply if it is intended to use the data for marketing by mail.

and tax) which apply to Articles 10 and 11 and other provisions such as those relating to subject access under Article 12. The exemptions and restrictions are discussed later.

It may be difficult to predict the situations when a controller will be excused giving the further information referred to Article 10(c) and 11(1)(c). By continuing to raise public awareness through publicity drives the Office of the Data Protection Registrar could eliminate the need to inform the data subject of his rights of access and rectification. As far as other information is concerned, the guiding principle is fairness of processing and this should be attained through a policy of openness. If there is any doubt as to whether the data subject should be given further information, it is surely better to give that information. There should be very good reasons for not giving further information such that the controller would feel confident about defending his position if it was argued that failure to give it was unfair to the data subject. Factors such as cost and effort will not suffice except where covered by Article 11(2) - such as processing for statistical purposes or historical or scientific research where impossibility or disproportionality of effort are factors[1]. If the data user has something to hide, the chances are it will be unfair to the data subject.

Data subjects' consent

Article 7 allows processing of personal data only if one of a list of criteria are satisfied. The first is that the data subject has given his unambiguous consent, which by the definition of data subject's consent, must be a freely given specific and informed indication of his agreement. The cost of seeking such consent from existing data subjects would be prohibitive for many organisations. The situation may not be particularly onerous in terms of "new" data subjects as consent can be obtained in many cases simply by asking the data subject to read a description of the processing activities and recording his assent by means of signing a form. The Directive is silent on whether a once and for all assent will suffice or whether the data subject should be asked periodically. Factors to take into account would include the test of fairness and, of course, whether the controller intends to use the personal data for new uses which the data subject has not specifically agreed to.

The requirement of consent under Article 7(a) should be applicable only in very rare cases as one or more of the other criteria (b) to (f) usually

---

1   Not only in respect of further information but in terms of the basic information to be given to the data subject.

will apply, as discussed earlier. It is not an easy matter to think of any processing activities which are fair and lawful but which are outside paragraphs (b) to (f) of Article 7 and not otherwise permitted by Article 8[1].

A possible example might be list trading for commercial gain. However, this is by no means certain as it could be deemed to fall within the legitimate interests of the controller. The reader is left to ponder whether a retail organisation whose main business is selling goods and offering credit facilities which decides to sell a list of its customers to another commercial organisation such as a package holiday company is acting within its legitimate interests. If it is, what about a hospital that decides to sell data relating to patients with walking difficulties to a company selling walking sticks? What about a charity selling details of donees to another charity or to a business organisation?

There are other situations where consent to processing is required. One is in respect of the exemptions to the general prohibition over processing of sensitive personal data. Such processing is permitted if the data subject has given his explicit consent by Article 8(2)(a), providing national law does not permit the data subject's consent to negate the general prohibition. Processing by non-profit-seeking bodies only requires the consent of data subjects if the data are to be disclosed to a third party; Article 8(2)(d).

Article 26 contains a further example. The data subject's unambiguous consent[2] is required in respect of transfers of personal data to a third country (that is, a country outside the European Community) which does not ensure adequate levels of protection. However, there are other criteria allowing transfer without the data subject's consent, for example, where it is a necessary part of fulfilling a contract with the data subject.

Data subjects' rights to object

In a number of instances, the data subject is given a right to object to the processing of his personal data. It must be said at once, however, that the data subject does not have a blanket right to prevent processing of his data under any circumstances. The rights to object are not as extensive as that.

---

1   By Article 6(1)(a) personal data must be processed fairly and lawfully.
2   It is unfortunate that the Directive is not consistent in its language. The data subject's consent may be explicit (Article 8(2)(a)), unambiguous (Articles 7(a) and 26(1)(a)) or just plain consent (Article 8(2)(d)). However, all should be read with the definition of data subject's consent in Article 1.

Considering the volume of "junk mail" received by most of us in the United Kingdom, arguably, the most important occasion when a data subject has a right to object is in relation to direct marketing. This right is provided for by Article 14(b) and would appear not to be limited to such marketing by mail[1]. It could apply also to direct marketing by "cold calling" by telephone, for example.

The 1992 proposal for the Directive was very restrictive in this respect and would have had serious consequences for this form of advertising and selling. Each time personal data were to be disclosed to third parties for marketing by mail purposes, the data subject would have had to be informed and offered the opportunity to have his data blocked[2]. If Company A wished to sell its list of customers to Company B, Company A would have to inform all the data subjects, giving them the right to have their data blocked free of charge. Company B, who would now become a controller, would have to inform the data subjects that it now held their data and also, as a potential junk mailer, give them the right to have their data blocked. In effect, the data subject would be told in advance that he was about to receive some junk mail but he could prevent this by submitting a request to have his data blocked. Bearing in mind the right of blocking was to be free of charge, it is unlikely that many would not have taken the opportunity to have their data blocked. This could have sounded the death knell of the direct marketing industry which is particularly active in the United Kingdom compared to other EC Member States[3].

The Directive has addressed this problem (although not many sympathise with junk mail or cold calling telephone marketing) and Article 14(b) contains a curious but important option. The data subject has the right:

— to object on request and free of charge to the processing of his personal data which the data user anticipates will be used for direct marketing; or

— to be informed before his data are disclosed for the first time to a third party for the purposes of direct marketing and to be

---

1   The 1992 text was limited to marketing by mail, OJ C311 27.11.92 p30, Article 15(b).
2   The 1992 text used the term "blocking". Presumably this meant that a person's data would not have to be erased as such from a database but would have to be flagged in such a way that it would not be used in a mailshot.
3   Even so, the provisions of Articles 10 and 11 must still be complied with and this may require, at least, informing the data subject before the data are disclosed for direct marketing purposes.

expressly offered the right to object free of charge to such disclosures or use.

These are alternatives and, crucially, Member States are charged with the duty of taking necessary measures to make data subjects aware of their right under the first alternative. Therefore, the controller will not have to inform the data subject if his awareness of the existence of the right has been achieved by appropriate measures. This may be realised by appropriate publicity, for example, by raising awareness of the existing mailing preference scheme under which data subjects can apply to have their names removed from mailing lists. This change in the text of the Directive represents something of a victory for the direct marketing industry. An equivalent scheme will be required for other forms of direct marketing, for example by telephone. Most people will rejoice in the opportunity to object to this latter intrusive method of marketing[1].

Article 14(a) gives data subjects the right to object to the processing of their personal data on "compelling legitimate grounds relating to his particular situation", at least where the processing is carried out under the criteria contained in Article 7(e) or (f) (public interest processing or necessary for the legitimate interests of the controller) "save where otherwise provided by national legislation". Article 14(a) goes on to say that processing may no longer involve the data subject's data if the objection is justified. The word "compelling" is a late addition to the text as is the requirement that the objection be justified. There are a number of difficulties with this provision. Apart from wondering what "compelling legitimate grounds" are, this begs the question "justified by whom"? The controller, data subject or the supervisory authority?

This provision could have a number of meanings, arguably the two most plausible being as follows:

— the data subject can object if he can show that he has a really good reason for not wanting his data processed although such processing is otherwise lawful, regardless of whether the processing is in the public interest or necessary for the legitimate interests of the data user; or

---

1   A proposal for a Directive for the protection of personal data in the context of telecommunications networks may give control over unsolicited calls by means of an opt out. Its full title is "Amended proposal for a European Parliament and Council Directive concerning the protection of personal data and privacy in the context of digital telecommunications networks, in particular the Integrated Services Digital Network (ISDN) and digital mobile networks", COM(94) 128 final COD 288, OJ C200 22.7.94 p4.

— the data subject can object only if the processing is shown to be unlawful, whether on the basis of the provisions of data protection law or otherwise.

Much depends on the meaning of "legitimate" - does it mean "lawful" or does it mean "justifiable" or "logically admissible"[1]. As we are dealing with legal provisions, it would seem reasonable to suppose that objecting on "legitimate grounds" must mean when the processing envisaged is contrary to the provisions of the Directive and not simply because the data subject does not want his data processed. But, if this is so, the best and most effective approach would be to alert the Data Protection Registrar who could bring his enforcement powers to bear[2].

The recitals do not help in understanding the meaning or purpose of Article 14(a). Recital 45 is expressed in very similar wording. It is submitted that this provision is just so much gobbledygook. The former of the meanings above would be impossible to legislate for in a satisfactory or predictable manner and the latter is simply unnecessary. If it was intended to give data subjects carte blanche to object to the processing of their data, it could have done so in much simpler language so, obviously, this was not the intention. The saving grace is that the Directive allows Member States to provide otherwise by national legislation. It is possible that the United Kingdom will provide otherwise by choosing to ignore Article 14(a)[3].

The government has indicated that it has no wish to extend the provision beyond processing under Article 7(e) or (f) and admits to having no experience of situations where the provision could be invoked by the data subject. One example given is where the data are to be disclosed to a person known to the data subject[4].

Automated individual decisions

Computers may be used to assist in decision making in a number of ways; for example, simply by providing the decision maker with more and superior information and, secondly by suggesting appropriate action or solutions. Of more concern is where the computer is used to make a decision which will be acted upon unquestionably by the operator. The computer has transcended the divide between assisting decision making to taking decisions. A computer database may contain

---

1   All of these meanings, and more, are in the Oxford Concise Dictionary.
2   The data subject's rights of access give a right to rectification, erasure or blocking of data only if the data are incomplete or inaccurate, Article 12.
3   Is it possible to "provide otherwise" by omission?
4   Home Office, *Consultation Paper on the EC Data Protection Directive*, 1996 p30.

a number of factors relating to individuals which are used in an automatic analysis to determine whether particular individuals should be granted or refused credit. The factors might concern past records of individuals' bank accounts, previous debts and records of payment, postcode, income, etc. The Directive aims to strictly control such automated decision making precisely because of the dangers that it could pose. For example, persons with a particular postal address could be refused credit not because they themselves have a history of bad debt but because, on average, persons living in that area are more likely to default on loan payments than is the case with other areas.

Article 15 seeks to control automated decisions. Paragraph 1 effectively prohibits such automated decision making by granting to a data subject a right not to be subject to a decision which produces legal effects or significantly affects him and which is based solely on automated processing of data intended to evaluate certain of their personal aspects such as performance at work, creditworthiness, reliability and conduct, etc. The list of personal aspects is not exhaustive and the recitals give no further clue. In view of the examples given, it is reasonable to suppose that it is limited to aspects related to the data subject's likely future behaviour or propensities.

To be caught, the decision must be based *solely* on automated decision-making. If there is some human input into the decision-making process, the prohibition does not apply although it is likely that the word solely is not used in a strong sense. Simply getting the computer operator to rubber stamp the decision probably would not be sufficient to avoid the provision. It is submitted that a more than trivial contribution to the decision must be made by a person who has some discretion to query or overrule the decision.

A complete ban on automated decisions would be unrealistic and, by Article 15(2) and subject to the other provisions of the Directive, it is allowed in the course of entering into or performing a contract with the data subject providing any request by the data subject has been satisfied or there are suitable measures to safeguard his legitimate interests, such as by allowing him to put his point of view. For example, Peter has asked to buy goods on credit from Bumper Stores. Before concluding the contract, the store assistant uses a computer, either personally or vicariously, by telephone, to check Peter's creditworthiness. However, the computer states that Peter is a bad credit risk and, on the basis of that automated decision, the assistant refuses to sell the goods to Peter on credit. In such a case, Peter should be allowed to put his point of view forward. This he might do in a number of ways, perhaps by claiming that the computer is wrong or by shouting obscenities at the assistant before storming out. Article 15 is silent about whether the other party has to do anything after hearing the data subject's point of view (such as verifying the correctness of the data or replying to a letter). However, the other provisions of the Directive are still available and the most appropriate steps for Peter would be to carry out a subject access request and use his powers to have the relevant data rectified or erased. However, this all takes time and expense.

Automated decisions are also allowed if authorised by law providing the data subject's legitimate interests are safeguarded. It would seem that specific legislation would be required to take advantage of this derogation unless the common law would allow the decision-making. It is not easy to think of an example although a decision about an individual made on the basis of confidential data relating to that individual might fall within the public interest defence under the law of breach of confidence. Would this allow processing, by means of an expert system using weighted criteria, of data concerning individuals' characteristics to produce a list of persons suspected of a serious crime[1]?

Present law in the United Kingdom is already able to control automated decisions within Article 15. The primary principle relating to data quality is that data should be processed fairly and lawfully[2]. Indeed, it could be claimed that this principle is all that is required in terms of data protection law as everything else flows from it, even the other principles[3]. The utility of this principle has been seen in *Equifax Europe Ltd v Data Protection Registrar*[4]. In that case, credit reference agencies were determining credit-worthiness on the basis of, *inter alia*, the applicant's address. If a previous occupant was a bad credit risk, this would count against the present applicant even though he may not have had any connection with the previous occupant - the stigma of risk of default attached to the property thereby affecting future occupants. The Tribunal agreed with the Registrar that such decision-making, being based on data relating to third parties, was unfair even

---

1   There must be measures to safeguard the data subject's legitimate interests. Thus, a conviction based on an automated decision only is unthinkable. (Such evidence is extremely unlikely to be admissible because its prejudicial effect would considerably outweigh its probative value.)
2   First Data Protection Principle, Schedule 1 to the Data Protection Act 1984 and Article 6(1)(a) of the Directive.
3   Of course, it would be very unsatisfactory to leave things there. Differences in judicial interpretation of such a phrase could lead to a very uneven data protection law throughout the Community. The detailed provisions are required to provide a detailed and workable framework for fair and lawful processing.
4   (unreported) 28 February 1992, Data Protection Tribunal.

though the credit reference agencies argued that it was significant in a statistically predictive way[1].

As noted above, the Directive goes further in that automated decisions of the type described in Article 15 are prohibited altogether unless concerning a contract or otherwise authorised by law. Thus, automated decisions will be prohibited even if they are "fair". This can be seen as over-restrictive especially as the use of automated decision-making has the potential of increasing fairness by removing human prejudice. For example, decisions made by an automated benefits assessment system could provide a useful element of objectivity in the performance of a complicated and difficult task.

Transfer of data to third countries

Article 1(2) states the second of the twin objectives of the Directive which is the freedom of movement of personal data throughout the Community. The free movement principle is a direct consequence of having an effective data protection law in place throughout the Community. However, transfers of personal data to destinations outside the Community may present dangers to the freedoms and rights to privacy, particularly where the standard of data protection in the receiving country is poor or non-existent. Another problem is that Community-based data users may be tempted to store and process their holdings of personal data outside the Community to take advantage of lax data protection laws. Plainly, in view of the growth of computer and telecommunications networks, the transfer of data outside the Community cannot be prohibited altogether.

The basic principle is that transfer to countries outside the Community of personal data that are undergoing processing or are intended for processing after transfer[2] will be allowed only if the third country in question ensures an adequate level of protection; Article 25(1). This must be without prejudice to the provisions of the Directive. Therefore, the processing envisaged in the third country must comply with data protection law in the Member State from which the data are transferred. Article 25(2) gives an indication of the factors to be taken into account in the assessment of the adequacy of protection required in the third country being:

---

1   An agreement was reached so as to allow the use of some such data, for example, where the applicant is related to the previous occupant or there is some financial dependency between the two.

2   An example of data intended to be processed after transfer is where the data are stored on paper in an unstructured way and it is intended that, after transfer, they will be extracted and placed in structured paper files or keyed into a computer.

— the circumstances surrounding the data transfer;

— the nature of the data;

— the purpose and duration of the proposed processing;

— the country of origin and country of final destination;

— the general and sectoral rules of law in place in the third country;

— the professional rules and security measures complied with in the third country.

However, with a touch of commercial pragmatism, if the third country in question does not reach the required standards of adequacy of protection, there is the possibility of derogation. By Article 26(1), save where otherwise provided by domestic law governing particular cases, Member States *shall* provide that transfer may take place on condition that:

— the data subject has given his unambiguous consent;

— it is necessary for the performance of a contract between the data subject and the controller (or pre-contractual measures in response to the data subject's request);

— it is necessary for the conclusion or performance of a contract between the controller and a third party which has been concluded in the data subject's interests;

— it is necessary or legally required on important public interest grounds or for the establishment, exercise or defence of legal claims;

— it is necessary to protect the vital interests of the data subject; or

— it is made from a register intended to provide information to the public and which is available for inspection by the public generally or those members of the public showing a legitimate interest.

Furthermore, by Article 26(2), Member States may authorise transfer to countries not ensuring an adequate level of protection where the controller "adduces adequate safeguards with respect to the protection of the privacy and fundamental rights and freedoms of individuals and, as regards the exercise of corresponding rights, such safeguards may in particular result from appropriate contractual clauses"; Article 26(3)[1]. There is provision for the Commission to stipulate that certain standard contractual clauses offer sufficient safeguards[2]. Appropriate clauses could include prohibitions on subsequent disclosure to others by recipients in third countries; laying down minimum levels of security measures and requiring the return or verifiable destruction of the data following completion of the relevant purposes. Taking all these derogations into account, transfer to third countries should not be unduly onerous. Many countries already should be deemed to have adequate levels of security (for example, Australia and the United States) whilst, for others, transfer will be possible in many cases.

There are provisions for communication between Member States and the Commission where a third country does not ensure an adequate level of protection in respect of a particular type of data and, if necessary, the Commission may require Member States to take measures to prevent the transfer of data of the same type to the country in question[3]. This is not an absolute prohibition on the transfer of data as it will only apply to specified types of data and, in any case, the derogations in Article 26 will be available.

There are a number of issues relating to adequacy. First, it is clear that it is a variable concept, depending on the circumstances surrounding the transfer such as the nature of the data, purpose, duration etc. Thus, a third country may have an adequate level of protection for certain types of data and processing operations but not for others. Secondly, how does the controller determine adequacy? There are three possible ways:

— the controller decides on the basis of his own judgment only;

— the controller decides on the basis of guidance produced by the supervisory authority;

— prior authorisation is required from the supervisory authority.

---

1   The Commission must be informed of such authorisations.
2   In accordance with the procedure laid down in Article 31(2) - measures adopted in accordance with the opinion of a committee of representatives of Member States.
3   Articles 25(3)-(6) and Article 31.

The second is the most likely in the United Kingdom[1]. The third option would be unthinkable because of the delay and disruption it would cause bearing in mind the growing global transfer of computer data.

When the growth of telecommunications is taken into account, in particular, networks such as the Internet, it is hard to see just how effective these provisions will be in practice. Whilst it might be relatively easy to police the use of personal data by public authorities and large business organisations established within the Community, it will be much harder to control misuse of personal data by others. For example, a computer hacker might breach the security of a computer which has sensitive personal data stored on it, download that data and then place it on the Internet. What is worse is that all this might be done in a country with no satisfactory data protection laws and which is outside the jurisdiction of the courts in the Community and where there are no appropriate extradition laws. Of course, the controller must have appropriate levels of security but, however good computer security is, experience shows us that all computer systems are vulnerable.

The territorial provisions make applicable the national law of the Member State in which the controller is established and, where the controller is established in a number of Member States, he must comply with the national law applicable in each Member State; Article 4. This may cause difficulties because of variance in the use of derogations and options in different Member States. For example, a controller might be established both in the United Kingdom and Italy. Say that Italy has not taken advantage of the derogations in Article 26 but the United Kingdom has. The controller finds that he can transfer data to a third country not having an adequate level of protection from the United Kingdom but not from Italy. Of course, all the controller has to do is transfer the personal data from Italy to the United Kingdom and from there to the third country in question. By Article 1(2), the Italian implementation of the Directive cannot be used to prevent the transfer from Italy to the United Kingdom. But circumventing the Italian prohibition in this way is unsatisfactory. These provisions could make it tempting for large organisations to have an additional establishment in the Member State that has taken advantage of all the derogations in Article 26 and other provisions of the Directive. This could be a factor in Member States' approach to the derogations. Taking advantage of them might increase the number of organisations seeking to establish there.

---

1   The government favours this option; Home Office, *Consultation Paper on the EC Data Protection Directive*, 1996 p45.

Manual processing

In principle, there should be no reason why personal data stored in paper files or other traditional form (for example, a photograph) should be treated any differently to personal data stored on computers. This was the conclusion of the House of Lords select committee which looked at data protection law[1]. Although the processing power of computers is a factor, if manual files are appropriately structured, information relating to a particular individual can be retrieved very quickly. The omission of manual records from the ambit of data protection law would do nothing to encourage the greater use of information technology. In retrospect, the focus of the Data Protection Act 1984 on automatic processing was misplaced and it is possible that a number of organisations deliberately retained sensitive information on paper to avoid the provisions of the Act[2]. Individuals can have their interests, freedoms and privacy harmed or compromised just as easily by information stored on paper as by computer data.

It is important to understand what type of manual data are within the scope of the Directive. It applies to "... the processing of personal data [within the scope of Community law] wholly or partly by automatic means, and to the processing otherwise than by automatic means of personal data which form part of a filing system or are intended to form part of a filing system"; Article 3(1). A personal data filing system, being the target of control over manual processing, is "... any structured set of personal data which are accessible according to specific criteria, whether centralised, decentralised or dispersed on a functional or geographical basis"; Article 1(c).

A card index system, where each card bears an identifier relating to an individual, such as a name, national insurance number or passport photograph, will be a personal data filing system. The same can be said for a filing system where each person has his or her own distinct file or folder. The fact that the filing system is not located at a single site or if the person requiring the information accesses it vicariously (for example, by instructing a clerk by telephone to retrieve the data) does not take it out of the definition. The basic test would seem to be whether it is possible to search for the relevant personal information by means of an identifier which, because of the way the filing system is

---

1   House of Lords, *Protection of Personal Data*, Session 1992/93, 20th Report: HMSO, 1993.
2   The Economic League which kept, *inter alia,* details of persons who were members of the Communist Party or involved in industrial disputes used manual records. The application of data protection law could have been quite serious for the League.

structured, facilitates access to it[1]. It would not, for example, apply to a general correspondence file arranged in date order.

Most organisations, whether or not they also use computer technology, hold considerable amounts of data in paper files, some of which may go back for many years. Employee files are an obvious example and these may be retained long after employees leave. There may be very good reasons for this. An ex-employee may request a reference for a new job, the Inland Revenue may require information relating to earnings or the information may be important in case an employee takes legal action in respect of an industrial injury or disease. For example, an employee who worked many years ago in a factory, part of which was notorious for choking clouds of airborne dust, might have recently developed a lung disease. He will need evidence of when and for how long he worked in the appropriate part of the factory and whether others have developed similar diseases. The retention for a long period of time of such information is important for both employer and employee alike. The law on limitation of actions has provisions to extend the normal periods where, for example, the injured person has no knowledge of the injury for a period of time. The court also has a discretion to disapply the normal limitation period. Thus, a miner who contracted pneumoconiosis but whose symptoms did not appear for many years was able to sue within three years of becoming aware of the disease[2].

It is highly likely that the United Kingdom will exempt all or most types of manual records from formal registration. Notwithstanding this, personal data in manual filing systems must comply with the principles relating to data quality and with the security provisions. The principles are stated earlier in the section on processing but when applied to manual records, they could require substantial work to be done. Existing manual records will have to be checked for compliance. Controllers will have to trawl through their existing (and archived) structured files, examining each and every one, perhaps destroying some files, or documents in files and making corrections and/or deletions. This could be very time-consuming, bearing in mind that, in the past, very robust statements may have been made about individuals and placed in files. Greater awareness of information quality, data protection law, the law of breach of confidence and the law of defamation has made many organisations examine and reflect on the content of their information systems. Matters that would have been

---

1   This is confirmed by recital 27, which stresses ease of access to individuals' personal data.
2   *Cartledge v E Jopling & Sons Ltd* [1963] AC 758. See also the Limitation Act 1980, s 11.

recorded in the past without concern are now toned down or not recorded at all.

Sectors particularly likely to be affected by the application of data protection law to manual processing include insurance[1], banking, health service providers, local authorities and organisations with large numbers of employees. Not only would checking existing files involve massive effort and expense but there is also the spectre of large scale subject access to manual records. In view of these problems, the Directive allows Member States to delay the provisions relating to data quality and processing (though not in relation to subject access and other provisions) for 12 years from the data of adoption of the Directive; Article 32(2). This gives controllers until 24 October 2007 to comply though this applies only in respect of manual filing systems in existence on the date the Directive is implemented by national law, which should be 24 October 1998. Controllers would be wise to put systems into place quickly so that any new data collected or recorded in paper files complies with the provisions affecting manual processing.

Many paper filing systems are incomplete, inaccurate or simply badly organised. The Directive, by extending data protection law to manual processing, may bring significant benefits. For many organisations the Directive will provide a stimulus for a rationalisation of paper filing systems with an opportunity to discard large quantities of irrelevant and outdated information. Some controllers will take the opportunity to convert the remaining information to computer readable form. The resulting efficiency gains may well outweigh the costs involved. At present The Audit Commission concluded that the automation of manual files in the health service could result in enormous savings and benefits[2].

Subject access

Article 12 deals with subject access. The purpose of providing subject access is stated in recital 41 as being to enable the data subject to verify in particular the accuracy of the data and the lawfulness of the processing. Article 12(a) requires Member States to give data subjects, without constraint and at reasonable intervals, a right of access to the following information:

---

1   The UK insurance industry holds some 195 million personal files, most of which are manual. House of Lords, *Protection of Personal Data*, HL Paper 75, HMSO, 1993 p62.
2   Annual information handling costs in the Health Service is in the order of £2.8bn; Audit Commission, *Setting the records straight*, HMSO, 1995.

—   confirmation as to whether data relating to him are being processed, the purpose of that processing, the categories of data concerned and the recipients or categories of recipients to whom the data are disclosed;

—   communication of the data (presumably a "copy of the data" is intended) in an intelligible form and any available information as to the source of the data;

—   knowledge of the logic involved in any automatic processing of data concerning him, at least where automated decisions within Article 15(1) are involved (recital 41 states that this right must not adversely affect trade secrets or intellectual property, in particular, software copyright, but this must not mean that the data subject is refused all information. In such cases, a generalised statement should suffice).

The data subject also has a right, by Article 12(b) to have data rectified, erased or blocked if the processing is contrary to the provisions of the Directive with particular emphasis on incomplete or inaccurate data. By Article 12(c), unless it proves impossible or involves a disproportionate effort, third parties to whom such data have been disclosed should be notified. If a controller keeps a record of all disclosures this should be easy to do. A computer system containing personal data could incorporate an audit trail, recording all disclosures. In some cases, this could require the writing of additional software, the modification of existing software and/or the creation of additional fields in records of personal data and could be an expensive proposition. Article 12 does not appear to place a positive duty on controllers to keep records of disclosures and, if they do not, notification to third parties may well prove impossible or require a disproportionate effort and hence be excepted. The recitals do not help in determining whether records should be kept but keeping comprehensive records of processing is, simply, good computing practice. In most cases, it would be in the interests of the third party to be notified so that he can make the necessary erasures or corrections otherwise he is processing in a manner contrary to the Directive. In any contract governing any disclosure of personal data, the recipient would be advised to insist on the inclusion of a term requiring notification of incomplete or inaccurate data. This may be coupled with an indemnity.

The subject access provisions go a little further than present United Kingdom law which simply requires, in most cases, that a copy of the relevant personal data be given to the data subject. In spite of this, the provisions in the Directive should be easy to comply with by taking of suitable measures. It also has to be borne in mind that relatively few subject access requests are made presently under the 1984 Act. Nevertheless, there is some concern about subject access to manual files as compliance with such requests could prove to be very expensive. Extending access to manual files may result in an increase in the numbers of subject access requests. However, experience suggests otherwise. Access to data in some categories of manual files is available already under specific legislation such as the Access to Health Records Act 1990 and the Access to Personal Files Act 1987 and, in practice, these rights of access are exercised in relatively few cases. The only major exception to the generally low traffic of subject access requests is under section 158 of the Consumer Credit Act 1974 which gives access to personal data held by credit reference agencies (whether on paper or as computer data)[1]. Large numbers of subject access requests are made under this provision but this may be a reflection of the small fee of £1 and the serious consequences of a refusal of credit. This suggests that, in the United Kingdom, people are more concerned about their credit-worthiness than about their general freedoms and privacy.

One reason why the volume of subject access requests under the 1984 Act is low is that data users can charge a fee of up to £10 for providing a copy of the personal data. Many do charge the full amount probably on the grounds that the fee acts as a large disincentive[2]. The possibility of charging a fee is likely to be retained in the United Kingdom. It even may be increased slightly.

Exemptions and derogations

The Data Protection Act 1984 contains a great many complex exemptions from some or all of its provisions. In most respects, these can be continued as the Directive contains optional exemptions in Article 13 which are similar in broad terms. It seems reasonable to assume that the United Kingdom will want to take maximum advantage of these so that the present range of exemptions can be retained in much the same form.

By Article 3(2), exemption from the whole of the Directive's provisions applies where the processing is:

---

1   Section 158 does not distinguish between paper files and computer files. Of course, credit reference agencies make full use of computers to store and process personal data.
2   *A fortiori* where the data user has a number of separate registrations so that the data subject has to make a number of subject access requests (unless the data user is prepared to be helpful and suggest which is the appropriate registration for the data subject).

— in the course of an activity outside the scope of Community law;

— concerning public security, defence and State security (including the economic well-being of the State when the processing relates to State security matters);

— within the activities of the State in areas of criminal law;

— by natural persons in the course of a purely personal or household activity.

Other exemptions are contained in Article 13 but are not absolute. They apply in respect of the rights provided by Article 6(1) (principles relating to data quality), Articles 10 and 11(1) (informing data subjects), Article 12 (subject access) and Article 21 (publicising processing operations). The particular exemptions provided for by Article 13(1) may be taken to safeguard:

— national security;

— defence;

— public security;

— the prevention, investigation, detection and prosecution of criminal offences, or of breaches of ethics for regulated professions;

— an important economic or financial interest of a Member State or of the European Union including monetary, budgetary and taxation matters;

— a monitoring, inspection or regulatory function connected, even occasionally, with the exercise of official authority the cases above except the first two;

— the protection of the data subject or of the rights or freedoms of others.

There is the possibility of a further limited exemption for data used solely for the purposes of research or are kept in personal form for a period that does not exceed the period necessary for the sole purpose of creating statistics; Article 13(2). This option is only possible subject to adequate legal safeguards (in particular that the data are not used to take measures or decisions in relation to any particular individual) and where there is clearly no risk of breaching the privacy of the data subject. Additionally, the exemption must be provided for by legislation.

There is a curious provision in Article 9 (curious from the point of view of the United Kingdom) which requires Member States to lay down exemptions or derogations from most of the provisions of the Directive where personal data are processed solely for journalistic purposes or for the purpose of artistic or literary expression[1]. But this is only to the extent that the exemptions or derogations are necessary to reconcile the right to privacy with the rules governing freedom of expression. This provision is unnecessary in the context of the United Kingdom, given the on-going debate about the excesses of media reporting. Some would argue that the freedom of expression presently exercised by the press should be constrained somewhat rather than reinforced. As regards artistic and literary expression this is balanced with privacy already, for example, by the law of defamation with its defences of fair comment and justification.

There is a general prohibition on processing sensitive data except in certain cases though it is possible for Member States to enlarge the occasions when such data can be processed by Article 8. Particularly relevant are the possibilities of allowing processing of data relating to criminal convictions or civil judgments, health care and "for reasons of substantial public interest". These are discussed earlier in the section on processing.

Article 32(2) requires processing already under way at the time the Directive is implemented to be brought into conformity with the Directive's provisions within three years of that date. Implementation of the Directive can be at any time before the end of three years from the date of adoption (24 October 1995). Therefore, if national legislation implementing the Directive comes into force on, say 1 January 1998, all processing activities in existence at that time must comply with the Directive's provisions by 1 January 2001. Of course, all new processing activities commencing after 1 January 1998 must comply immediately. It would appear, notwithstanding the complication of the direct effect of Directives or parts thereof[2], if a Member State is late in complying, that lateness will benefit those carrying out existing processing activities at the date of compliance. Thus, if Member State X

---

1   Recital 37 emphasises the audiovisual field. The derogation relates to Chapter II, IV and VI of the Directive.
2   See Case 148/78 *Publico Ministero v Ratti* [1980] 1 CMLR 96, joined Cases C-6/90 and C-9/90 *Francovich and Bonifaci v Italy* [1993] 2 CMLR 66 and Case C-106/89 *Marleasing v La Comercial Internacional de Alimentacion* [1990] ECR I-4135.

does not comply until 1 November 1999 (over 1 year late), pre-existing processing will not have to comply until 1 November 2002.

The Directive recognises the difficulties of applying all its provisions in a relatively short time to manual processing and Member States may derogate by providing that existing processing of data already held in manual filing systems does not have to brought into conformity with Articles 6, 7 and 8 until a maximum of 12 years following the date of adoption of the Directive as noted above. This is without prejudice to subject access rights and processing new data must comply in any case. It is likely that the United Kingdom will take advantage of this to give organisations with large amounts of existing paper files containing personal data a breathing space and time to phase in compliance[1].

Supervisory authority

The supervisory authority's duties and powers are laid down in Article 28. It is to be expected that the function will remain with the Office of the Data Protection Registrar. The supervisory authority will be responsible for monitoring the application of the national provisions adopted in pursuance of the Directive and will act with complete independence. It also has a right to be consulted in the drawing up of administrative measures or regulations concerning individuals' rights and freedoms with regard to the processing of personal data.

The powers are, to some extent, implicit in the Directive. For example, the power to accept or reject registration and the power to enter into negotiations with various bodies representing data subjects and controllers. Specific powers are set out in Article 28(3), being investigative powers, effective powers of intervention and the power to engage in legal proceedings. Any decisions of the supervisory authority will be subject to appeal to the courts. The authority will also have a duty to hear complaints from or on behalf of data subjects and to hear claims in respect of matters such as the lawfulness of processing where a controller seeks to rely on an exemption. The supervisory authority must publish a report of its activities at regular intervals. These provisions restate and re-inforce the Registrar's present powers and duties.

There are provisions for supervisory authorities of all the Member States to co-operate with each other. A Working Party on the protection of individuals with regard to the processing of personal data will be set

---

1   The government tacitly acknowledges the need for delaying the full impact of the Directive on manual files and even considers that the 12 year period is inadequate; Home Office, *Consultation Paper on the EC Data Protection Directive*, 1996 p48.

up; Article 29. It will have an advisory status, act independently and be comprised of representatives of supervisory authorities. By Article 30, the Working Party will look at uniformity of approach, the protection afforded in third countries, advise on possible changes to data protection law and on codes of conduct drawn up at Community level.

The Office of the Data Protection Registrar already takes an active and effective part in terms of international co-operation and this function will be enhanced. The possibility of a substantial reduction in the volume of registrations should enable more resources to be directed towards investigation and enforcement work. Although it is by no means a foregone conclusion that the Office will retain its present level of staffing of around 110, the extension of data protection law to manual files and the increased links with other supervisory authorities and the Working Party should ensure that the Registrar and her Office continue to have an important role to play in data protection.

Chapter 4 : Perspectives on the Directive: The Controller

Introduction

To a significantly greater extent than the Data Protection Act 1984, the Directive creates, modifies and controls relationships between the various persons involved directly or indirectly with personal data. The main categories of persons are as follows:

— controllers;

— processors;

— recipients;

— third parties;

— data subjects;

— supervisory authority.

For the meaning of these terms see the definitions section in Chapter 3. There may be some overlap, for example, a processor who is processing personal data on behalf of a controller is also likely to be a controller in his own right. Thus, a computer bureau processing personal data for a number of clients will be a controller in respect of its own holding of personal data, for example, in respect of employee files.

A useful insight into the workings of the Directive can be obtained by viewing its provisions, in a practical manner, from the viewpoint of each of these types of person. this will breathe life into the Directive's provisions. This chapter looks at the Directive's provisions in a practical manner from the perspective of the controller. Following chapters concentrate on the implications for processors, recipients and third parties and, finally, data subjects.

Controller

The controller[1] is the key person and the major thrust of the Directive (and indeed the Data Protection Act 1984) is to set standards in a regulatory framework to ensure that processing of personal data is carried out in a fair and lawful manner, to maintain the integrity of the data and to prevent harmful abuses of personal data. It is not surprising, therefore, that controllers tend to regard data protection law as an unwelcome constraint on their use of personal data and responsible for imposing onerous administrative duties. This is not to say that data protection law is lacking in benefits for controllers. For example, compliance with the data quality principles in Article 6 and other aspects such as the provisions relating to security of processing is largely a matter of implementing and maintaining good data management practices. Having accurate and up-to-date personal data is for the benefit of the controller just as it is for the data subjects concerned. The overall efficiency of data processing operations will be maximised by having personal data that are accurate, relevant and up to date.

To assess the impact on controllers of data protection law as set out in the Directive, the context of a group of companies is used. It may, for example, be a group of companies involved in the construction industry or in manufacturing. The processing of personal data by such organisations is unlikely to be "sensitive" or particularly controversial but the data protection issues and the obligations imposed upon such a group will be typical of those experienced by the considerable number of companies and other organisations in their handling of personal data. The rights and duties identified in relation to such a group of companies will be those facing the majority of controllers. The proportion of data users processing "sensitive" data will be relatively small.

Processing Activities

First, it will be useful to identify and analyse the operations performed by or on behalf of the companies within the group. The table below lists the general type of personal data that might be held, what they might be used for, from whom they are likely to have been obtained and to whom they are likely to be disclosed and, finally, to whom and where they may be transferred. Of course, much of the data will not be personal data and will concern companies such as clients, sub-contractors and suppliers but, even here, there will be personal data associated with it such as data relating to individuals employed by

---

1   Equivalent to "data user" under the present law.

those companies. For example, details in a database of suppliers will contain, typically, names of contacts, their telephone number or extension and their position within the company.

Table 4.1 Personal data in a company within a group of companies

Activity/operation	Description
holding data comprising or including personal data	employees (including past employees), clients, suppliers, sub-contractors, consultants
purpose of holding or processing personal data	payments to employees, suppliers, sub-contractors, consultants, payment from clients, pensions, statistics, marketing, legal, tax and administrative purposes
obtaining from	employees, clients, suppliers and sub-contractors trade directories, journals, magazines, etc
disclosing to	employees, banks, building societies, pensions companies, health care providers, etc potential clients (often want CVs of employees) organisations seeking job references parent, subsidiary or sister companies government agencies and public bodies (eg CBI) Inland Revenue and Customs and Excise "processors" (eg computer bureaux)
transfer to	parent, subsidiary or sister companies, take-over or merger companies unconnected companies for marketing (list trading)

To take an example, consider that one company within the group is a building contractor. It builds offices, light industrial units and speculative housing. Its clients include local authorities, companies and private individuals. The types of data it is likely to process[1] are set out below. Bear in mind that "paper-based" personal data is within the scope of the Directive if it is contained in structured files.

1. Client-based data

(a) Local authority clients - names of authorities and contact staff for present and past building contracts. Records of individuals will include architects, quantity surveyors, engineers, planners, clerks of works, administrators (especially clerks in the Treasurer's department - important for chasing up late payments). Not all these persons may be employed directly by the local authority and some may be self-employed consultants engaged by the local authority.

(b) Companies - there may be minimal information concerning the company-client and its employees particularly, as is usual, where the design of the scheme and the supervision of its construction is undertaken by a private firm of architects. The building contractor is likely to keep details of relevant individuals working for the firm.

Information about companies' boards of directors and financial standing may also be kept. It is common practice to take out financial references for new clients so that a building contractor can satisfy itself that the client is likely to be in a position to pay. Conversely, the client may need financial guarantees, typically in the form of a bond, in respect of the contractor's performance. In either case, such information is likely to contain at least some personal data.

(c) Private clients buying speculative housing - details of individual persons and couples buying or inquiring about new houses. Details are likely to include information about such persons' solicitors, banks or building societies, some of which will be personal data.

Apart from immediate use for purposes associated with construction or sale, some of the information above may be used later for marketing purposes, for statistical purposes or for list trading.

2. Employees and Consultants

(a) Salaried employees - the company will have a database of salaried employees. This will include details such as name, address, date of birth, sex, marital status, PAYE code, National Insurance Number, date appointed, job title, grade, holiday entitlement, overtime worked, bank details, sick leave, pension, attachment of earnings orders, etc. Some of

---

1   "Process" is used in the wide sense as defined in the Directive; see Chapter 3.

this information may be disclosed to the company's bank which will make payments to individual employees' bank accounts. Disclosure to pension companies is also likely (it may be that the group has its own pensions company).

(b) Non-salaried employees - where employees are non-salaried and paid in cash, the wages department will hold similar information.

Employee details may be held by the company itself or by the parent company or both. Apart from disclosure to banks and building societies, relevant information will be passed on to the Inland Revenue and to organisations seeking financial references in respect of employees.

Employee information may also be disclosed to government departments and trade organisations in statistical form.

When an employee retires or resigns, the company will have to consider what to do with that individual's personal data.

3.   Suppliers and Sub-contractors
The company is likely to have numerous suppliers of materials and equipment and sub-contractors. All the suppliers are likely to be companies but a number of sub-contractors may be self-employed individuals or partnerships. Even where suppliers and sub-contractors are corporate beings, details held by the building contractor will be certain to include information about individuals working for the companies.

In some cases, the personal data held is likely to be fairly sparse, for example, a database of ready-mix concrete suppliers may contain location of mixing plants, types of concrete supplied, name of person(s) who can give quotes and names of persons who take orders by telephone. It is possible that other information may be contained such as a comment about a particular individual's helpfulness or otherwise. For example, an entry might say:

Supplier:	Acme Ready-Mix Concrete Ltd.
Goods/material supplied:	All types of ready-mix concrete
Depot 1:	Middlesbrough (slag aggregate)
Telephone:	0123-345675
Fax:	0123-365743
Contacts:	Joy Spack (don't try before 3 in
afternoons -	in pub)
	Horace Fish (shout when ordering -
	he's deaf)

etc.

It is questionable whether such comments ought to be included and this is discussed later.

The contractor will also maintain databases containing details of the companies or individuals certified work to date, payments made, payments due, retention, etc. This is likely to contain information relating to the contractor's site agent (in charge of the particular contract), and the financial controller of the supplier or sub-contractor.

Where sub-contractors are self-employed or partnerships, details will include more personal data such as home address, where they work from home, and tax exemption details.

4.   *Marketing*
The contractor is likely to keep several databases relating to marketing. It will have a number of client databases - say one for local authorities, one for private corporate clients and one for purchasers of its houses. The former two may be used for future advertising and mailshots, addressed to the appropriate persons at the organisations. The latter may have some commercial value which can be realised by selling copies. For example, by selling a sub-set of persons who have recently bought one of the more expensive houses built by the company to a dealer in luxury cars or manufacturer of garden statuary.

The value of such lists may be enhanced by collecting more data at the time of sale of the house, for example, whether the purchasers have any children. Whether such information should be collected and/or transferred is discussed later.

The contractor is also likely to have marketing databases comprising potential clients. It may obtain the relevant information from a number of sources, including its sister companies, trade literature or by buying it in.

Mode of storage

Much of the information described above is likely to be stored electronically. Some will be stored on paper. The significance is that electronically stored data can be retrieved by reference to particular identifiers. For example, a list of employees who have been off-sick for more than one week in the last year can be retrieved almost instantly. In many cases, there is no need to pre-define the identifiers used to retrieve information. Some database systems allow new forms of query to be designed by the user or easily programmed in.

With the increasing power of computers, there are few restrictions on what can be held. A few years ago, designers of electronic databases would have been careful to try to limit the overall size. Only 40 spaces might have been allocated for a name, for example. Nowadays, space considerations are less important and besides having ample space to store textual information, it is now feasible to store visual and sound data digitally. For example, an employee record might include a digitised photograph or even video footage of each employee. Imagine that our building contractor wishes to win a prestige contract on a "design and build" basis. It may send the potential client a video showing its previous work and including profiles of its key employees who will design and manage the project and who appear on the video and introduce themselves and outline their experience. Such data may also be available on the contractor's "web page" on the Internet if it has one[1].

Many companies also have a number of electronic address books which may be tied into their facsimile machines or email systems. Typically, these will contain personal information such as name, email address, postal address, telephone, company and position.

The distinction between electronic data and paper-based systems is that the latter will be caught by the provisions of the Directive only if they are structured in such a way as to allow easy access to personal data[2]. This will have required, at the outset, a conscious decision to structure the data, such as by having a card index or separate files for each individual. By their very nature, all electronic databases containing personal data are within the provisions of the Directive unless exempt.

Notification

A group of companies as described above can benefit from no longer having to comply with formal registration requirements. Article 18(2) of the Directive allows Member States to provide for simplification of or exemption from the notification requirements where the "rights and freedoms of data subjects are unlikely to be affected adversely". This phrase must be the key test.

---

1   If it does not have a Web Page now it probably will in the future.
2   "Personal data filing system" is defined in Article 2(c). Recital 27 indicates that important factors in whether manual processing is within data protection law is structure and ease of access to personal data.

It is almost certain that the United Kingdom will provide for exemption from registration for non-sensitive processing of non-sensitive data.[1] Further, it is possible that all manual processing will be exempt. However, as will be seen later, there is a price to be paid for exemption and some organisations which would otherwise be exempt from registration might find it more convenient to notify its processing operations formally, if this is an option[2].

Article 8 which prohibits the processing of sensitive data subject to limited exceptions gives an imperfect clue as to the likely extent of exemption but is unlikely to provide an exhaustive test. Generally, it is unlikely that there will be exemption from registration where data processed by computer reveal "racial or ethnic origin, political opinions, religious or philosophical beliefs, trade union membership or where the processing concerns health or sex life". However, many employers will keep details of union membership (and, indeed, make the necessary deduction from salary or wages to pay over to the union) and processing this data for appropriate purposes should not adversely affect the rights and freedoms of the employees.

Of course, in determining whether the rights and freedoms of data subjects are affected adversely, consideration must be given not just to the nature of the data held but also to the nature of the processing, disclosure and transfer. In the most cases, smaller companies in sectors such as construction and manufacturing should be exempt from notification. However, this could be prejudiced if additional information is collected for purposes not directly associated with the current interaction between the company and the individual. Data collected and retained for marketing purposes could easily fall into this category. An example is where house purchasers are asked to give details of children or birthdays or hobbies, etc. For example, a house builder might publish a glossy magazine which it makes available "free" to purchasers of its houses and which contains many items of interest about furnishings, gardening and cooking. Obtaining the magazine might entail completing an application form where such information is elicited. If such information is requested, it should be clear what it is required for (for example, direct marketing) and the applicant should be asked to give consent to such uses. Furthermore, it is likely that formal notification of such processing will be required.

---

1   "Consistent with the needs of business and other data users, the Government intends to make full use of the scope which the Directive offers for easing still further the burden of registration", Home Office, *Consultation Paper on the EC Data Protection Directive*, 1996 p35.

2   It may be that, if the exemption from notification route is chosen by the United Kingdom, applications to register will not be accepted if all the processing thus notified is exempt from formal notification.

For organisations which will have to notify the supervisory authority under the new rules, it is likely that a similar form will be used to that currently used under the 1984 Act. At the present time, there are two types of forms, DPR1 which has two parts and form DPR4 which is intended for smaller data users and covers four specified purposes only[1]. Part A of DPR1 asks for basic information such as the data user's or computer bureau's name and address, the period for which registration is required and one or more addresses for subject access requests[2]. For every purpose that a data user processes personal data, he or she must complete one Part B of DPR1. Part B elicits information about the data subjects, data classes, sources and disclosure and countries outside the United Kingdom to which it is intended to transfer the data. It is a question of ticking boxes and, if there are no appropriate boxes, describing the particular information.

For notification under the Directive's provisions there will be some differences to the form. The Directive does not require the source of data to be notified but a general description of security measures must be given so that a preliminary assessment of their appropriateness can be made[3]. This information need not, however, be placed on the register. It will be for the Data Protection Registrar's eyes only. There is genuine concern amongst controllers about divulging any information relating to their security measures as this could itself jeopardise security. However, only a general description has to be given and controllers having to register should find some suitable form of words. An example is:

"The controller takes appropriate technical and organisational measures to protect personal data from accidental or unlawful destruction or accidental loss, alteration unauthorised disclosure or access. In particular, the controller maintains several generations of back-up copies of personal data which are kept in securely locked fireproof safes; uses and changes at frequent intervals non-obvious passwords; trains and updates its staff in respect of security measures and the importance of such measures; restricts access to personal data to persons who have the controller's express permission to process the data and transmits personal data across non-local networks only in encrypted form. Furthermore, the

---

1   Personnel/Employee Administration, Marketing and Selling, Purchase/Supplier Administration and Customer/Client Administration. It follows the format of DPR1.
2   Computer bureaux are required only to give details of their name and address and period for which registration is required.
3   Article 19(1)(f).

controller regularly reviews and audits its security measures and monitors and evaluates new and developing security measures."[1]

Publicity for Exempt Controllers

Article 21 requires that processing operations are publicised and that a register of notified processing operations is maintained which must be available for public inspection. The current practice of the Office of the Data Protection Registrar will probably suffice. That is, occasional publicity campaigns by the Office, the publication of the index to the register, the ability to inspect register entries at the Office in Wilmslow and the purchase of copies of register entries[2].

However, where controllers are exempt from the notification requirements (and this could apply in a considerable number of cases) Article 21(3) requires that the controller[3] makes available to any person on request the information referred to in Article 19(1)(a) to (e), being:

— the name and address of controller and representative, if any;

— the purpose or purposes of processing;

— a description of the category or categories or data subject and of the data or categories of data relating to them;

— the recipients or categories of recipient to whom the data might be disclosed;

— proposed transfers of data to third countries.

Exempt controllers must consider how to publicise their processing operations and prepare a form containing the relevant information to be shown to any person on request. Publicity could be achieved through printing an appropriate notice on forms and advertising literature, for example:

"*Data Protection:* In relation to its processing of personal data, Acme Ltd is exempt from registration under the Data Protection Act, as amended. In accordance with the Act, Acme will make available for inspection details of such processing, to the extent required under

---

1 This is a suggestion only. There is no guarantee that it will be acceptable or appropriate.
2 The current fee is £2 per copy. The register is also available on the Internet.
3 Article 21(3) allows another body appointed by Member States to make the information available. This would seem to defeat the object of exempting controllers from formal notification. It is unlikely to be used in the United Kingdom.

the Act, to any person on request calling at Acme's Head Office during normal office hours."

A typical form setting out the relevant information should, ideally, follow the format used by the Data Protection Register, using the same codes and descriptions. The following (incomplete) example is given. It will need modification in the light of changes to categories, descriptions and other details resulting from the implementation of the Directive.

Details of Acme Ltd's Processing Operations

Data Protection Act, as amended

Name: Acme Limited   Company registration No   2093245

Address: 123 New Street
              Old Town
              Rutland. RT9 1ZZ

Address for receipt of subject access requests: (as above)

PURPOSE 1

P001   Personnel/Employee Administration

          The administration of prospective, current and past employees, including, where applicable, self-employed or contract personnel, secondees, temporary staff or voluntary workers.

          Typical activities are: recruitment, recording of working time, administration and payment of wages, salaries, ... (and so on)

          Description of Data Subjects or Categories of Data Subject
          S001   Employees, trainees, voluntary workers
          S002   Employees of associated companies
          S003   Employees of other organisations

          Description of Data or Data Categories
          C001   Personal identifiers
          C002   Financial identifiers
          C003   Identifiers issued by public bodies
          C011   Personal details
          C051   Academic record
          C052   Qualifications and skills
          C053   Membership of professional bodies

C068   Payments, deductions

Recipients or Categories of Recipient to whom data might be disclosed
D101   The data subjects themselves
D104   Employers - prospective
D202   Other companies in the same group
D301   Inland Revenue
D302   Customs and Excise
D305   Department of Social Security
D306   Department of Employment
D362   Banks

Proposed Transfers to Third Countries
None

PURPOSE 2

P003   Marketing and Selling (Excluding Direct Marketing to Individuals)

...

(and so on)

Note that there is no requirement to give information about sources of the data[1], unlike there is at present and the statement of security measures is not required to be publicly available.

It can be seen that, in most cases, there will be little to be gained by being exempt. Producing the necessary information will require almost as much effort as applying for registration. Indeed, having to provide the information on request will require training of staff such as receptionists and it could prove less expensive simply to register if this is possible.

It would seem that, within a group of companies each company, having its own separate and distinct legal personality, must satisfy the notification requirements individually, whether exempt from formal registration or not. In terms of groups of companies, it is likely that the parent or holding company will provide a centralised service in terms of data protection and carry out the necessary work for each subsidiary company. Most large and medium sized companies and other organisations will have a person or department responsible for data

---

1   The provisions for notifying the data subject in the Directive will, in most cases, make this information otiose.

protection. However, recital 19 suggests that a parent company can be a controller in respect of all its subsidiary companies. At the end of the day, it may boil down to a matter of convenience.

In-House Data Protection Official

An option open to Member States in respect of simplification of or exemption from notification is to require controllers to appoint a personal data protection official charged with ensuring compliance and with keeping a register of processing operations[1]. Whilst this is unlikely to be a requirement in the United Kingdom for commercial organisations, it could be used in the public sector or in private companies operating in that sector. In any case, as mentioned above, most organisations that are exempt from formal notification will appoint someone charged with the tasks required of a data protection official. It is simply good data processing practice.

Our hypothetical group of companies will probably have a manager and team employed by the parent company with, *inter alia*, data protection duties for the group. Their remit could easily be combined with training employees throughout the group in good data processing practice including raising awareness of the dangers of computer hacking and fraud in addition to auditing and checking the use of data, personal and otherwise, throughout the group.

Security

The Data Protection Act 1984 in its present form requires appropriate security measures to be taken against unauthorised access to, or alteration, disclosure or destruction of, personal data and against accidental loss or destruction of personal data. Guidelines on interpretation in Schedule 1 to the Act state that regard shall be had to the nature of the data and the harm that might result from such access, alteration, disclosure, destruction and to the place where the data are stored, security measures programmed into the relevant equipment and measures taken to ensure the reliability of staff having access to the data.

In respect of in-house processing, the Directive places similar obligations on the controller, in particular, the measures taken must be commensurate with the nature of the data and the risks represented by the processing[2].

---

1   Article 18(2).
2   Article 17(1).

Security should not be an issue as it is in the interests of every organisation to implement, maintain and monitor adequate levels of security. However, the Directive applies also to data on paper or other form structured to facilitate access and this will require organisations to consider security aspects in relation to paper files, card indexes and the like. Bearing in mind that security covers accidental loss or destruction, there could be a significant upturn in demand for lockable fireproof cabinets.

Consider a typical company in the construction or manufacturing sector. Most of the data it processes will not be particularly sensitive. It is suggested that appropriate security measures should include:

—   the use of an appropriate hierarchical password system which is changed at frequent intervals;

—   access to data (whether automatically or manually processed) limited to those members of staff requiring access to perform their assigned duties;

—   personal data stored on paper stored in locked cabinets, locked rooms, etc;

—   not allowing employees to remove personal data from offices;

—   training staff in the application of data protection law.

The Directive mentions networks as an area of particular concern. There may be two aspects to this as regards a typical controller. First, it may have a local area network of computers. The use of suitable passwording systems should be used, as above, with staff being instructed to use non-obvious passwords, to change them frequently and not, for example, to write their passwords on a piece of paper stuck on the computer (it happens). Additionally, staff should be trained not to leave terminals logged on in their absence, for example, if a member of staff goes for a coffee break, he or she ought to log off the network. Again, all this is simply good data processing practice.

As far as other networks are concerned, even more care should be taken. A company may have access to a wide area network operated throughout the group, giving access to databases in other companies within a group of companies. It may also have access to electronic mail and the Internet. It is essential that staff are made aware of the implications of using such systems for a number of reasons, including issues related to data protection, confidence, copyright and defamation.

Where a controller makes use of the services of a "processor", being someone who processes data on behalf of the controller, Article 17(2) requires that the processor must provide sufficient guarantees in respect of security and ensure compliance with measures taken. This must be formally provided for by written contract or legal act.

Within a group of companies, it is likely that the parent company carries out some processing activities on behalf of the individual subsidiary companies. This must be carried out under a formal written contract. The contract, which will deal with other matters such as payment and liability for delays, must include a term imposing the relevant duty on the parent company. The following is an example which might be appropriate. A duty of confidence should also be imposed, as required by Article 16.

"Security of processing

Acme Holdings plc warrants that it will implement appropriate technical and organisational measures to protect personal data processed on behalf of Acme Contracting Ltd against accidental or unlawful destruction or accidental loss, alteration, unauthorised disclosure or access and all other forms of unlawful processing of such data. Acme Contracting Ltd is entitled to, without notice and at reasonable intervals, to inspect and evaluate the above mentioned technical and organisational measures to satisfy itself as to their appropriateness and efficacy. Should the measures fail to reach the standard required under data protection law, Acme Holdings plc warrants that it will modify, improve or enhance the measures to reach that standard as soon as is practicable and in no event later than further processing of the said data is performed.

Confidentiality

Acme Holdings plc agrees that personal data processed on behalf of Acme Contracting Ltd will only be processed in accordance with Acme Contracting Ltd's express instructions unless required to process those data by law. Furthermore, Acme Holdings plc agrees that it is under a duty of confidence to Acme Contracting Ltd in relation to such personal data and other data associated with it."[1]

Such contractual provision may need the addition of an arbitration clause to deal with a situation where the two companies disagree over

---

1   There is no need to include a lengthy confidence clause prohibiting express acts such as disclosure to third parties because of the scope of the definition of processing in the Directive.

the required level of security. This could be another reason to appoint an in-house "data protection official" who, perhaps after consulting the Office of the Data Protection Registrar, could give a ruling on whether the contemplated security measures are satisfactory. Additionally, unlike the contract term above which leaves, at first instance, the choice of measures to the processor, the controller may wish to particularise the precise measures to the taken in the context of the actual data to be processed.

There may be many others processing personal data on behalf of controllers, such as public bodies, auditors, sub-contractors, computer bureaux and the like. Contractual terms will be required in most cases. In other cases, a "legal act" is required; this could be in the context of the imposition of an express duty of confidence. It may be provided for by legislation, for example, imposing the relevant duties on a public body.

A group of companies should check and evaluate all the flows of personal data between the companies within the group and to outside organisations. Existing arrangements must then be checked to ensure that the appropriate contractual guarantees are included in the contracts or other formal notices or documentation. When doing this, consideration must be given to the scope of processing for the purposes of the Directive. For example, the parent company may use a waste disposal company to collect and destroy old computer print-out from time to time. It may use the services of a company providing facilities management. It may have a contract with a disaster recovery company which holds back-up copies of all the group's computer software. All of these activities require the necessary contractual guarantees.

Informing Data Subjects

The Data Protection Act 1984 makes no express provision for informing data subjects as to the controller's processing of personal data relating to them, apart from providing a copy of their personal data to comply with a subject access request. However, in some circumstances, fair and lawful obtaining and processing of personal data under the First Data Protection Principle requires that the data subject is informed of the proposed use of his or her data at the time of its collection[1]. Nevertheless, the Directive sets out what appears at first sight to be more onerous duties to inform data subjects.

The data subject must be informed at the time the data are collected[2] and, if the data have not been obtained from the data subject, he or she must be informed at the time of recording or, if disclosure to a third party is envisaged, no later than the time of first disclosure[3]. A saving grace is that the data subject need not be informed if he or she already has the relevant information. Nor need the data subject be informed on recording or disclosure where the processing is, in particular, for statistical or research purposes and would involve a disproportionate effort or where provided for by law. In such cases, Member States must lay down appropriate safeguards.

The information to be given must include the identity of the controller and representative, if any, and the purposes of the processing. Further information may be required to guarantee fair processing. Articles 10 and 11 set out what further information may be required[4].

The implications of the obligations to inform data subjects can best be seen in the context of different categories of individuals whose personal data an organisation is likely to process. Those categories are:

— employees and consultants;

— individuals working for other organisations such as suppliers, sub-contractors and clients;

— individual consumers.

Employees and Consultants

The first category, employees and consultants is easily dealt with. There is formal contact between the controller and the data subjects. In the case of employees there must, by law, be a written contract of employment and this can contain the necessary information. Better still, the information can be included in a letter offering employment, for example:

---

1   As, for example, in relation to uses that are not obvious at the time of collection; see
     ● *Innovations (Mail Order) Ltd v Data Protection Registrar* (unreported) 29 September
     1993, Data Protection Tribunal.
2   Article 10.
3   Article 11.
4   See Chapter 3 for details of this further information.

"Acme Manufacturing Ltd maintain and process personal data relating to all its employees for the purposes of employee administration and pensions administration. The data are obtained from the employee directly, from the Inland Revenue, DSS and other statutory and public bodies. The data will be processed by Acme Manufacturing Ltd and its parent company Acme Holdings plc, disclosed to employees and agents of the Acme groups of companies, the companies' banks and, if you become a member of the company pension scheme, to Acme Pensions Ltd. You have rights of access and rectification in relation to your personal data. It is Acme Manufacturing Ltd's policy to charge a fee for access to personal data. Contact the Human Resources Department for further details.

If you decide to accept this offer of employment, please complete the attached form. Failure to complete the form fully and return it promptly may result in a delay in payment of salary or in an emergency tax code being assigned to you."

The fact that some data has not been obtained from the controller is mentioned above (in practice, there may be other sources of data), and, although mention of the source is not required[1], it is probably just as easy to mention the obvious sources. Alternatively, the information could simply say "... some of the data are obtained directly from the employee whilst other data necessary to carry out processing for the above-mentioned purposes are obtained from other sources".

Less obviously, personal data may be disclosed to the controller from an unexpected source. An employee may have an attachment of earnings order made against him by a court, for example, resulting from a failure to make maintenance payments to a former spouse. However, the employer should not have to inform the employee about this as the court should have already told the employee that the relevant information will be disclosed to his or her employer.

Note that the data subject must be informed at the time of collection of the data. Putting the notice in a contract of employment will not do if, as tends to be normal practice, the employee is not given his or her formal written contract of employment until after he or she has been working for a few days (or even weeks!).

•

---

1   Available information as to the sources of data is required for the purposes of subject access.

Individuals Employed by Other Organisations

Imagine that George, an employee of a firm of accountants, telephones the sales department of a stationery supplies company and speaks to Angela, the sales manager, asking her for a quotation for photocopying paper. George finds Angela particularly helpful and obtains the following information from her:

— name;

— position in company;

— telephone number and extension;

— mobile phone number;

— prices for photocopying paper.

The firm of accountants has a database of its suppliers and George decides to enter Angela's name, telephone numbers and fact that she is sales manager into this database. He also writes her name and telephone numbers in his diary.

Perhaps without realising it, George has obtained personal data from Angela[1]. What is more, he has recorded it with the intention of further processing it. Simply consulting the information at some future date is processing, as is recording, as is storage (sic). Article 10 clearly requires that Angela is told at least the purpose of the processing (she should know the identity of the controller, unless George has failed to tell her). Although easily done, for example by George telling Angela that he hopes she does not mind if he records her name and telephone numbers so that he can speak to her again to place an order or to obtain further quotes, it is equally easy to forget.

In the main, it is a matter of developing appropriate attitudes to the use of personal data so that informing such persons becomes second nature. However, it does illustrate the Directive's tendency to overkill. Employees in different organisations dealing with each other know that the person they are dealing with will keep a record of such mundane information. They would be surprised if it were otherwise. Collection of

---

1   Personal data means any information relating to an identified or identifiable natural person; Article 2(a).

data of this sort cannot, under any reasonable view, be prejudicial to the "fundamental rights and freedoms of natural persons"[1].

Incidentally, writing names and addresses in a diary or address book could be within the Directive's control because the data will be structured (for example, in alphabetical order[2]) in such a way as to allow easy access to information relating to a given individual. The Directive does not apply to data processed for purely personal activities so address books containing nothing more than information about friends and relatives are unaffected. In practice, however, most people have entries in their personal address books (paper-based or computer-based) that are related to work.

Individual "Consumers"

A large proportion of organisations have dealings with private individuals, whether as a consumer, client or in the performance of public duties. These are surely the persons the Directive is particularly aimed at. Perhaps because the main thrust of the Directive is to protect such persons vis-à-vis their personal data, it is arguable that the Directive will have some onerous and unfortunate implications with respect to other categories of individuals, as suggested above.

Informing individual clients or customers on collection of their personal data should not be a particular problem in most cases. Where the individual and controller are in a contractual relationship or the controller is performing some public duty, there will usually be some "paperwork" which can include the relevant information. A form of words should be chosen appropriate to the business operations carried on by or duties owed by the organisation. Particular care must be taken however, where the controller is collecting personal data indirectly, for example, where the controller asks for information about a spouse or other family members. Article 11 requires that that other person is informed at the time the data are recorded or no later than disclosure to a third party if this is envisaged.

Imagine that a brewery owns a number of public houses, many of which serve food. The public houses are managed by persons directly employed by the brewery. In order to encourage customers to dine at its public houses, the brewery has introduced a points scheme using its own "gold food card" and each time the holder of the card buys a meal at one of the brewery's public houses, the number of points on the

---

1   Part of the basic statement of data protection in Article 1(1).
2   It may also have internal structure, for example, information arranged by name, address, telephone number.

card is increased. This is done by "swiping" the card along a slot in the till which is also connected via the telecommunications network to the brewery's main computer. Points on the card can be exchanged later for free meals or entitle the holder to a reduction in the price of a meal.

To apply for the card, the customer has to complete a form which asks for his or her name, address and date of birth in addition to some simple questions about "lifestyle" (for example, how often the customer eats out, whether he or she drinks wine or is vegetarian, etc. There is also a section to be completed in respect of the applicant's spouse or partner in which the same information is elicited. The application form has to be signed by the proposed card holder only and, in some cases, details of the spouse or partner are given without his or her knowledge. Additional points are awarded for completing details of the spouse or partner. The reason why date of birth is asked for is so that the brewery can send details of special birthday meal offers and the lifestyle information is needed for the breweries own marketing efforts and to sell on to other organisations. For example, florists might be very keen to have a database of birthdays.

The brewery must inform the customer of the purposes for which the information is required. Some of this will be obvious and, after all, is the reason why the customer is completing the application form. But other purposes, such as selling on its lists of customers, must be made clear to the customer. Other information, such as the identity of recipients or categories of recipients also must be given. The Directive does not expressly state that the information must be given to the data subject at the time of collection. However, in the light of the *Innovations* case, the customer must be informed of non-obvious uses at the time of collection and not later. This is on the basis of what constitutes fair obtaining of data and is implicit in the principles relating to data quality in Article 6(1).

As regards the spouse or partner (who might not be very pleased when he or she discovers that his or her date of birth has been divulged), the brewery must give the necessary information at the time of undertaking the recording of the data. A problem here is where the spouse or partner is not present when the form is completed and the card issued. As the card will be swiped through the till, the information will be recorded immediately on the main computer. The question then is whether the concept of informing a data subject vicariously, by informing the spouse or partner will do. The United Kingdom government's view is that it probably will[1]. Even then, it would seem sensible for the controller to ask the person providing the information to inform any other persons whose data are collected as to the identity of the controller and the purposes of the processing.

The working of Article 11 is unclear where the data are recorded and then disclosed to a third party, as in the brewery example above. As regards those two activities the wording of Article 11(1) is in the disjunctive. That is, the information should be given "... at the time of undertaking the recording of personal data *or if a disclosure to a third party is envisaged,* no later than the time the data are first disclosed ..." (emphasis added). The following interpretations are possible in the context of the brewery and data subjects from whom the data have not been directly obtained, such as spouses or partners:

— the spouse or partner must be informed, expressly or vicariously, the instant the data are recorded (that is, when the data are entered into the main computer[2]); or

— as the brewery envisage selling a copy of the data to other organisations, the spouse of partner need not be informed until such disclosure is made or is imminent; or

— the spouse of partner must be informed both when the data are recorded and when the data are disclosed.

What if the controller does not envisage disclosure at the time of collection but later, suddenly appreciating that it has commercial value, decides to sell a copy of its customer database? The wording of Article 11 would seem to suggest that the data subject need not be given the information. However, the recipient of personal data is under a duty to inform the data subjects, at least of its identity and the purposes of processing. The only time this is not required is when the data subject already has the information. The controller who collects the data and the recipient to whom the data are disclosed must decide between themselves which has responsibility for providing the data subjects with the necessary information. Note that Article 11(1) requires the identify of the controller to be given and simply giving a general description of categories of controllers will not do.

---

1   Home Office, *Consultation Paper on the EC Data Protection Directive,* 1996. At p21, the paper suggests that where a survey is carried out house to house, the controller's responsibility may be discharged by providing the information through the person from whom the data are collected.
2   *Quaere,* whether the form itself could be seen as part of a personal data filing system if forms are retained and kept in alphabetical order.

Returning to the brewery. Suppose one of the organisations it wishes to sell a copy of its customer details to is a jewellery company. The following options are possible:

—   when the brewery collects the personal data, apart from giving the basic information it may also state that it will pass on the personal data to the jewellery company, naming it specifically; or

—   when the brewery collects the personal data, it will give the basic information plus a statement to the effect that the data may be "given to other companies who have products which we consider might be of interest to you"; when a copy of the data is given to the jewellery company it will have to inform the data subjects under Article 11.

In either case, the form should, as is now standard practice, give the data subject the opportunity to request that his or her personal data are not disclosed to other organisations. The usual method is to ask the data subject to tick a box if he or she does not want the data so disclosed.

The contract between the immediate controller and organisations to whom the data will be disclosed, which will become controllers in their own right, should deal with the question of informing data subjects. This will directly affect the value of the data. Imagine a database containing information about 100,000 individuals. The controller may have been in a position to give the necessary information to data subjects when it collected the data, for example, by including an appropriate statement on application forms. The cost would thus be minimal. But imagine if the recipient of a copy of the database had to inform each of the data subjects individually. Even allowing for discounts for posting such volumes, the cost would be considerable.

Article 11(2) allows exception from the notification on recording or disclosure to third parties of data not obtained directly from the data subject if the provision of the information proves impossible or involves a disproportionate effort or where the recording or disclosure is expressly laid down by law. Particular examples of processing for statistical and research purposes are mentioned but it is possible that further exceptions may be provided.

An assessment of whether effort is disproportionate can take into account the number of data subjects, the age of the data and any compensation measures adopted[1]. Legislative provision may be required to give effect to this exception. A situation where it could prove useful is where a company has a database of customers which it has collected over a period of time. In the light of the Directive's provisions, the company might re-design its forms to include a suitable statement as to future disclosures of personal data. However, some of the longer established customers of the company might not have seen these newer forms. It could involve a disproportionate effort to identify these customers now.

Other Occasions when Data Subjects must be Informed

Data subjects must be informed in situations other than those described above. Data may be transferred to a third country, for example, where the controller, although established in the United Kingdom, has foreign subsidiaries or associated organisations. Alternatively, the organisation may transfer the data to a foreign sub-contractor for processing. Given the existence of global networks, this may be done simply by transmitting the data across telecommunications systems. For example, a company established in the United Kingdom may transmit its holding of personal data to, say, Venezuela where it is processed and returned with the results of the processing.

Where the "third country" (being a country that is not a Member State of the EC) fails to provide adequate levels of protection in relation to personal data, the data may only be transferred under certain circumstances, by way of derogation from the Directive, as set out in Article 26. Unless within the other conditions set out in Article 26, the data subject must be informed and his unambiguous consent obtained before transfer.

Nevertheless, this is unlikely to be required in most cases, in particular where the transfer is in connection with a contract with the data subject or the data are from a publicly available register, such as the register of electors. Even so, there may be occasions when express consent is required and controllers must be aware of this and check whether this is the case before going ahead with the proposed transfer. It is possible that the Office of the Data Protection Registrar will keep a "black list" of countries which do not afford adequate protection for personal data in specified circumstances. It is expected that the number of countries thus classified will be small. However, a major difficulty is that Article 25(2) describes adequacy in terms of considerations such as the nature of the data, the purpose and duration of processing, etc. Thus,

---

1   Recital 40.

adequacy of protection will vary from case to case and all that can be given is guidance. In many cases, it will be up to the controller to decide for himself or herself[1].

A possible pre-condition of transfers of personal data to third countries not having an adequate level of protection is for the controller to adduce adequate safeguards in terms of the protection of the privacy and fundamental rights and freedoms of individuals and the exercise of their corresponding rights[2]. Such safeguards may be provided for by contractual clauses which may be adopted by and required by the Commission under Article 26(4). At this stage it is impossible to say how this will work in practice. The Office of the Data Protection Registrar may prove helpful as a source of guidance. It is not inconceivable that these provisions could be implemented in such a way that individual clearance from the Registrar is required before transfer. This is unlikely, however, particularly in view of the Commission's experience of granting individual exemption under Article 85(3) of the EC Treaty[3]. Of course, where the Commission adopts approved contractual clauses, controllers must ensure that they include them in the legal agreement under which data are to be transferred to the third country in question[4].

The data subject must give his or her consent if none of the grounds for processing in Article 7(b) to 7(f) apply. In practice this is likely to be quite rare. Finally, consent may be required in terms of processing of sensitive data.

Subject Access

The Data Protection Act 1984 presently provides for subject access. Under the Act, data users must, within 40 days of a request, inform the data subject whether the data user holds data which include personal data relating to that data subject and, if so, to supply the data subject with a copy of those data[5]. Where the information is expressed in terms which are not intelligible without explanation, such explanation must also accompany that information. The data user is entitled to charge the data subject up to £10 for complying with the subject access

---

1   The Home Office favour this approach to requiring clearance from the Data Protection Registrar; Home Office, *Consultation Paper on the EC Data Protection Directive*, 1996, p45.
2   Article 26(2). however, this is without prejudice to paragraph 1 which provides the basic derogation.
3   The Commission quickly found it was unable to cope with the volume of agreements notified to it and was forced to adopt the very unsatisfactory procedure of issuing "comfort letters".
4   Article 26(2) is not limited to occasions when data are transferred under a contract.
5   Section 21.

request. The data user does not have to provide other information such as the purposes of the processing, the source or recipients of the data. If the data user holds no personal data relating to the data subject, or holds data which are exempt from the subject access provisions, he can simply respond with an unhelpful form of words such as "I hold no personal data relating to you which I am obliged to give you a copy of".

For most organisations subject access requests are made infrequently. In some measure the possibility of charging a fee probably accounts for this. On the whole, individuals are likely to make a subject access request only when they suspect something is wrong which has or could have serious implications. The most obvious example is where a person has been denied credit although applications to obtain a copy of data from a credit reference agency is specifically covered by section 158 of the Consumer Credit Act 1974 and outside the ambit of the Data Protection Act.

Most organisations have to deal with only the occasional subject access request and, because of this, it is tempting not to bother to set up the mechanisms to deal with them efficiently nor to train appropriate members of staff in complying with subject access requests. This will have to change under the new law. More information must be given to the data subject by the controller and, because data protection law will extend to manual processing, an increase in volume of requests is anticipated. Rightly or wrongly, many individuals might suspect that far more interesting (and potentially damaging) information is stored on paper than in a computer. Although the increase in requests may be marked, it is unlikely to be very substantial, as experience in relation to medical records, where subject access to paper files is already available, demonstrates[1]. Nevertheless, organisations are advised to be aware of the new requirements for subject access and adopt appropriate measures. Otherwise, the cost of complying, especially where an individual's data are stored in part on computer and in part in a number of disparate and scattered paper files, could be significant.

The Directive requires that, without excessive delay or expense, the data subject must be furnished with confirmation as to whether the controller is processing personal data relating to the data subject and, if so, the following information in addition to communication of the data undergoing processing in an intelligible form[2]:

— the purposes of the processing;

---

1   Access is provided for under the Access to Health Records Act 1990.
2   It is submitted that a copy of the data, rather than the actual data, will suffice at present.

— the categories of data concerned;

— the recipients or categories of recipients to whom the data are disclosed;

— any available information as to the source of the data;

— knowledge of the logic involved in any automatic processing (at least those within Article 15(1)).

The data subject also has rights of rectification, erasure or blocking of incomplete or inaccurate data and a further duty is placed on the controller to notify third parties[1] of the fact that the data subject has exercised these rights and the controller has complied, unless this proves impossible or involves a disproportionate effort. The implications of these provisions, apart from responding to subject access requests is that the controller should consider keeping a record of the obtaining and disclosure of personal data.

Consider the house building company in our group of companies. In respect of sales of its houses to private individuals, the company keeps the following personal data:

— index cards held at site offices with details of buyers' name and address, telephone number, solicitor, building society, whether the buyer has a house to sell, approximate completion date of the house, preferences for options such as colour of bathroom suite, extras required, etc;

— individual files at head office containing an "order form" containing much of the above information in addition to correspondence with the buyers, their solicitors, etc. The files are stored in filling cabinets in alphabetical order;

— a computer database of persons buying houses or having bought houses from the company in the past containing name, age, approximate salary (in a band, for example, "£30,000 to £40,000"), address, telephone number, solicitor, house type and plot number, stage (that is, whether deposit paid, stage payments, etc), size of mortgage, etc.

The company obtains the data mainly from the persons buying the houses. Further information may be obtained from solicitors, banks and

---

1   Note that this applies not just to recipients but to all third parties.

building societies and the like. The company discloses the data to the legal department in the parent company, to sub-contractors (for example, the plumbing sub-contractor needs to know which colour of bathroom suite is wanted), public utility companies (gas, water, electric companies) and some of the data in the computer database is extracted and sold on to a number of companies selling furniture, carpets, curtains, and gardening equipment. Data is extracted on the basis of a number of parameters concerning individuals so that appropriate lists can be sold to different companies. For example, for a company selling expensive hand-crafted furniture, a list is derived based on those persons having the larger, more expensive houses who are aged over 40 and have a salary of at least £40,000.

Imagine that a certain Mr Peter Wiley recently bought one of the company's houses. After moving in, he has been annoyed because he has received a lot of junk mail with his name incorrectly spelt as "Willey". He suspects that the mistake may emanate from the house building company and, therefore, he decides to carry out a subject access request.

The company will have to provide a print-out of his data from the computer database and a copy of the relevant index card. Furthermore, a copy of the order form in his personal file would have to be given to him. Copies of correspondence in his personal file would not have to be given to him as such data are not a structured set of personal data unlike the order form itself.

Any reference to personal data relating to other individuals would have to be "blocked" (that is, suppressed from the print-out or blacked out) unless they have given their express consent. Additional information would have to be provided along the following lines:

Statement of Processing of Personal Data

I confirm that Acme Housing Ltd processes personal data relating to *Peter Wiley* of *123 Station Road, Newcliffe on Sea,* a copy of which is attached to this statement.

Your personal data are processed for the following purposes:
Customer/client administration - the administration of orders and accounts relating to customers and clients. Typical activities include recording and processing of orders and payments, credit checking or rating, control and monitoring of after sales service or maintenance, dealing with customer complaints or enquiries, analysis for management purposes and statutory returns

Marketing and selling. Typical activities include the classification, rating or checking of individuals' credit-rating, distribution of promotional materials by mail, door to door delivery or other means, telephone or face to face marketing or canvassing, dealing with complaints or enquiries, analysis for management purposes and statutory returns.

Trading in personal information. Typical activities include the maintenance and distribution, as a business activity, of information or data banks consisting primarily of data about individuals, analysis for management purposes and statutory returns.

Categories of data concerned:
Name, address and telephone number, legal representative, mortgagee and mortgage details (if any), completion date (actual or anticipated), choices of options and extras for properties under construction, present property ownership, details of property bought or ordered, deposit and stage payment details, income band.

Recipients or categories of recipients:
Employees, servants and agents of the Acme group of companies. Relevant departments in other companies within the Acme group of companies, sub-contractors, public utility companies, statutory bodies and public authorities.

Commercial organisations having products or services which are considered might be of interest (unless you have intimated your wish not to have your personal data disclosed to such organisations, either by ticking the appropriate box on the order form or by informing us in writing).

Current status
You have not informed Acme Contracting Ltd that you do not wish your personal data to be disclosed to such commercial organisations

Source of data:
Your personal data have been obtained, primarily, from information supplied by you. Information has or may be obtained, with your express approval, from your legal advisor and mortgagee, if any. Further information has been or may be obtained from statutory bodies and public authorities.

Automatic Processing:
Acme Contracting Ltd makes use of automatic processing to derive lists of data or databases concerning valued customers which it makes available to commercial organisations having products and services considered to be of interest to you, unless you have asked for your personal data not to be so disclosed as mentioned above.

In deriving the lists or databases, Acme Housing Ltd uses computer expert systems software that selects appropriate customers on the basis of property type and location, mortgage and income bracket.

Signed   Joe Ninety, Esq   Date
                Information Technology Manager
                Acme Housing Ltd

Controllers should also prepare appropriate statements for employees making subject access requests. Although the exercise of preparing to meet subject access requests may seem an unnecessary chore, it can and should be usefully incorporated in an objective study of the controller's entire data processing activities. For example, it may be found that some data are being stored but are never used again whilst other data that would prove extremely useful in future operations are not being obtained at an early opportunity, thereby significantly increasing the costs of data collection.

Summary

The framework of data protection law in the Directive is more complex and imposes more duties on controllers than does the present law. Controllers must make themselves fully aware of the implications of the Directive in a timely fashion because, to minimise the cost and disruption to data processing activities, it is of little use waiting until the day the new law comes into force. The processing of personal data under the new regime requires, in particular, detailed consideration of the notification, security, informing data subjects and subject access provisions of the Directive. Controllers would be advised to take the opportunity to review the whole range of information handling activities performed, whether in relation to personal data or otherwise. In this way, compliance mechanisms and procedures can be assimilated within the context of all the controller's information processing.

Apart from thinking about the particular provisions discussed in this chapter, controllers should also be aware of the following points and make appropriate provision:

—   There will be some important exemptions from some of the important provisions of the Directive (in relation to data quality, informing data subjects, subject access and publicising processing operations[1]). The extent and scope will not be known precisely until the specific legislative measures are drawn up[2].

—   Data subjects have a right to object to processing of data relating to them on "compelling legitimate grounds"[3]. Whether this extends to processing which the data subject has really good grounds to object to or simply to unlawful processing is impossible to tell at this stage[4]. If the latter, there should be no problem for controllers - they cannot complain if their processing is contrary to the Directive's provisions as implemented or other legal provision such as the law of breach of confidence. If the former interpretation is used, controllers must consider how they should deal with such objections which have to be "justified". Perhaps controllers should allow the data subject to put his objection, without delay, before a panel of senior officers of the controller's organisation or the in-house data protection official, if there is one. Speed could be of the essence because delay in dealing with what turns out to be a justified objection could give rise to compensation.

---

1   Articles 6(1), 10, 11(1), 12 and 21.
2   Article 13 states that Member States may adopt legislative measures to restrict the scope of the relevant obligations.
3   Article 14. This is primarily aimed at processing within Article 7(e) and (f). Member States may legislate to narrow down the right. The United Kingdom is unlikely to extend it to processing carried out on other grounds, Home Office, *Consultation Paper on the EC Data Protection Directive*, 1996, p30.
4   In the Home Office paper, p30, an example of a data subject objecting to disclosure of his or her data to a person known to him or her is used.

Chapter 5 : Perspectives on the Directive: Recipients and Third Parties

Introduction

The controller is the person who determines the purposes and means of processing and is the key player in terms of imposing obligations in respect of processing personal data. However, there are a number of other persons who handle personal data and who may have obligations and constraints placed upon them in relation to these data. Those other persons of particular interest for the purposes of this chapter are processors, recipients and third parties. Article 2 of the Directive contains definitions of these persons.

A "processor" is a person processing data on behalf of a controller. A typical example is an independent computer bureau which performs the physical processing of the data for the controller. Usually, the processing will be carried out in the context of a contract between the controller and processor but this may not always be so as the definition is in terms of "natural or legal person, public authority, agency or any other body which processes personal data on behalf of the controller". Although it appears that employees of the controller could be classed as processors, the definition of "third party" suggests otherwise as does the language of Article 17 on security of processing.

"Recipient" is defined as a natural or legal person, public authority, agency or any other body to whom data are disclosed, whether a third party or not. Basically, this means anyone to whom the data are disclosed, including the employees and agents of the controller and processor, if there is one. There is, however, one curious exception and that is authorities which receive data in the framework of an inquiry. Presumably, this could mean the Inland Revenue asking for information about an employee's earnings or about payments made to a consultant or sub-contractor. The consequence of this is that information about recipients or categories of recipients which is given when notifying processing activities or to data subjects does not have to include a description of such authorities.

A "third party" is any natural or legal person, public authority, agency or any other body other than the data subject, the controller, the processor and persons who, under the direct authority of the controller or processor, are authorised to process the data. If an employee of the controller makes a copy on magnetic disk of the controller's database which contains personal data and then sends it to a computer bureau for processing, neither the employee nor the bureau or its employees are third parties. Figure 5.1 illustrates the identity of various persons to whom, for example, the data are disclosed.

The definitions are important in determining the scope of data protection law and in the relevant person's perception of how the law affects him or her and what measures should be put in place to ensure compliance with the ensuing obligations. Of course, in many cases, controllers will also be processors and recipients in respect of personal data. For example, a parent company in a group of companies will be a controller in respect of its own employees, clients and customers; it may process personal data on behalf of its subsidiary companies and it will have personal data disclosed to it from a number of other sources.

The way in which the Directive imposes obligations on processors, recipients and third parties is discussed below, commencing with processors.

Duties imposed on processors

A processor is a natural or legal person, public authority, agency or any other body which processes personal data on behalf of the controller. A computer bureau is a processor as is a bank processing personal data for a client company so that the necessary salary payments can be made. In a group of companies, one company may act as a processor in respect of the other companies' personal data. However, it may be that the parent company is deemed to be the controller in respect of itself and all its subsidiary companies[1], although this contradicts present practice in the United Kingdom and legal reality as each company in a group of companies is a separate legal entity.

---

1   Recital 19 dealing with the position where a controller is established in a number of Member States, particularly by virtue of subsidiary companies, suggests this is possible.

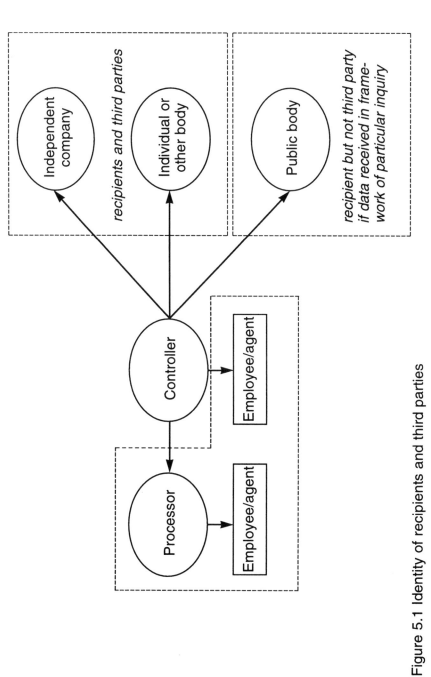

Figure 5.1 Identity of recipients and third parties

Local authorities and other bodies run along similar lines present problems in determining the identity of and distinction between controllers and processors. Local authorities have departments headed by chief officers, such as the treasurer's department, town clerk's department, etc. Two possibilities arise. Either each department is a controller in respect of its own data which may be processed by another department or the local authority is the controller of all the personal data processed by all its departments.

It would be sensible if the acid test of who should be controller was based on legal personality. However, this may not always be appropriate. A local authority has but one legal personality, as a corporation. This is unlike a group of companies where each has its distinct and separate legal personality. On the other hand, a partnership does not have its own legal personality distinct from its partners[1] and it would be ridiculous if each partner had to register separately as a controller. In practice, there may be some leeway and it may be up to organisations with complex structures to decide how to approach the issue. To some extent this is in line with current United Kingdom practice which is[2]:

— each company in a group must register separately in respect of its own processing of personal data;

— if processing is done by one company on behalf of another within a group of companies, it must register as a computer bureau;

— a large organisation, albeit only having one legal personality, may find it more convenient to have separate registrations, for example, on a departmental basis;

— partnerships register as such giving names of individual partners;

— sole traders register giving details of their own name and trading name, if any.

It is submitted that this practice will continue. In particular, large organisations which are a single legal entity but have branches or substantial departments may choose whether to operate the whole organisation as a single controller or to set up each branch office or

---

1   Unless a rare limited partnership.
2   Office of the Data Protection Registrar, *The Guidelines*, Third Series, November 1994, pp43ff.

department as a controller in its own right[1]. If the latter approach is used, this will have important implications, including:

—   the notification requirements could be more onerous;

—   information about disclosures to other branches and departments may have to be given to data subjects;

—   each branch or department will be a processor if it processes personal data on behalf of other branches or departments.

Large single entity organisations must give some careful thought to which would be the best approach for them. This will require an in-depth analysis of present and future data flows within the organisation and to outside persons and bodies. A further factor will be how organisational responsibility for personal data is assigned.

The Directive imposes the following explicit obligations on processors:

—   in respect of confidentiality of processing under Article 16;

—   implementing measures in relation to security of processing; Article 17.

Furthermore, the controller must ensure that the data quality principles in Article 6(1) are complied with and contractual guarantees may be required in relation to transfers to third countries (in which a processor may be established) under Article 26. How these obligations affect processors is considered below.

Confidentiality of Processing

Confidentiality of processing is provided for by requiring standards of security as set out in Article 17, discussed later, and by Article 16 which states that any person acting under the authority of the controller who has access to personal data must not process those data except as instructed by the controller. An exception is where processing is required by law. The restriction on processing only in accordance with the controller's instructions applies to "any person" and, although the processor is specifically included, it will also apply to employees and agents of both the controller and the processor.

For the avoidance of doubt as to the scope of the controller's instructions, processors should obtain a formal written statement of

---

1   It may have to do this if it has branches in other EC Member States; see recital 19.

those instructions. The processor also must ensure that its employees, agents and consultants who have access to the data are aware of the instructions as to processing. It would be advisable to restrict access to the data by means of appropriate passwords so that only those persons carrying out the controller's instructions have access to the data.

Processing required by law could include compliance with a search warrant or an Anton Piller Order. The Data Protection Registrar presently may apply to a circuit judge for a search warrant which includes the power to inspect and seize any documents or other materials which may be evidence of the commission of any offence under the Data Protection Act or contravention of any of the data protection principles. This power will be retained under the law, with appropriate modification and extension.

Anton Piller Orders instruct a potential defendant to allow the plaintiff accompanied by his or her solicitor to enter his or her premises and inspect, copy or remove relevant materials. For example, consider a company which can show a strong *prima facie* case that ex-employees, who have set up business in competition with the company, have taken a copy of the company's customer database without permission. The company may be granted an Anton Piller Order, allowing it to search the ex-employees premises for the database and to take it or a copy of it to retain as evidence of a breach of confidence and/or copyright infringement for the trial.

Disclosure to bodies such as the Inland Revenue, DSS and Customs and Excise will also fall within the "required by law" exception. Of course, apart from the above specific obligations, the law of breach of confidence will be highly relevant. Even though the personal data are not particularly secret or sensitive, the law of confidence imposes obligations on recipients of confidential information not to use it or disclose it without the permission of the "owner" of the information[1].

Security of Processing

Article 17 lays down obligations on controllers in respect of security. It also requires controllers to choose processors who can provide sufficient guarantees in terms of technical security measures and organisational measures. Further, the processing carried out by a processor must be governed by a contract or legal act binding the

---

1   Relatively mundane information such as customer lists have been accepted by the courts as protected by the law of confidence. See, for example, *Thomas Marshall (Exports) v Guinle* [1976] FSR 345.

processor to the controller. In particular, such contract or legal act must stipulate that:

— the processor shall act only on instructions from the controller; and

— the obligations placed on the controller are also incumbent on the processor[1].

For evidential purposes, the relevant part of the contract or legal act must be in writing or equivalent form[2]. Article 17(1) spells out the nature of the obligation. It requires appropriate technical and organisational measures to protect personal data against accidental or unlawful destruction or accidental loss, alteration, unauthorised disclosure or access, in particular where the processing involves the transmission of data over a network, and all other unlawful forms of processing. Having regard to the state of the art and the cost of implementing the measures, the level of security must be commensurate with the risks represented by the processing and the nature of the data. In other words, the more sensitive the data, the better the security measures to be adopted.

As far as the relationship between the controller and the processor is concerned, three aspects are important. First, the processor has the same duty and standard of care in relation to the personal data as does the controller. Secondly, the imposition of this duty must be evidenced in writing (or other permanent form such as an electronic document). Finally, the processor should indemnify the controller against the consequences of any breach of the duty of care. Providing an indemnity does not absolve the controller from responsibility and the controller appears to be jointly and severally liable with the processor[3]. However, it does enable the controller to recoup any compensation paid to an aggrieved data subject. It will also concentrate the mind of the processor on the importance of security. A typical contractual clause is given below.

Security and Confidentiality of Processing

The processor agrees to implement, maintain and monitor appropriate technical and organisational measures to protect personal data processed on behalf of the controller. The measures taken shall be in accordance with those required under

---

1   Incumbent means imposed as a duty.
2   Article 17(4).
3   Article 17(3) states that the obligations shall also be incumbent on the processor.

the [Data Protection Act 1984, as amended[1]], and as supplemented by this agreement. The processor agrees to process the data only in accordance with the controller's written instructions and, in particular, agrees not to disclose the data or give access to the data to any person other than the processor's employees and agents charged with the task of processing the data. The processor agrees to inform such employees and agents of the confidential nature of the data, the restrictions on processing them and the requirements for security of processing.

The processor warrants that it is aware of the requirements of data protection law in relation to processing personal data (including the principles relating to data quality), security and confidentiality and that it will comply with all such requirements. Furthermore, the processor agrees to save harmless and indemnify the controller in the event of any breach of its obligations in respect of security and confidentiality of processing howsoever caused.

Similar formalities will be required as between companies within a group of companies or departments of large organisations where the companies or departments operate as individual controllers.

Note that the sample clause makes reference to confidentiality of processing and to other obligations under data protection law. The processor must, apart from anything else, comply with the principles relating to data quality as discussed below.

Data Quality Principles

The principles relating to data quality are set out in Article 6(1) and are broadly equivalent to most of the data protection principles in the Data Protection Act 1984[2]. After all, both sets of principles have a common origin in the European Convention on Data Protection. The principles in the Directive require that personal data shall be:

(a)   processed fairly and lawfully;

(b)   collected for specified, explicit and legitimate purposes and not further processed in a way incompatible with those purposes ...;

(c)   adequate, relevant and not excessive in relation to the purposes for which they are collected and/or further processed;

---

1   Assuming the Directive is implemented by amending the present Act.
2   Other principles, such as that relating to security are dealt with separately elsewhere in the Directive.

(d) accurate and, where necessary, kept up to date; every reasonable step must be taken to ensure that data which are inaccurate or incomplete, having regard to the purposes for which they were collected or for which they are further processed, are erased or rectified;

(e) kept in a form which permits identification of data subjects for no longer than is necessary for the purposes for which the data were collected or for which they are further processed ...

Article 6(2) requires the controller to ensure that these principles are complied with. Therefore, the controller must be satisfied that any processing carried out on his or her behalf by a processor is done in accordance with the principles. The controller can do this by making reference to the principles in his or her instructions to the processor. Ideally, as above, this can be incorporated in the relevant contractual term and backed by an indemnity.

Processor Established in Other Member States and Third Countries

It is possible, especially given the ease of transmitting massive amounts of data anywhere in the world at little cost, that the processor will be located outside the United Kingdom. Where the processor is in another EC Member State, the applicable law in relation to processing will be that of the controller[1]. However, this is not so clear cut where the controller is established in more than one Member State. Article 4 states that the applicable law is the national law in each of the Member States in which the controller is established. Consider that a company in the United Kingdom has a French subsidiary company which carries out some of the United Kingdom company's data processing. Recital 19 contemplates that a single controller may be established in a number of Member States by virtue of subsidiaries and, if so, each subsidiary will be subject to the national law in which it is established. If the French company is a processor, the applicable law will be English or Scots as the case may be. However, if the French company is deemed to be simply part of the controller, French law will be the applicable law. This distinction could be important because of the possibility of differing approaches between Member States as to derogations and options contained in the Directive. Also, there could be differences of interpretation of the Directive's provisions.

---

1   The applicable national law provisions in Article 4 make no mention of processors. The controller is governed by the national law in the State in which it is established or, where established in more than one Member State, the relevant national law in

In other cases, a United Kingdom controller may engage a processor located outside the EC. As now, if the data are used or to be used in the United Kingdom, such processing clearly must be governed by the relevant United Kingdom law[1]. Thus, if the controller fails to obtain the necessary contractual guarantees concerning security or fails to ensure that the principles relating to data quality are complied with, he or she will be in breach of the United Kingdom's data protection law.

The transfer of personal data for processing to a third country may take place only if the third country ensures an adequate level of protection[2]. This is without prejudice to the provisions adopted in compliance with the Directive by the Member State from which the data are transferred. Where the third country does not afford an adequate level of protection, the controller may only transfer personal data subject to one of the conditions laid down in Article 26[3]. Whilst the onus is on the controller to see that the conditions are present, processors may find themselves providing contractual assurances that the required safeguards are in place.

To summarise, processors in third countries will have obligations, in most cases of a contractual nature, placed on them in respect of:

—   confidentiality of processing;

—   security of processing;

—   the principles relating to data quality.

In addition, where the third country itself does not afford an adequate level of security, transfer may only be permitted provided contractual guarantees are in place. Appropriate contractual clauses may be approved by the Commission, in which case, the appropriate clause must be used[4]. However, the Directive is silent on applicable law in such a case. Consider a contract between a controller established in England which sub-contracts its processing to a processor established in, for the sake of argument, Taiwan[5]. Realistically, the contract could be subject to English law or Taiwanese law and whichever is used, this

---

each. Recital 18 suggests that the applicable law will be that in the Member State in which the controller is established.

1   This is the effect of section 39(5) of the Data Protection Act 1984.
2   Article 25(1).
3   Even then, there must be full compliance with national law adopted in pursuance of the Directive, in particular Article 8; see recital 60. Other domestic laws may prevent the transfer.
4   Article 26(4).
5   It is not suggested that Taiwan will be a third country failing to provide adequate safeguards. It is simply used for the purposes of illustration.

could have a significant effect on the interpretation, value and enforcement of the contractual guarantee[1]. The importance of the contractual guarantee is that it "encourages" the processor to reach an acceptable standard of processing because he or she would be in breach of contract otherwise. It is important that its impact is not diluted and it would be sensible for the controller to insist that the contract is subject to the law of the relevant EC Member State rather than some third country law where the enforceability of the contractual guarantee could be in doubt.

Controllers in Third Countries

It may be that the processor is established within the EC but the controller is established in a third country. For example, a United States' company may transfer its personal data to Ireland or Wales for processing[2]. Whilst the American company will be subject to United States data protection law, by virtue of Article 4(1), the Irish or Welsh processor will be subject to Irish and United Kingdom implementations of the Directive, as appropriate. This is because the controller is making use of equipment situated in an EC Member State. At once, it can be seen that the manner in which Member States implement the Directive is very important. Member States making maximum use of possible derogations and choosing the least onerous options are likely to be more attractive processing "havens" than those which implement a more restrictive version of the Directive.

Article 4(2) requires that, in cases where the controller is not established in the EC but makes use of equipment for the purposes of processing personal data within the EC, a representative established within the territory of the Member State must be designated. Of course, this is most likely to be the processor. This has implications in respect of the notification requirements and there are two possibilities where formal notification is necessary:

—   the controller will notify, naming the processor as representative; or

—   the processor, as the controller's representative will notify, also naming the controller.

Processors carrying out processing on behalf of controllers situated in third countries must check whether the processing activities have to be formally notified to the relevant supervisory authority and, if so make

1   Of course, in many such cases, the contract will be subject to English law.
2   A common occurrence.

sure that the controller carries out the necessary formalities or, if the processor does so as the controller's representative contractual provision is made for this. For example, if the processor registers the processing activity, there should be a clause in the contract empowering the processor to act as the controller's representative, requiring the controller to furnish the necessary information. The representative and controller are likely to be jointly and severally liable for breaches of data protection law[1].

As at present, data protection law imposes statutory duties on controllers and in some circumstances, breach of a duty will give rise to personal claims by individual data subjects for compensation. Some, if not all, of those statutory duties will also be placed on processors. How will this operate where the controller is in a third country and the processor is in, for the sake of argument, England or Wales?

Imagine that a processor, BBS (Bedfordshire Bureau Services) is based in Luton and it processes data for a number of controllers based in different countries. Imagine that BBS processes personal data relating to Karen who lives in London on behalf of Data-CD Inc, (a company incorporated in the United States), Kömputer GmbH (a German company) and OsloData (a Norwegian marketing firm). Due to a lapse in security at BBS, Karen's data, from all three sources, are modified and then disclosed to an English credit reference agency, all without authorisation of any of the controllers. Karen suffers loss and distress as a result of being unable to obtain credit because the modified data indicate, incorrectly, that she is a bad credit risk, having several county court judgments for debt against her.

There has been both an unauthorised modification of Karen's data, which are now inaccurate, and an unauthorised disclosure of her data. First, it will be important to establish which law applies as regards the processing of Karen's data[2].

—   BBS is the representative of Data-CD and its processing for Data-CD is subject to the United Kingdom's implementation of the Directive;

---

1   Article 4(2) requires controllers established outside the EC (or the territory of a Member State in which it law applies) to designate a representative without prejudice to legal actions which could be initiated against the controller himself. Of course, suing a controller established in another country could prove difficult and expensive. Suing a foreign controller in the United Kingdom may require leave of the court before service of proceedings.
2   Article 4, when read with recitals 18 to 21, is not notable for its clarity and other interpretations may be possible. Home Office, *Consultation Paper on the EC Data Protection Directive*, 1996, p16.

— BBS's processing for Kömputer GmbH should be subject to the German implementation of the Directive;

— BBS's processing for OsloData is subject to the United Kingdom's implementation of the Directive.

If Karen wishes to sue for compensation, where can she sue issue legal proceedings? She is likely to want to sue in London. Looking at the three controllers of her data in turn:

— Data-CD is not domiciled in any of the EC or EFTA countries. Normally, the English courts have no jurisdiction over it. However, it is possible that Karen could be granted leave to serve proceedings abroad[1]. The court has discretion in such cases and if the processor, being the man on the spot, is liable for compensation in such circumstances, leave of an English Court to serve proceedings in the United States is unlikely;

— Kömputer GmbH is domiciled in Germany which is a Member State of the EC. Therefore, the Civil Jurisdiction and Judgments Act 1982, based on the Brussels Convention on jurisdiction and enforcement of judgments in civil matters, applies[2]. The basic rule is that the defendant can only be sued in the State in which he is domiciled. However, there are a number of exceptions. For a tort, the defendant can be sued in the State in which the harmful event occurred - in this case, England;

— similar principles apply to the Norwegian firm on the basis of the Lugano Convention which extends to EFTA countries[3]. The Norwegian firm can be sued in England and leave to issue proceedings against it would not be required.

From this analysis it would seem that, as processor, BBS is only liable for compensation in respect of its processing on behalf of controller's based outside the EC. It should seek an indemnity from such controllers in respect of acts or omission of the controller which might give rise to a claim against BBS for compensation. On the other hand, where the controller is established within the EC, it can easily find itself being sued in the English courts for compensation resulting from the acts or omissions of BBS. It would be wise for controllers established in

---

1   Order 11, Rules of the Supreme Court. Rule 1(1) sets out categories of claims where service outside jurisdiction may be possible. This includes a tort committed within the jurisdiction.
2   Implementing Article 220 of the EC Treaty.
3   Implemented in the United Kingdom by the Civil Jurisdiction and Judgments Act 1991.

other EC Member States to obtain appropriate contractual indemnities against processors established in other Member States.

Of course, the new data protection law, as now is the case, is likely to be backed by a number of criminal offences. Foreign criminal law cannot be applied in the English Courts. However, processors established in the United Kingdom will be subject to the full weight of the criminal law, notwithstanding that they are processing personal data on behalf of a foreign controller.

Another factor to be borne in mind is that the definition of "processing" in the Directive is very wide. For example, a person who simply collects or organises personal data on behalf of the controller is a processor and such persons must be aware of the data protection implications of what they do. A typical example of such processing is where a publisher of a magazine available in England agrees to insert a form into an issue of the magazine seeking personal information from readers who then return the completed form to the publisher, perhaps encouraged by a chance in a competition. The publisher then forwards the completed forms to the marketing department of a foreign commercial organisation.

Finally, if the processor decides the purposes and means of processing jointly with the controller, the processor is himself a controller with all this implies. The Directive is unclear where the controller decides the purposes but the processor decides the means of processing. Suppose a marketing consultancy has collected enquiry forms from a large number of prospective customers. It engages a computer bureau to enter the data onto computer and to generate a list of those potential customers arranged by "an appropriate credit-scoring system" of the processor's choice. The marketing consultancy has determined the purposes of the processing but the computer bureau has determined the means. Who is the controller? The marketing consultancy, the computer bureau, both or neither? Would it have been better to identify the controller based on who determines the purposes only?

Duties imposed on recipients

A recipient is a natural or legal person[1], public authority, agency or any other body to whom the data are disclosed whether a third party or not. Public authorities receiving data in the framework of a particular inquiry are excepted from the definition. The meaning of "recipient"

---

1   In English law, a natural person is a legal person. The term "legal person" includes
     natural persons and juristic persons such as companies and corporations.

appears to be very wide, including employees and agents of the controller or processor. The definition is important as information as to the identity of recipients or categories of recipients is amongst that to be given to the data subject on relevant occasions.

The Directive places obligations of confidentiality and security on some recipients. Any person (for example, employees, agents and consultants) acting under the authority of the controller or processor, including the processor himself or herself, must not process personal data except on instructions from the controller[1]. In addition to this duty, the law of confidence will apply in many cases and will control, in particular, unauthorised disclosure and use.

Under Article 17, the controller has an obligation in relation to security of processing and it will be sensible for the controller to impose an equivalent duty on persons acting for the controller. For example, the contract of employment between the controller and its employees should explicitly state that the employee must only process personal data in accordance with the controller's express instructions; must not disclosure them to anyone else within the controller's organisation or otherwise and must take all precautions to maintain the security of personal data. It should also draw employees' attention to the fact that failure to comply will be treated very seriously and may result in dismissal or other disciplinary action against the employee. Equivalent warnings should be given to consultants and the like and a processor should be required to use similar provisions in its dealings with employees and consultants.

The operational measures implemented by the controller can be usefully supplemented or reinforced by drawing employees' attention to the importance of security. The seriousness of security in relation to computer data has been acknowledged by the courts in the context of employees in *Denco Ltd v Joinson*[2], before the Employment Appeal Tribunal. The Tribunal held that, in a modern industrial world, a deliberate use of an unauthorised password by an employee to gain access to information to which he was not entitled and which was stored in a computer was, *prima facie*, gross misconduct which could result in summary dismissal unless there were exceptional circumstances making such a response unreasonable. The Tribunal recognised the importance of maintaining the integrity of computer stored information and it was said that management should make it very

---

1   Article 16.
2   [1991] IRLR 63.

clear that unauthorised interference would result in the imposition of severe penalties.

Employees may be liable to prosecution in a number of ways. The Data Protection Act 1984 presently contains a number of criminal offences which may be committed by employees. These are likely to remain and may be extended. For example, in their role as recipients, employees and agents may be liable to prosecution for unauthorised disclosure of personal data[1]. Procuring the disclosure of personal data is also an offence[2] whether carried out by an employee or any other person. Directors, managers, secretaries and similar officers of corporate bodies may be liable to prosecution if the relevant offence is committed with their consent or connivance or is attributable to their default[3].

In many respects the present law imposes far more duties on most of the persons who would be classed as recipients under the Directive which is concerned with civil law not criminal law[4].

Third Parties

Some recipients, such as outside organisations to which personal data are disclosed are third parties. In many cases, third parties may owe a duty of confidence in respect of the data disclosed to them. Of course if they then process the data, deciding the purposes and the means of processing, they will become controllers in their own right. Otherwise, the Directive will have little direct impact on third parties.

Article 12, governing data subjects' right of access to their personal data, places a duty on controllers to inform third parties to whom personal data have been disclosed of the fact that the data have been rectified, erased or blocked in particular because of the incomplete or inaccurate nature of the data unless this proves impossible or involves a disproportionate effort. The Directive is silent as to what the third party is meant to do in such a case. Presumably, if the third party has recorded or stored the data, he or she should make the correction so as to comply with the principles relating to data quality. If the third party did not record the data or has subsequently passed it on to another, there would seem to be little the third party can be expected to do.

---

1   Section 5(3) of the Data Protection Act 1984 imposes criminal liability of employees and agents.
2   Section 5(6) of the Data Protection Act 1984.
3   Section 20(1) of the Data Protection Act 1984.
4   Criminal law is outside the ambit of Community law.

Chapter 6 : Perspectives on the Directive: Data Subjects

Introduction

Under the present law, data subjects are ill served in terms of the information available to them concerning processing of their personal data by data users or computer bureaux. Apart from the subject access provisions and being informed of non-obvious uses of their data when they are collected from them, data subjects are not informed about who holds their data and for what purposes it is held. It is possible to glean some potential uses from forms completed by data users, either having the ubiquitous "tick box" to prevent further processing of their data for marketing purposes or requiring the data subject to write in to prevent such further processing. Furthermore, the Data Protection Act 1984 only applies to the automatic processing of personal data[1]. Unless access to personal data in manually processed files is available under specific legislation, such as the Access to Health Records Act 1990, individuals have no general right of access to personal data relating to them stored on paper.

Individuals will know the identity of a number of data users who hold their personal data. For example, employees will know that their employer is likely to have information about them on computer. Their bank, building society, club or mail order companies they deal with will have personal data relating to them. Public authorities and bodies such as local authorities, tax authorities, health service providers, DSS, DVLC and others have massive amounts of personal data which are processed automatically. But how many other organisations hold their personal data? The difficulty is that personal data are valuable and a significant amount of "list trading" goes on (that is, selling copies of databases containing personal data). Personal data also may be disclosed in a number of ways. Literally hundreds, if not thousands, of organisations could hold personal data relating to one particular individual.

---

1   The Economic League, which provided information to enquirers including membership of the Communist Party, kept all its personal data on index cards.

How does the data subject find out about these other organisations that may hold their personal data? It could prove quite a task for a detective, let alone an ordinary individual. Inspecting the Data Protection Register is not helpful in this respect. An individual may find out when he or she starts to receive mailings from an organisation not previously dealt with. Another, less pleasant way to find out is when the individual is refused credit, perhaps inexplicably. Or, like the unfortunate man with an impeccable character and without any previous convictions whatsoever was arrested and charged with driving whilst disqualified because of incorrect information stored on the police national computer. Details about the disqualification had been entered against his name by mistake. He lost his job and had his car impounded. It took him four months to trace the man to whom the previous conviction related and who had a very similar name before he could clear his name[1].

The difficulties do not stop at finding the identity of the data user. Some data users have a considerable number of registrations; perhaps 30 or 40. In respect of which registration does the data subject carry out a subject access request? Checking the register entries (available from The Office of the Data Protection Registrar at Wilmslow[2]) may give some clue as to which are likely to contain the individual's personal data. In some cases, the data user may prove helpful but there is no statutory duty for the data user to assist. In an extreme case if there are, say, 30 entries on the register, the data subject may have to make 30 subject access requests and pay 30 times the fee which may be up to £10! A further problem with the current provisions is that the data user has up to 40 days to respond. To say the very least, the present arrangements for subject access are cumbersome, inadequate and unsatisfactory.

An important feature of the Directive is its emphasis on transparency of processing, keeping the data subject informed about the processing of his personal data. Together with the Directive's stated goal of protecting fundamental rights and freedoms of individuals, in particular their right of privacy in respect of processing their personal data, this sounds like good news for data subjects. We should all welcome this - we are all data subjects, whether we like it or not. How these provisions will be applied in practice and just how effective they will be in achieving the first of the Directive's twin aims is discussed below[3].

---

1   *The Times*, 8 May 1990 p4.
2   Copies may be purchased at £2 each. The register is now also available on the Internet.
3   The other, somewhat contradictory, aim is the free movement of data; Article 1.

The Data Subject's Perspective

What does the typical data subject (the man on the Clapham Omnibus, perhaps) want from data protection law? In an ideal world, a data subject might want only those controllers to process his or her data who have the data subject's express permission to do so, and then only for declared purposes the data subject has agreed to. Clearly, this would be unworkable in practice. It would be unduly restrictive and make the cost of processing personal data, in many circumstances, prohibitively expensive. The Directive does not seek to introduce too many obstacles on controllers processing personal data but attempts, perhaps imperfectly, to strike a balance between the interests of the various players in the processing of personal data.

Realistically, a data subject's expectations of data protection law should allow him or her to find the answers to the following questions:

—   Who has my personal data?

—   How do I get to see a copy of it?

—   How do I get it rectified if it is wrong (and can I get compensation if I suffer damage)?

—   Under what circumstances can I stop my data being processed?

The provisions in the Directive which require information to be given to data subjects on the collection, recording or disclosure of personal data relating to them should help increase data subjects' awareness of controllers processing their data. In this respect, the Directive appears more satisfactory than the present law. Subject access is similar to that presently provided for though there are some important changes. Rights of data subjects to have incorrect data dealt with together with compensation are in the Directive and are not dissimilar to the present arrangements. The data subject is given a new "right to object" to processing which, depending on its manner of implementation in the United Kingdom, could be quite important and, as far as the data subject is concerned, empowering. It is also possible that, in some circumstances, the data subject will have to expressly consent to the processing of his or her personal data. Another important issue which may not immediately occur to data subjects is how secure personal data relating to them is. These issues are now considered in more detail.

Informing data subjects

We have seen that there are a number of occasions when the data subject must be given information being, primarily, when data are collected from him[1] and, when the data have not been obtained from the data subject, when they are recorded or disclosed to a third party[2]. However, the information need not be given when the data subject already has it and this fact is very important for controllers who are likely to adopt systems of data gathering that will inform the data subject contemporaneously. This can be expected to be done at the point of contact between the data subject and the controller.

Where the data subject is, for example, opening a bank account, applying for hire purchase, registering with a health service provider or completing an official return, he or she will complete or sign a form. That form, or a printed statement accompanying it, can carry the necessary information which may be no more than the identity of the controller and the purposes of processing. An example is:

> "Acme Bank plc is a controller processing personal data under the [Data Protection Act]. Your personal data will be used for the administration and servicing of your accounts, including any form of deposit, savings or current account, borrowing or credit accounts and investment accounts, and the provision of other personal banking services to you and all associated and related activities. A full statement of our data protection policy is available on request. Unless you advise us in writing to the contrary, we may send you details of services offered by ourselves and our associated companies from time to time."

Article 10 on informing data subjects on collection of data from them is expressed in the imperative. The controller must provide the data subject with the information unless he already has it. Further information may be required to be given if necessary to guarantee fair processing. Thus, if the personal data is to be disclosed or processed in a manner which would not be immediately apparent to the data subject, this should be mentioned at the time of collection. Individuals would not expect to be told that the data will be disclosed to and processed by employees of the controller. But, if the data are to be sold on for commercial purposes, this fact should be mentioned and, as is present practice, the data subject should be given an opportunity to object to this.

---

1   Article 10.
2   Article 11.

In most cases, the new provisions on informing the data subject on collection will not have any significant effect. A great many data users currently make use of appropriate statements and, in any case, very few individuals actually read them.

Including appropriate statements on forms or on accompanying leaflets is a relatively easy and inexpensive way of informing data subjects but there are occasions when personal data are collected in the absence of a form. Placing orders by telephone is a particular example. If the order is placed in response to an advertisement in a newspaper or magazine, it may be possible to include the statement in the advertisement. If not, would the person placing the order be happy to listen to a statement on the telephone before his or her personal details are asked for? Probably not if that person is paying for the call. However, the Directive does not stipulate that the information is given at the time of collection, it may be printed on a confirmation of order form, for example[1].

Where the data have not been collected from the data subject, he or she must be informed at the time the data are recorded or before disclosure to a third party[2]. The wording of Article 11(1) lacks clarity. Are data that have been obtained indirectly from the data subject covered? What is the position as regards informing the data subject no later than the time the data are disclosed to a third party - must such disclosure be envisaged before, at or after the time the data are collected? Fortunately, recital 39 is very helpful in determining the meaning of Article 11(1). It indicates that the necessary information must be provided on recording the data where the data have not been collected directly from the data subject. Furthermore, the requirement for giving information prior to disclosure to a third party is intended to extend to situations where such disclosure was not anticipated at the time the data were first collected from the data subject[3].

Thus, the relevant information must be given to the data subject:

— when personal data which have not been collected directly from the data subject are recorded; or

— when such personal data are disclosed to a third party whether or not such disclosure was anticipated at the time of collecting the data.

---

1   However, in respect of non-obvious uses, this would not comply with the present law; see *Innovations (Mail Order) Ltd v Data Protection Registrar* (unreported) 29 September 1993.
2   Article 11.
3   Anticipated by whom? The data subject or the controller?

The information need not be given where the data subject already has it. Therefore, if disclosure to a third party is envisaged at the time the data are collected, it may be possible to give the information at this stage even though disclosure may not occur for some time. This is something the controller and third party should work out between themselves.

To show how this could work in practice, consider the example indicated in Figure 6.1. Controller #1 has collected personal data directly from the data subject and intends to disclose the data to controller #4 in due course. Controller #2 collects personal data relating to the data subject indirectly, from a relative of the data subject. At this stage, controller #2 does not intend to disclose the data to a third party. Controller #3 has as least some data relating to the data subject that have not been collected, directly or indirectly, from the data subject[1]. Controller #3 later discloses the data to controller #4.

The basic information that must be given includes the identity of the controller and representative, if any, and the purposes of the processing. Further information must be given if necessary to guarantee fair processing, for example, categories of data, recipients or categories of recipients and the existence of subject access rights. It is suggested that, in the example, the following information should be given to the data subject:

— controller #1 will, at the time the data are collected, provide information (possibly by including an appropriate statement on a form) relating to:

    — the controller's identity (and representative, if any);

    — the purposes for which the data are being collected;

    — a description of categories of recipients into which controller #4 falls;

---

1   The personal data could have been generated by the controller. For example, the controller could be a body such as the NHS assigning a national insurance number to the individual.

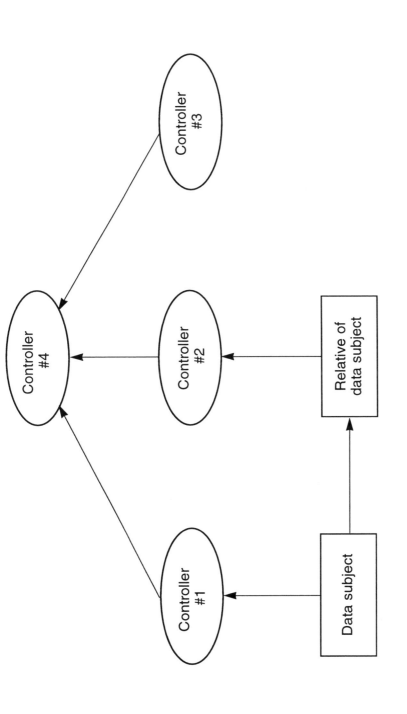

Figure 6.1 Informing data subjects on recording or disclosure

—   controller #2 will, at the time the data are recorded give information (which may be given through the person from whom the data are collected, especially if that person is a relative or colleague) as to:

  —   the identity of the controller (and representative, if any);

  —   the purposes for which the data are being collected;

—   when controller #2 decides to disclose the data to controller #4, the following information should be given to the data subject no later than the time the data are disclosed:

  —   the identity of the controller (and representative, if any);

  —   the identity of the third party recipient;

  —   the purposes for which the third party will process the data.

Controller #3 is in the worst position as it may have no direct or indirect contact with the data subject. It will have to give appropriate information, probably by post, to the data subject. It should also try to predict future disclosures to third parties and provide that information at the same time. If the data are "sensitive", it may also have to seek the data subject's consent. If controllers #1, #2 and #3 provide the necessary information, controller #4, in the normal run of things, will not have to provide information to the data subject, unless it later decides to process for purposes not previously notified to the data subject or discloses the data to other third parties.

Article 13 contains exemptions from a number of provisions including the requirement to give information and subject access. Controllers may come to the conclusion that they are within the exemption and simply not give any information at all. Unlike subject access requests where it may be plain that the controller is attempting to make use of an exemption[1], this may be difficult to pick up by data subjects.

A further exception from providing information under Article 11 is where, in particular in the context of processing for statistical or research (scientific or historic) purposes, the provision of information

---

1   For example, see *The Agreement in the Enforcement Action against the Halifax Building Society*, (unreported) 6 January 1992 where the building society claimed to be exempt disclosing some personal data in response to a subject access request on the basis of prevention of crime.

proves impossible or would require a disproportionate effort. Provision of information would be impossible if the data have been converted to a form suitable for statistical analysis such that there are no longer any personal identifiers. For example, in a household survey of leisure preferences, the name and address of each interviewee may not have been stored in the database to be analysed. Provision may prove to require a disproportionate effort if such a database contains data which could allow extraction of identifiable personal data only after considerable work. For example, the database may contain information as to age (in banded ranges), sex and address but does not contain names. Again, in many cases, it will be the controller who will make the initial decision whether providing the information proves impossible or involves a disproportionate effort[1].

The above exception may apply in wider circumstances than statistical or research purposes. Article 11(2) allows exception if the recording or disclosure is expressly laid down by law. As Member States may restrict the scope of the right to receive information by virtue of Article 13, it is difficult to envisage why further exception would be required under Article 11(2). However, it should be noted that the first limb of the Article is not limited to the stated purposes of statistics and research and it could cover other purposes. The acid test must be whether data subjects' "rights of privacy" are likely to be unfairly prejudiced by the recording or disclosure envisaged. One way this could be addressed is to consider whether personal data will end up being processed in a way or by a controller which the data subject would not expect and such that the data subject's right of access effectively is defeated by his or her ignorance of the processing.

In applying Article 11, the golden rule should be that, apart from express and limited exceptions based on Article 13, the data subject should always know or be able to find out about processing of his or her data, to obtain a copy of it and, if it is incorrect, have it rectified or erased. Too great a reliance of the exception in Article 11(2) by controllers and third parties will prevent or hinder this and, from the data subject's point of view, transparency of processing operations will be lost. Policing this aspect of data protection law will be very difficult.

---

1   However, Member States are to provide appropriate safeguards, whatever they might be! Could the existence of subject access provisions be deemed to be an appropriate safeguard?

Subject Access

Under present data protection law subject access requests are not made in large numbers. A number of changes may stimulate subject access requests such as:

— the provision of more extensive information than is now given;

— the extension of subject access to manually processed personal data files;

— possible changes to subject access procedures;

— an increase in publicity.

In addition to gaining access to his or her personal data, under the new law, a data subject also will be given information concerning the purposes of processing, the categories of data, recipients or categories of recipients and the logic involved in any automatic processing for automated decisions. As this further information is likely to be expressed in general form, for example, by making use of standard descriptions currently used for registration purposes, it will not, of itself, lead to a significant increase in subject access requests. An employee making a subject access request to his or her employer is likely to receive information such as that below, in addition to receiving a copy of his or her data:

Your personal data (a copy of which is attached) are used for the following purposes:

1.   personnel/employee administration

2.   work planning and management

The categories of data concerned are as indicated on the attached copy of your personal data and include name, title, age, PAYE code, NHS No, address, bank details, job title, salary grade, start date and any special needs.

Your data are disclosed routinely to our holding company which carries out processing of data on our behalf, to banks and financial institutions for payment of salary, to the trustees of the group pension scheme, to statutory bodies and public authorities including the Inland Revenue, DSS and Health and Safety Executive and otherwise as required by law. We will not disclose your personal data to any other third party unless required by law without your prior consent.

None of your personal data are subject to decisions which may affect you which are made solely by automatic means

In compiling such information, controllers will bear in mind the rationale for subject access being, by recital 41, to enable the data subject to verify the accuracy of the data and the lawfulness of processing. Unless an individual suspects that there is a mistake in the data, he or she is unlikely to want to go to the trouble of making a subject access request. Certainly, in many cases, the nature of the data and the processing will be reasonably apparent.

Organisations granting credit may be concerned at having to provide knowledge of the logic involved in automatic processing, particularly within Article 15(1). The danger is that would-be fraudsters will be able to find out the basis for granting credit and modify their credit applications accordingly. There are two reasons why the information given regarding automatic processing is unlikely to compromise the fight against fraud.

First, the basic rationale is, as for other information provided in respect of subject access, to enable the data subject to verify the accuracy of the data and the lawfulness of the processing. However, recital 41 goes on to say that this right to know must not adversely affect intellectual property rights including trade secrets, providing this does not result in the provision of no information whatsoever. The techniques used in automated decision-making, such as the factors to be used and their relative weighting, are likely to be trade secrets. It is arguable that any complex formulae used may also be subject to copyright in addition to being protected by the law of confidence[1].

The second reason is connected with the exceptions to a number of provisions of the Directive including providing information to the data subject and the right of access. One of these exceptions which may be provided for by Member States is the prevention, investigation, detection and prosecution of criminal offences. This will almost certainly be seized upon by the United Kingdom and, consequently, controllers may refuse to give any information relating to automated decision-making where the prevention of crime is appropriate - as it will be in terms of credit-giving organisations which consider that they would

---

1   In *Bookmakers Afternoon Greyhound Services Ltd v Wilf Gilbert (Staffordshire) Ltd* [1994] FSR 723, Aldous J seemed to accept that a formula could be an original literary work in which copyright subsisted.

increase their vulnerability to fraud if the relevant knowledge was disclosed to data subjects.

It is likely that the controller will respond to this aspect of subject access requests with a bland and generalised statement of the logic involved or, where the prevention of crime exception is relied on, with no mention at all.

Although derogation from certain provisions of the Directive is possible for manually processed files for up to 12 years from the date of adoption, this does not extend to the subject access provisions. However, data subjects should not expect to receive copies of every reference to the data subject held by the controller as the Directive's provisions apply only to manually processed files that fall within the definition of a personal data file. Recital 27 indicates that the Directive applies only to files that are structured so as to allow easy access to personal data. Controllers will not have to trawl through all their general and correspondence files looking for incidences of personal data relating to the individual making the subject access request.

Although there is no express mention in the articles of the Directive, recital 42 makes it clear that subject access to health data may be restricted, for example, that access may be obtained only through a health professional. There are other provisions dealing with personal data held in manual files. To some extent this mirrors present practice under the Data Protection (Subject Access Modification) (Health) Order 1987 and, for manually processed files, the Access to Health Records Act 1990. For example, by section 5(1) of the 1990 Act there is exemption from subject access if there is a likelihood of causing serious harm to the physical or mental health of the patient or any other individual. The basis of such an exemption can be seen in *Sidaway v Board of Governors of the Bethlem Royal Hospital*[1] in which the House of Lords made it clear that a doctor's duty, as with the health authority, was to act at all times in the best interests of the patient. In appropriate circumstances this could justify withholding information from the patient.

In *R v Mid-Glamorgan Family Health Services, ex parte Martin*[2], a patient had been refused access to his health records going back to before the 1990 Act came into force. It was argued that it would be detrimental for the patient to see those records directly. An offer was made to disclose the records conditionally to a medical expert

---

1   [1985] AC 871.
2   (unreported) 29 July 1994.

appointed by the patient but this was not accepted by the patient who claimed that there was a common law right of access. The Court of Appeal refused to grant access on the "best interests" principle, rejecting that there was any such common law right.

Equivalent provisions have been made under the Data Protection Act 1984 in respect of social work data[1]. There is no express equivalent in the Directive. However, Article 13 allows exemption and restriction from subject access to safeguard the protection of the data subject or the rights and freedoms of others. This should allow the United Kingdom to retain its present approach both to health and social work data as regards subject access.

Incorrect or Incomplete Data

Assuming that the data subject has been able to determine that a controller is processing data relating to him or her which are incorrect or incomplete, that data subject will be keenly interested to have those data modified quickly. The individual will also want to know whether compensation is available in respect of any harm suffered as a result.

Under the present Data Protection Act 1984, data users holding or processing personal data that are inaccurate or not up-to-date are in breach of the data protection principles and could be subject to enforcement action taken by the Registrar. Also, depending on the circumstances, the data user could commit a criminal offence under section 5 of the Act. The unauthorised disclosure of personal data is also a breach of the principles and can attract criminal penalties. Apart from these provisions encouraging data users and, in some cases, computer bureaux, to comply with the Act, individuals also are given certain rights to have data rectified or erased and may be in a position to obtain compensation from data users or computer bureaux.

Under section 24 of the Act, a person who finds that a data user holds inaccurate data about him or her can apply to either a County Court or the High Court for an order for the rectification or erasure of the inaccurate data[2]. The Court will issue an order if it is satisfied that the data are inaccurate. There are certain options available to the court. If the inaccurate data were received or obtained from a third party or from the data subject himself then the Court may instead order that the data be supplemented by a statement of the true facts as approved by

---

1   Data Protection (Subject Access Modification) (Social Work) Order 1987, SI 1987/1904.
2   Of course, in many cases, the data subject may prefer to complain to the Data Protection Registrar instead, in which case, he or she cannot receive compensation.

the Court. Erasure is likely where the data subject has suffered damage by reason of unauthorised disclosure or access to the data and there is a substantial risk of further unauthorised disclosure or access.

There are two forms of compensation available to data subjects under the Data Protection Act 1984. Section 22(1) provides for compensation for damage suffered as a result of inaccuracy of personal data. Data are inaccurate if they are incorrect or misleading as to any matter of fact[1]. Compensation is also available in respect of any distress also suffered. For example, consider an ambitious young man trying to obtain a better job. He is called for interview at a prestigious company only to be told that he cannot be offered the appointment because of a bad reference from his current employer. When pressed, the interviewers say that the reference suggests that he is dishonest and not to be trusted. He makes a subject access request to his current employer and finds his personal details in the employer's computer include a statement that he has been disciplined for "fiddling his expenses". This is a mistake and applies to another employee with a very similar name. The individual may sue under section 22(1) for compensation for the loss of opportunity (the lost chance of obtaining a better job) and could also expect to receive an award for the distress he would suffer from hearing of the allegation of dishonesty[2]. The total award could be substantial.

Data subjects may also obtain compensation for loss or unauthorised disclosure of personal data relating to them under section 23 of the Act. The authority referred to is that of the data user or the computer bureau, as the case may be. Apart from this it should be noted that, in the absence of some other legal obligation such as imposed by contract, a data user has every right to deliberately erase personal data. Section 23 is concerned with accidental or negligent loss of data (perhaps because of poor security measures) or disclosure to or access by persons not specified in the register entry. Again, in addition to compensation for damage suffered, compensation is available for distress[3].

There is a statutory defence against claims for compensation by data subjects. This applies where the data user has taken such care as in all the circumstances was reasonably required to ensure accuracy or to prevent the loss, destruction, disclosure or access in question.

---

1   Section 22(4) of the Data Protection Act 1984.
2   The author is not aware of any significant actions taken under the compensation provisions of the Act.
3   It would seem that there must be actual damage to sustain a claim in respect of distress.

The Directive does not go into great detail as regards the rights of individuals to have data rectified or erased or as to compensation provisions. The fine detail is left to Member States. However, Article 12(b) does require that data subjects have the right to obtain from the controller "as appropriate the rectification, erasure or blocking of data the processing of which does not comply with the provisions of this Directive, in particular because of the incomplete or inaccurate nature of them".

"Blocking" is a new concept and means that the data are not erased but are not processed for the purposes of a particular activity[1]. For example, an organisation may have a database of customers, copies of which it makes available to other organisations from time to time. If a particular individual objects to this, his or her personal data can be "flagged" accordingly so that they are suppressed when compiling copies of the database to give to other organisations but the data still exist and may be used for the organisation's own internal requirements.

The Directive mentions incomplete data. The Fourth Principle in the Data Protection Act requires data to be adequate, relevant and not excessive in relation to the purpose or purposes for which the data are held. Incomplete data are inadequate and thus will breach the Fourth Principle. However, the Act does not specifically give any direct right to the data subject in respect of incomplete (or inadequate) data unless, by virtue of their inadequacy, they are deemed to be inaccurate.

Article 23 of the Directive requires Member States to provide for compensation for data subjects who suffer damage as a result of any unlawful processing operation or act incompatible with the national provisions adopted in pursuance of the Directive. It is possible that controllers will be given a statutory defence if the controller proves that he or she was not responsible for the event giving rise to the damage. In respect of the controller's defence, recital 55 emphasises fault on the part of the data subject or *force majeure.*

Although somewhat vague, the Directive appears to provide for compensation in wider circumstances than in the Act as it refers to "unlawful processing". Presumably this means processing contrary to the provisions of the Directive[2]. There should be no particular reason why United Kingdom law cannot respond accordingly. It is unlikely to

---

1   The Home Office take "blocking" to mean retaining the data but preventing their further active processing; Home Office, *Consultation Paper on the EC Data Protection Directive,* 1996 p23.
2   Harry Cohen's *Data Protection and Privacy Bill,* 1996, bases compensation on breach of the data protection principles. This is, arguably, too narrow.

lead to a plethora of compensation claims as the burden of proof in respect of damage suffered will remain with the complainant. If the United Kingdom fails to enlarge the circumstances when compensation is available, the data subject may be able to bring an action on the basis of a breach of statutory duty[1] if the relevant provisions in the Directive are deemed to be of direct effect.

The right to subject access, like a number of other important provisions of the Directive, may be excluded or restricted by Member States by virtue of Article 13 but this does not appear to extend to the right to compensation for unlawful processing. However, in practice, without subject access, it will be difficult, if not impossible, for data subjects to find out whether the processing is unlawful. The co-operation of the supervisory authority may be useful in such a situation.

To take an example, say that Henry, a teacher, has a twin brother named Harry who was indicted and tried for indecent assault on a child. Harry was acquitted. However, Henry, who has recently completed a teacher training course, finds that he is unable to secure a teaching appointment. He suspects that the fact that Harry has been accused of such a crime, involving a child, has been wrongly noted on his file held by the local education authority. He makes a subject access request but the copy of his data contain no information about the indictment. Suspecting that the authority has suppressed this information, Henry complains to the Data Protection Registrar who investigates the matter and finds that the authority does indeed have a note on Henry's file about the indictment. The authority explains that it did not supply this information to Henry on the basis of the prevention of crime and/or public security exception. The authority apologises to the Registrar for the mistake and corrects Henry's file. Even assuming the exemption from subject access was applicable, Henry can now sue for the damage he has suffered (for example, his inability to obtain a teaching post[2]) resulting from the error.

Other areas of law may be appropriate in cases where compensation is available under data protection law. For example, the law of breach of confidence (unauthorised disclosure or access to personal data) or

---

1   See *Garden Cottage Foods v Milk Marketing Board* [1984] AC 130 in relation to Article 86 of the EC Treaty.

2   In practice, as it would be by no means certain that Henry would have gained a teaching post, the court will only award him a proportion, based on his loss of chance of appropriate employment. Thus, if the court considers it 75% likely that he would have been offered a post, damages will be assessed accordingly.

defamation (publication of incorrect data) may be relevant depending on the nature of the data and the circumstances[1].

Objecting to Processing

A data subject may know of a controller processing personal data relating to him or her but be unhappy about this even though the processing otherwise appears to be lawful. Examples could include processing of:

—   "white" data; this is data indicating that the data subject has a good credit record;

—   "grey" data indicating that the data subject has been or is in default of some credit arrangement for a period of time not exceeding, say, three months;

—   lifestyle data for marketing purposes;

—   endangered life data, for example, indicating that the data subject is terminally ill or has a limited life expectancy.

The Data Protection Registrar has voiced concern over processing such data under the present Data Protection Act[2]. Much was done, mainly by way of co-operation with the relevant bodies but much remains to be done in this field. However, apart from the intervention of the Registrar in some of these difficult areas, under the 1984 Act the data subject has no right to object to the processing of such data providing it complies in all respects with the Act. Will the Directive change this, inconvenient though it might be to give individual data subjects rights to object to processing?

The following provisions of the Directive appear to give the data subject a right to object or provide for the data subject's consent to be obtained (which could be withheld):

—   Article 14(a) - compelling legitimate grounds;

—   Article 14(b) - direct marketing;

—   Article 7(a) - consent required for processing;

---

1   Legal aid is not available for defamation but might be for an action under data protection law.
2   In particular, see the *Tenth Report of the Data Protection Registrar*, HMSO, 1994, pp7-30. This was Eric Howe's last report.

— Article 8(2)(a) - consent required for processing sensitive data;

— Article 8(2)(e) - consent required in respect of disclosure by certain bodies;

— Article 26(1)(a) - consent required for transfer of data to a third country.

These instances seem to be a significant improvement over the 1984 Act and appear to give the data subject much more control on the processing of his or her personal data.

Article 14(a) gives the data subject a right to object, at least where processing is carried out under Article 7(e) and (f)[1], at any time on compelling legitimate grounds relating to his particular situation, except where otherwise provided by national legislation. Where the objection is justified data relating to the data subject can no longer be processed by or on behalf of the controller. It has been suggested in Chapter 3 that various interpretations of this provision were possible. On the one hand it could give a data subject a right to object for "good reason" only. Alternatively, it might only be applicable when the processing is outwith that permitted by the Directive.

The Home Office quote an example where the right to object might be appropriate being where the personal data was likely to come into the hands of a person known to the data subject[2]. This could be a particular problem in the United Kingdom because of the lack of any general law of privacy. However, Member States may whittle down this particular right to object. It is submitted that, either this provision will be ignored when implementing the Directive, or the right to object to processing that is otherwise lawful will be restricted to situations where the processing will cause distress to the data subject.

Article 14(b) contains two variants. The first is simply to give the data subject a right to object to his or her data being used for direct marketing purposes. Member States must take steps to ensure that data subjects are aware of this right. It is almost certain that, given the level of direct marketing in the United Kingdom, this variant will be adopted. In many ways it mirrors the present approach where data subjects are usually given an opportunity to object to their data being passed on to

---

1   Public interest or official authority processing or processing necessary for the legitimate interests of the controller , etc. The right could be extended to other forms of processing but the government does not intend to do so; Home Office, *Consultation Paper on the EC Data Protection Directive*, 1996, p30.

2   Ibid.

other organisations. The existence of the Mailing Preference Scheme, allowing individuals to make known their desire not to receive "junk mailings" is another reason for using this variant. Thus, there should be little, if any, change to present practices.

The second variant is, as mentioned in Chapter 3, so cumbersome and potentially expensive that it could so seriously jeopardise the direct marketing industry that its adoption in the United Kingdom would be unthinkable.

Article 7(a) allows processing if the data subject has unambiguously given his or her consent. In practice, it is almost certain that one or more of the other grounds for processing in Article 7(b) to (f) will apply and consent under Article 7(a) will rarely, if ever, be required. It can be seen as no more than a safety net to catch any processing not covered by the other grounds. The author cannot think of a good example when it would apply apart, perhaps, in terms of list trading.

On the other hand, consent to processing sensitive data is more likely to be required. Article 8(2)(a) allows processing of sensitive data with the data subject's explicit consent[1]. An example could be where an employer uses ethnic monitoring or collects information relating to disabilities as part of its equal opportunities policy[2]. The relevant form should make it clear that the information is to be given only if the data subject consents and it would be advisable to require the data subject to sign the form signifying his consent. The other situation when the data subject's consent is required in respect of sensitive data is where a non-profit making body, such as a trade union, wishes to disclose the data to a third party; Article 8(2)(e). The body does not need consent for processing in the course of its legitimate activities.

A situation where consent may be required is where a trade union has negotiated a special deal with a life assurance provider and wants to disclose its member list accordingly. The data subject may be asked to signify his consent on the annual membership renewal form, by means of the ubiquitous box. The provision does not say that the consent must be explicit or unambiguous. Notwithstanding the definition of the data subject's consent in Article 1, it is possible that ticking the box to prevent disclosure will be acceptable rather than the other way round.

---

1   Member States may prohibit processing of sensitive data in some circumstances notwithstanding the data subject's consent.
2   Arguably, this could be within Article 8(2)(b) - employment law obligations and rights. However, the employer's policy may go beyond that required by law.

Finally, the data subject may be asked to consent to the transfer of personal data relating to him or her to a third country not having an adequate level of protection under Article 26(1)(a). The consent must be unambiguous and it is clear that it must be obtained before transfer. However, there are a number of other conditions which will, in most cases, apply. In particular transfer in the context of a contract between the data subject and the controller will be the most common.

Part III : How the Directive Impacts on Different Types of Organisation

In the following chapters the impact on controllers of the Directive's provisions, as they are likely to be implemented in the United Kingdom, are examined. Where there is potential in the Directive for derogation from a particular provision or where Member States may choose from a number of options, the resulting effects of differing approaches by the government are compared. Assessment of the most likely choices is also given with an overall view of the impact of the Directive as the author considers it is most likely to be implemented ("best case") together with a "worst case scenario". The worst case scenario is, even then, based on the most onerous implementation that may realistically be implemented in the United Kingdom. There is little to be gained by delving into the realms of fantasy and considering options that are, frankly, totally unrealistic.

Generally, the author's view of the most likely manner of implementation is based on a minimalist approach, being the least onerous for controllers to comply with. This accords with the current government's view, being to "... implement the Directive in the least burdensome way for data users, whilst protecting individuals"[1].

For the purposes of the following chapters, a standard format is used. After an introduction describing the nature of the category of organisation dealt with, there is a discussion of the processing of personal data by such organisations, including an examination of the flows of personal data, both internally and externally, depending on the nature of the organisation. Next, the data protection environment affecting processing of personal data is considered, concentrating on the notification and publicity aspects of the Directive and constraints on the processing of "normal data" and "sensitive data". The distinction between normal and sensitive data is based upon whether the data falls within Article 8 of the Directive - the processing of special categories of data.

---

1   Home Office, *Consultation Paper on the EC Data Protection Directive*, 1996 p5.

Links with data subjects are examined, in particular, those relating to informing data subjects on collection, recording or disclosure to third parties, subject access and situations where data subjects' consent may be required or where data subjects are likely to raise objections to processing. Transfers to third countries are then examined in the context of the categories of organisation concerned. Finally, there is a summary which emphasises some of the main issues for the type of controller under consideration.

Given the complexity and variety of processing operations carried out in respect of personal data, a comprehensive and detailed examination of every form of processing of personal data by varying organisations is not possible. The author's intention is to concentrate on the most common and important forms of processing in the context of the Directive, highlighting some of the most important issues for controllers.

As issues relating to employees and consultants engaged by organisations are broadly similar to all forms of organisations, they are dealt with separately in Chapter 16.

Chapter 7 : Banking and Financial Services

Introduction

Most of us have dealings with banks and other providers of financial services and have regular contact with them. From the familiar bank or building society in the High Street to the investment broker, the range of financial services now available is quite dazzling. Until recently, however, a significant number of individuals did not have a bank account or building society account but, since the abolition of the Truck Acts 1831-1940[1], employees no longer have a right to be paid in cash and, in most cases, payment is made by crediting employees' bank or building society accounts or by cheque.

The types of services provided by, say, a typical bank, include:

—   deposit and current account facilities;

—   credit facilities such as overdraft facilities, loan accounts, credit cards;

—   mortgage facilities;

—   share broking;

—   investment advice and financial planning services.

Other services might be offered such as insurance and pensions, PEPs (personal equity plans) and such like[2]. Indemnities and bonds may be arranged for parties to contracts as a form of guarantee for performance.

Clients and customers range from private individuals to large corporate bodies such as public limited companies and public authorities. Other clients include partnerships and sole traders.

---

1   Repealed by the Wages Act 1986.
2   Some services may be offered by associated or subsidiary companies.

A typical bank is used for the purposes of examining the implications of the Directive. The issues and conclusions should be generally applicable to most other forms of organisation granting financial services. It should be remembered that, like many other organisations, banks owe a duty of confidence in respect of information relating to their clients. Exceptions are laid down for banks by the case of *Tournier v National Provincial*[1] and by the Code of Banking Practice, particularly with a view to protecting banks from fraud. Data protection law is both superimposed on and inter-twined with the duty of confidence.

Personal Data Processing

A large number of individuals have bank accounts. Those accounts will be held and administered at local branches of the bank and the sort of personal data held will include name, address, date of birth, title, age, employer in addition to considerable data relating to balances and transactions, current and historical, going back over some time. Other information will include details of personal loans, overdraft agreements, standing orders, direct debits, share ownership, mortgages, life and property insurance and, perhaps, some form of credit rating and details of previous handling of the accounts. For example, whether the individual has paid off loans in accordance with the form of agreement, whether the individual has attempted to exceed an overdraft limit, etc. Other information may be kept such as the existence of a county court judgment against the individual or conviction for a fraud offence. The rationale for keeping such data is that it will help the bank form a view as to risk in future lending and protect itself from fraudulent activities.

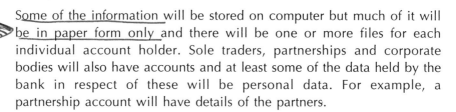

Some of the information will be stored on computer but much of it will be in paper form only and there will be one or more files for each individual account holder. Sole traders, partnerships and corporate bodies will also have accounts and at least some of the data held by the bank in respect of these will be personal data. For example, a partnership account will have details of the partners.

Each branch of the bank will have information about persons and organisations providing goods and services to the bank such as stationery supplies, window cleaning, etc. Again, though much of the information will not be personal data, some of it will be. Whether this information is subject to data protection law depends on whether it is processed automatically or, if not, whether it is stored in structured files for manual processing.

---

1   [1924] 1 KB 461.

Data flows

Figure 7.1 shows some of the most common data flows to and from banks. The data subject, the employer of the data subject[1] and organisations and bodies linked to the data subject, such as a party to a contract with the data subject or a mortgagee, will pass information to and receive information from the bank. The gateway for most of this information will be the data subject's branch of the bank but it will be the bank's head office that will handle data protection issues such as registration, developing and implementing policies and the like. Some of the data subject's data will be passed to the bank's head office, to other banks and through the bank clearing system. The bank may also provide financial references to third parties, typically other banks acting for clients, for example, on behalf of a potential party to a contract with a customer of the bank[2].

The data subject's branch may also, either directly or through the head office, pass on personal data to associated companies offering financial or related services such as insurance or investment advice. The bank may also pass on information to credit reference agencies, which keep records of individuals' credit worthiness, and to statutory bodies such as the Inland Revenue. Banks are likely to be involved in marketing in various ways. Some marketing may be generated in-house, some from associated companies and some may result from list trading, where the bank sells a database of clients to a third party organisation for marketing purposes. Other, *ad hoc* disclosures may be made, for example, in connection with the investigation of fraud. The extent to which data protection law constrains such processing is examined below.

---

1   The employer's bank paying the employee's salary also will pass data to the bank.
2   Apart from data protection law, this will be subject to the liability for negligent misstatement under the doctrine in *Hedley-Byrne v Heller & Partners* [1962] 2 All ER 575.

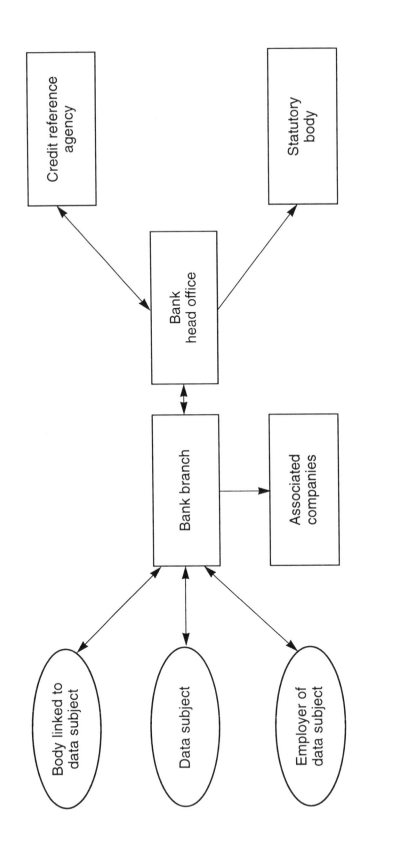

Figure 7.1 Data flows – banks

Processing under the Directive

Little, if any, personal data relating to clients or customers is likely to be sensitive within the meaning suggested by Article 8(1) of the Directive. However, information relating to an individual's finances is sensitive in a broader sense. Banks and other financial institutions should keep our personal information confidential and should not disclose it without good reason, for example, where disclosure is required by law. We expect banks to take care with our information but, in the past there have been examples of lapses of security in this respect. For example, there has been some concern about banks divulging customer data over the telephone.

Other current concerns relate to the disclosure of "white data" (data showing an account has been properly handled) and to the recording of personal data by banks which falls within the category of sensitive data within section 2 of the Data Protection Act 1984. It is arguable that such practices do not comply with the law as it presently stands[1]. The Directive is unlikely to provide an easy solution to such matters.

One major advantage a bank has over some other forms of controllers is that banks have regular contact with their customers and clients. This should mean that increased obligations to inform data subjects will be met easily and with little additional expense. Furthermore, banks already take data protection law very seriously and have adopted policies and mechanisms to comply. They are likely to adapt to the new regime of data protection law with minimal disruption.

Notification

Banks tend to have numerous different registrations for strategic purposes. It is easier to handle registration to deal separately with different categories of personal data being processed for different purposes. It is likely that banks will maintain this approach if formal notification is required. As has been noted earlier, exemption from or simplification of notification is a mixed blessing as the controller still has to have the relevant information available for any person on request and this could prove just as costly as formal registration. Banks are unlikely to welcome the requirement to give a general description of their security measures for fear that this could indeed jeopardise security. However, a very general bland statement should be acceptable.

---

1   *Tenth Report of the Data Protection Registrar,* HMSO, 1994, p20.
1   Ibid pp19-21.

One possibility is that exemption from notification is "bought" by the appointment of a personal data protection official. This should be welcomed by banks, most of which if not all, already employ persons responsible for dealing with data protection law.

Because notification (or publicising processing operation in the case of exemption from notification) will extend to structured manual files, the costs of notification could increase for banks which still have considerable amounts of personal data so stored. However, this may be an opportunity for them to critically analyse their manual processing of personal data and lead to modifications increasing efficiency. In some cases, it could encourage banks to review their manual processing with the object of automating it, wholly or partly, leading to considerable cost savings and increases in efficiency.

Best case - complete exemption from formal notification, probably coupled with the appointment of a personal data protection official (whether required by law or not) responsible for ensuring compliance and publicising processing operations in accordance with Article 19.

Worst case - formal notification of all the bank's processing operations required. Even so, it is unlikely that formal notification will be required for manually processed files.

The costs implications between the best and worst cases are likely to be insignificant. The savings in registration fees if exemption is permitted is tiny in proportion to the costs of deriving and monitoring the details and information required whether for formal notification or, if exempt from formal notification, so as to comply with the publicity requirements.

Constraints - "Normal" Data

In the normal run of things, there should be little constraint over the processing of the usual type of data held by banks. Processing will be permitted under Article 7(f), being necessary for the purpose of the legitimate interests of the controller or third party to whom the data are disclosed. Article 7(b) will also be applicable in respect of much of the bank's processing, being necessary for the performance of a contract with the data subject, etc.

Disclosure to statutory bodies is lawful under Article 7(c), compliance with a legal requirement, or Article 7(e), exercise of public authority.

Public interest disclosure will probably mirror that now permitted under the law of confidence.

The data subject's consent under Article 7(a) will be required where disclosure is made for other purposes, such as by passing on the data subject's details to an associated company or third party for the purposes of marketing[1]. As consent has to be unambiguous, it is questionable that the usual form of "tick box" will be acceptable and some positive form of indication of consent should be sought. For example, if the relevant form is to be signed by the data subject, it could carry a statement such as "I agree/do not agree that you may pass on my personal data to organisations which have products or services which you consider may be of interest to me" with an instruction to strike out accordingly.

Because the data subject's consent must be freely given, the practice adopted by some banks in the past that the provision of services to the customer was conditional upon giving consent to disclosure to other organisations (even within the same group of companies) is to be frowned on[2].

> Best case/worst case: there is no significant latitude for derogation in respect of processing normal data in this context.

Constraints - "Sensitive" Data

Apart from monitoring for discrimination amongst its own staff, banks should not need to process sensitive data within Article 8 of the Directive, being data revealing racial or ethnic origin, political opinions, religious or philosophical beliefs, trade union membership and data concerning health or sex life. One exception is perhaps trade union membership, where the data subject belongs to a trade union and pays his or her subscription by way of a standing order or direct debit. However, in that case, the data subject will have given his or her explicit consent and, accordingly, processing will be allowed under the Directive.

Prior checking of processing of personal data is unlikely to be required in the context of conventional banking and financial activities.

---

1   It is at least arguable that disclosure for marketing could fall within the "legitimate interests" of the bank or the third party to whom the data are disclosed.
2   *Tenth Report of the Data Protection Registrar,* HMSO, 1994, p19. Such practices are now contrary to the Code of Banking Practice.

Best case - there are no significant additional obligations imposed on banks and the like in respect of sensitive data.

Worst case - prior checking could be required for new and innovative forms of business developed by banks where sensitive data is involved. This could be burdensome, particularly as processing may not proceed until such prior checking, by the supervisory authority or sanctioned by it, has been carried out.

Links with Data Subjects

As mentioned above, banks are in regular contact with data subjects, so the provision of information required under data protection law and the obtaining of consent should not present insurmountable problems to banks and building societies and other organisations in the financial sector with a customer base.

This is not so with organisations such as credit reference agencies which do not obtain their data directly from data subjects. Such agencies receive information about individuals' credit worthiness from banks, hire purchase companies and the like. The wording of Article 11, which requires information to be given to the data subject on recording or disclosure to a third party of data not collected from him or her, is unclear. Recital 39 suggests that information regarding disclosure to a third party should be given to the data subject even when the data have been collected from him or her when such disclosure was not anticipated at the time of collection. To make sense of this "anticipated" must mean anticipated by the data subject. Thus, the data subject should be informed of the possible future disclosure of his or her data to a credit reference agency at the time the data are collected. Other disclosures should also be indicated at this time.

Ideally, the identity of the recipients, rather than categories of recipients, should be given. Otherwise, there is a danger that the data subject will be unable to find out which organisations are processing his data and transparency of processing is lost. This is important when consideration is given to the requirement for further information to be given under Article 10 to be such as to guarantee fair processing in respect of the data subject. If the bank fails to identify the credit reference agency or other third party specifically, there is a possibility that the agency or third party will have to supply this information direct to the data subject on the basis of the first limb of Article 11, recording data not collected from the data subject.

Informing Data Subjects

A bank's primary obligation to inform data subjects arises from Article 10. By giving further information, which may in any case be required in the circumstances, as to the future recipients of the data, the bank will save itself (and/or the recipient) the expense of having to do this at a later stage. The information should be given at the initial point of contact such as when an individual applies to open a bank account, completes a mortgage application form, etc. This should involve minimal expense, perhaps no more than redesigning the appropriate *pro formas* and agreements to include a suitable statement.

As indicated above, it is important to give some thought to the nature of the information to be given and the amount of detail. Giving sparse information at this stage may result in further information having to be given, either by the bank or a recipient to which the data are disclosed, in the future. Banks, building societies and the like should discuss the form of notice with potential recipients. It should be a matter for consideration in any contractual agreement under which data are disclosed or transferred.

> Best case/worst case: there is no significant latitude for differences resulting from the Directive. Much of the cost implications are dependant upon the bank's preferred method of informing data subjects.

Subject Access

Relatively few people exercise their right of subject access under the present law. There may be some increase under the new law because subject access will also extend to manually processed files. Whilst data users are likely to be able to charge a modest fee, as is now the case[1], satisfying a subject access request involving computer-held data and data in structured personal files is likely to be more expensive. Because Article 12 requires subject access to be "without excessive delay or expense", it is unlikely that either the 40 day limit for response under the Data Protection Act 1984 nor the current maximum fee of £10 will be increased significantly, if at all.

Because of the relatively low level of subject access requests, controllers such as banks have to weigh up the costs of implementing efficient procedures to deal with them with the staff training that that will entail or simply to respond to subject access on a one by one basis. In

---

1   The present maximum fee is £10.

either case, the cost of complying with a single request is likely to far outweigh the £10 fee.

More information must be given to the data subject exercising his or her right of access than before. Under the Directive, in addition to being furnished with a copy of the data[1], information must be given as to the purposes of processing, the categories of data concerned and the recipients and categories of recipients to whom the data are disclosed. Unlike Articles 10 and 11, there is no exemption from this where the data subject already has the information. Appropriate notices should be prepared by controllers. Further, and of some concern, is having to provide knowledge of the logic involved in any automatic processing, at least in the context of automated decision within Article 15(1). Although this must not prejudice trade secrets and intellectual property rights, some information must be given where such processing is performed.

Banks and other financial institutions may make use of computer software as a decision-making tool to evaluate whether, for example, to grant a loan to the data subject. If the decision generated by the software is the sole basis for approval or rejection of the application for a loan, the data subject must be given some information about the logic. Banks and other financial institutions must take great care to develop an appropriate statement which must be sufficient to give the data subject some inkling of the logic whilst not prejudicing security or making the institution more vulnerable to fraud.

> Best case/worst case: there is no latitude for derogation in the Directive apart from the exemptions in Article 13. Much will depend on how controllers approach compliance with subject access. Discussions between representatives of the banks and the like, such as the British Bankers' Association, and the Data Protection Registrar may help in the formulation of guidelines.

Consent and Objections

Set in a contractual environment as it is, the relationship between a bank or building society and its customer should provide for any necessary consents being granted by the data subject. The same applies to objecting to processing on compelling legitimate grounds. The formal agreement between the controller and the data subject must provide for any instances where consent may be required. "Compelling

---

1   Article 12(a) requires communication of the data in an intelligible form together with any available information as to their source.

legitimate grounds" are unlikely to be raised frequently but, if they are, the bank should consider putting a mechanism in place for dealing with them such as a senior executive or panel to whom the data subject can put his case. It will be rare that this provision will give rise to a justifiable objection. It might be where there is a possibility of undue influence or coercion on the part of the person to whom the data are to be disclosed. Banks and other organisations should treat reasonable objections sympathetically and responsively.

The only other occasion when the data subject may wish to interfere with the processing of his or her data are where they are used for direct marketing, either by the controller or some third party. Article 14(b) provides two alternative approaches for giving the data subject an opportunity to object. The first does not require specific action by the controller although Member States are charged with taking measures to ensure that data subjects are aware of their right to object. The second requires that data subjects are expressly offered the right to object before the data are used or disclosed for the first time for direct marketing purposes. The simple expedient of including an appropriate form of words to which the data subject can signify his or her consent to direct marketing either by the controller or a third party or both should be sufficient to deal with this at little cost to the controller.

> Best case/worst case: whichever of the alternative forms of objecting to direct marketing is adopted in the United Kingdom, the costs to banks and the like should be minimal, at worst requiring the inclusion of an appropriate form of words in agreements between the data subject and the bank.

Transfers of Data to Third Countries

Banks and other financial institutions may wish to transfer personal data to third countries for a number of reasons. A number of examples come to mind:

— the transfer may be in connection with a financial transaction made in the third country by one of its customers;

— a customer of a bank may be entering a contract with a person in a third country which requires financial references or a contractual bond;

— a bank may transmit data for analysis, modification or calculations to a processor in a third country which will return the data after carrying out the operation concerned;

— a bank may have collected personal data from new, existing or potential customers on forms which are to be sent to a third country for conversion to digital form and subsequent return.

Given the growth of networks and the ease of transmission the transborder flow of personal data is likely to increase substantially. Factors include the globalisation of markets and the ability to make use of data processing facilities in other countries, for example, where data entry is cheaper and more accurate. Of course, if the flow of data is within the European Community, there should be no problem whatsoever as Article 1(2) of the Directive breaks down barriers to data flows which are in place on the basis of protecting the rights and freedoms of individuals. It is conceivable that barriers could be erected on other grounds, for example, when the processing is not within the competency of Community law or the basis of the restriction or prohibition is for some other reason but, in practice, this should not be a significant problem.

Transfer to third countries is another matter where adequacy of protection is in issue. Bearing in mind the difficulty in determining adequacy, being dependant on a number of factors, such as the nature of the data, there could be restrictions or prohibitions on such transfers. Controllers in the United Kingdom can, however, take heart in the government's approach to transfers to third countries which include the issue of guidance from he Office of the Data Protection Registrar and its view that the question of adequacy should be determined by the controller and not require prior authorisation by the supervisory authority[1].

Other provisions in the Directive in Article 26 allowing derogation from the prohibition of transfer to third countries not having an adequate level of protection will prove most useful to controllers such as banks transferring personal data outside the Community. In particular, the derogation based on the data subject's consent will prove most useful. Further derogation is possible under Article 26(2) where adequate safeguards are in place such as by the use of appropriate contractual clauses. Standard clauses may be formulated by the Commission and it is possible that clauses appropriate to the banking industry are so drafted and which will have to be used in those cases where the third country does not afford an adequate level of protection and the other derogations in Article 26 do not apply.

---

1   Home Office, *Consultation Paper on the EC Data Protection Directive,* HMSO, 1996, p45.

Best case: problems of adequacy of protection will be raised in very few cases. The controller will determine adequacy in the light of published guidelines. Even where adequacy is in doubt, the use of the derogations and/or contractual guarantees will permit transfer in almost all cases.

Worst case: the Commission may find that a considerable number of third countries fail to meet the required standards of protection and may request that Member States takes steps to prevent transfers (see Article 25(4)). Otherwise, where adequacy of protection is an issue, prior authorisation from the supervisory authority will be required. Transborder data flows could be significantly restricted in such cases[1].

Summary

Banks and other financial service providers already have a reasonably good track record on the processing of personal data and compliance with the existing law. Most have appropriate procedures set up and have staff with expertise in data protection law and who oversee compliance with the 1984 Act in an effective and cost-effective manner.

The notification provisions in the Directive should pose a significant concern in this sector and there may even be small saving to be obtained from the possibility of exemption and simplification of notification. On the whole, there should be no substantial constraints on the processing of data in the normal course of the provision of banking and other financial services.

Informing data subjects and catering for subject access should not pose insurmountable problems as, in most cases, there is an on-going relationship between the controller and the data subjects. There may be some additional burdens in respect of marketing and list trading activities to the extent that they are carried out by the controller. There is also a possibility, though remote in view of the government's stated approach to this issue, that certain transborder data flows could be hampered or made more difficult.

Overall and in terms of traditional financial services, the financial sector has little to fear from the Directive's provisions providing they are addressed in a reasonable and thoughtful manner. Dealing with personal data as a commodity in its own right is likely to involve more

---

1   However, as noted above, the government of the United Kingdom can be expected to act in such a way as to minimise the difficulties and possible disruption to the free flow of data.

costly though, if properly thought through, these additional costs should not be prohibitive. In many cases, it will be a matter of forward planning and providing the necessary information and obtaining the necessary consents at a time when it is easy to do so.

Chapter 8 : Health Care

Introduction

Each and every one of us has information concerning ourselves held and processed by health care providers, whether they be part of the national health service[1], hospital trusts or in the private sector. A proportion of the personal data so stored or used is sensitive within the ambit of Article 8 of the Directive (data concerning health or sex life) and it is important that such data are processed with care, kept securely and not disclosed except in limited and appropriate circumstances. Imagine the harm that could be done if data relating to health or sex life came into the wrong hands. It could be personal data relating to HIV, genetic make-up, venereal disease, mental instability, abortions or simply information showing that the data subject suffers from severe ill health or has an incurable disease. Such information could expose the data subject to blackmail or ridicule or could make it difficult for him or her to obtain secure employment, credit or insurance.

Given the potential sensitivity of such data, it is not surprising that the Data Protection Registrar has expressed concern at the level of security in respect of computers in doctors' surgeries following a number of thefts of computers from them[2]. Security aspects are of considerable importance with the types of personal data processed by health care providers as are the need for controls over the disclosure of personal data to servants and agents of the controller, processors and to third parties. The data quality principles in this area are of the utmost importance, especially those requiring data to be accurate, up to date, not excessive and not kept longer than necessary.

Typically, in the context of the national health service, a particular individual will be registered with a general practice and may obtain medicines on prescription from time to time. Occasionally, that

---

1   Every individual has (or should have) a National Health Service Number.
2   *The Times,* 2 December 1992 p3.

individual may be referred to a hospital consultant for treatment or an operation, either as an out-patient or in-patient. Because of serious disease or illness, an individual may be in long term care in a hospital, local authority or private institution.

Many of us also have dealings with dentists, opticians, and other health providers such as acupuncturists and osteopaths. We have contact, directly or indirectly, with the Department of Health and National Health Service. It is apparent that there will be considerable processing of individuals' personal data in relation to the provision of health care services and a significant traffic in data flows between the various providers.

Apart from data protection law, this is an area where the law of confidence has an important role to play. The courts will be quick to impute an obligation of confidence in any relationship between health care professionals and their patients or clients. There is a strong public interest in maintaining the confidentiality of, say, the doctor-patient relationship. However, in some cases, this obligation can be overridden. In *W v Edgell*[1], W had killed five people and had been diagnosed as suffering from paranoid schizophrenia. His plea of guilty to manslaughter on the grounds of diminished responsibility was accepted by the trial court and he was detained without time limit under the Mental Health Act 1959[2]. Over time, W's condition improved and his doctor recommended that he be transferred to a regional secure unit, saying that his illness was under control and he was no longer a danger provided he remained on medication. Following refusal of consent by the Home Secretary, W applied to a mental health review tribunal for discharge or transfer. The defendant, Dr Edgell was instructed to examine W and make out a report which was unfavourable to W. However, on receiving the report, W's solicitor withdrew his client's application to the tribunal. When Dr Edgell heard of this, he sent a copy to the Medical Officer and further copies to the Home Secretary and the Department of Social Security. W complained that this was a breach of the confidential relationship between a patient and a doctor.

The Court of Appeal upheld the decision of Scott J in the Chancery Division. He said that Dr Edgell owed a duty of confidence to W which was created and circumscribed by the particular circumstances of the case. Dr Edgell considered that W had a psychopathic personality and

---

1   [1990] Ch 359.
2   Sections 60 and 65 (now replaced by the Mental Health Act 1983, sections 37 and 41).

he believed that W's solicitors intended to suppress the report. Because of this, Dr Edgell also owed a duty to the public which required him to place before the proper authorities the results of his examination of W who was, by no stretch of the imagination, an ordinary member of the public. Although W had a personal interest to see that the confidence he had reposed in Dr Edgell was not breached, the maintenance of a duty of confidence had to be balanced with the public interest in protecting others from possible violence. Thus, in this case, the public interest in restrictive disclosure outweighed the public interest that W's confidences should be respected.

It will be rare when the duty of confidence will be overridden by public interest and the facts of the above case are very unusual. However, there are other occasions when disclosure of personal health data may be undertaken in circumstances which have no direct bearing on the treatment of the patient. For example, health data may be used for medical research purposes. It may be that the data subjects can no longer be identified from the research data in that it has been stripped of all personal identifiers but this may not necessarily be so. In such cases, unless there is an overriding public interest in such research, the data subject's consent should be sought unless, controversially, such consent can be implied.

Personal Data Processing

Most doctors' surgeries, dental practices, opticians and other localised or specialised health care providers have computers. Except in the case of a health care professional operating alone, a practice will usually have a network of computers so that personal data can be called up from each terminal or computer in the network. Of course, major players such as hospitals have long had considerable computing facilities. Nevertheless, much personal data is not stored in or processed by computers. It is still held in paper form. A visit to a local general practitioner for a consultation will quickly verify this.

Consider a typical general practitioner's practice with a computer system. The computer will hold information about a given individual along the lines of that following:

— patient's name and address;

— age and sex;

— weight, height;

— current medicines taken, if any;

— known allergies;

— blood group, blood pressure and cholesterol count, where these have been checked;

— X-rays and the results of other tests, if any.

There will be also, for that given individual, paper files containing more extensive information going back over a period of time. For example, a record of previous visits, symptoms the patient presented with, diagnosis and treatment together with notes and comments made by the doctor. There will be information about referrals to specialists and consultants and their outcome. Such files can contain a substantial amount of information. Since the Access to Health Records Act 1990, individuals have a right to see their personal data even if they are kept and processed in paper form. Following the coming into force of that Act, it is entirely possible that doctors have been a little more guarded in the comments they choose to write in patients' files.

Data flows

Figure 8.1 shows the typical data flows that might take place in connection with the health care of an individual. Not all the data flows are connected directly with the well-being of the data subject and may relate, for example, to the acquisition of life assurance or payments for time off work through ill health. Some data flows may take place because they have been requested by the data subject. For example, a company offering life assurance policies may ask the data subject for the name and address of his or her general practitioner in order that a reference may be obtained. Alternatively, the company may require an applicant for life assurance to undergo a health check with a doctor nominated by the company, the results of which will be forwarded to the company with a copy going to the applicant's general practitioner.

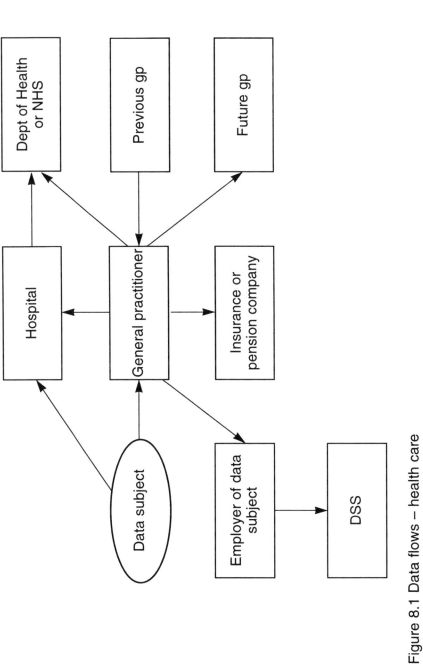

Figure 8.1 Data flows – health care

In the figure, the general practitioner will collect personal data from the patient and from observations and tests carried out in respect of him or her. When a new patient registers, information will be forwarded from the patient's previous general practitioner. If the patient is referred to a consultant at a hospital, some of his or her personal data will be disclosed to the consultant and other relevant staff such as technicians, radiographers, nursing staff and administrators. The hospital will add to the patient's data during his or her course of treatment by the consultant and retain the data for a pre-determined period of time following completion of the treatment. Both during and on completion of the treatment, there will be data flows back to the general practitioner.

A patient may, from time to time, require a doctor's note to show to an employer or educational institution at which the patient is enrolled as a student or to claim sickness benefit. That note will be disclosed to certain relevant staff at the organisation concerned. For example, a student missing an examination through ill-health may provide a doctor's note to a University examination board for its consideration. Personal data will be disclosed, usually via the patient to a pharmacist making up a doctor's or dentist's prescription. Increasingly, pharmacists hold computer information relating to those persons who use their prescribing services.

Both the general practice and the hospital may disclose personal data to the Department of Health, Department of Social Security or National Health Service, locally or nationally. These data may, in some cases, be in statistical form so that the data subject cannot be identified from the data but this will not always be the case.

Where the patient is a minor or mentally incompetent his or her personal data may be collected from and disclosed to a parent, guardian, relative or person with power of attorney.

Processing under the Directive

As much of the personal data processed by health care providers are likely to be of a highly sensitive (and confidential) nature, there is little scope for exemption from notification. Processing in this sector is also likely to attract the attention of the supervisory authority and be subject to careful scrutiny and monitoring. Dangers of lax security, poor data quality and inadequate controls over the processing of personal data are, arguably, heightened in the context of the recent development of an internal market in health care. The Data Protection Registrar has noted that, although the Data Protection Act 1984 gives the Secretary of State the power to modify or supplement the present data protection principles in relation to health care, no action has yet been taken[1].

Concerns over security following thefts of computers from doctor's surgeries has already been mentioned. Other concerns relate to ethnic data which may be collected and processed for a variety of reasons. It may be used to identify persons at risk from diseases prevalent or confined to a particular ethnic group, such as sickle cell anaemia. Alternatively, it may be used to monitor consistency of health care across ethnic groups or for research purposes, providing valuable information to enable targeting of health care. Another concern identified by the Data Protection Registrar relates to the storage, use and disclosure of genetic screening data[2].

Notification

Given the nature of much of the personal data processed in the health sector, it is certain that formal notification of processing will be required. However, the Directive does permit simplification of notification under two conditions[3], one of which being where the controller appoints a data protection official with specified responsibilities. This reflects the current position in Germany. Whilst this may not be practicable in terms of small medical or dental practices, it certainly is where the controller is a large hospital. Because of lack of experience in this area, the government has not expressed an opinion either way on such an approach[4]. Many health service providers already have officers responsible for data protection. Whether the requirement in the Directive that the appointed data protection official ensures the application of national provisions implementing the Directive in an independent manner can ever be reconciled with the official's duty of fidelity to his employer is another matter. There could be a conflict of interests unless, of course, compliance is deemed to be in the employer's best interests. Whilst this may be so in the vast majority of cases, it may not be so easy where there is ambiguity or difficulties in interpreting the national provisions. For example, what if the data protection official considers that the national provisions have failed to properly implement one of the key provisions of the Directive?

---

1   Data Protection Registrar, *Tenth Report of the Data Protection Registrar,* HMSO, 1994 p12.
2   Ibid p13.
3   Article 28(2). The two conditions may be conjunctive or disjunctive; it is up to Member States adopting simplification of or exemption from notification.
4   Home Office, *Consultation Paper on the EC Data Protection Directive,* 1996 p34.

Article 20 of the Directive requires prior checking of processing operations likely to pose specific risks to the rights and freedoms of individuals. Such prior checking may be performed by the supervisory authority or the in-house data protection official, if there is one. Recital 53 suggests prior checking should be carried out where the processing may exclude individuals from a right, benefit or a contract, or pose a threat by virtue of the specific use of new technologies. An example in the health sector is where a heart operation is denied to a smoker because, by reason of his or her inability to give up the habit, the surgeon considers it a better use of limited resources to perform the operation on a non-smoker. In practice, the situation may be more complex, involving the assessment of a number of criteria relating to the individual. It is just this sort of processing that the prior checking provision is designed for. Prior checking should ensure that such difficult decisions are made in a fair and objective manner but it is inevitable that there are likely to be differences of opinion in this area. Doctors and surgeons are likely to see such prior checking as an unwelcome intrusion into the exercise of their medical judgment.

Another area where prior checking may be envisaged is where "expert systems" or decision-support systems are used to aid decision-making, under the "specific use of new technology" head. Computer systems have been in use for some time to assist in diagnosis and it is inevitable that they will be used in other areas as a means of mitigating the scarcity of expert knowledge in the medical field[1]. For example, junior doctors may use a computer system containing rules and knowledge derived from experienced consultants as a means of improving the ability of the junior doctor to analyse symptoms and diagnose illnesses and diseases. This could be particularly important where there is no time to consult a more experienced doctor such as in a serious road traffic accident where the victim requires urgent treatment. In addition to data protection issues such systems have other legal implications, particularly in relation to negligence and negligent misstatement[2].

As prior checking is likely to impede processing operations, be cumbersome and bureaucratic, the government intend to limit it to situations where the risk is clear and real[3]. This may not fully reflect the

---

1   FT de Dombal, DJ Leaper, JR Staniland, JC Horrocks, AP McCann "Computer-aided diagnosis of acute abdominal pain" (1972) 2 *British Medical Journal* 9. The system designed by de Dombal and his colleagues has been in use in several hospitals in the United Kingdom for a number of years.
2   DI Bainbridge, "Computer Aided Diagnosis and Negligence: Legal Liability Arising from the Use of Medical Expert Systems", (1991) 31 *Medicine, Science and the Law* 127-136, and DI Bainbridge, "Legal Aspects of Computer-Aided Diagnosis of Expert Systems", (1992) 7 *Theoretical Surgery* 116.
3   Home Office, *Consultation Paper on the EC Data Protection Directive,* 1996 p36.

Directive as Article 20 is worded in terms of processing operations which are likely to present specific risks.

> Best case - simplified notification procedures with the appointment of a data protection official (likely to be the person presently responsible for data protection within the organisation) and prior checking only in limited cases where the envisaged processing poses obvious and real threats to individuals' rights and freedoms and, even then, such prior checking to be carried out by the data protection official.

> Worst case - no simplification of or exemption from notification with substantial prior checking carried out by the Office of the Data Protection Registrar accompanied by significant time delays and presenting serious hurdles in the efficient processing of data.

The best case scenario should result in minimal increases in costs. It may even be possible to achieve modest savings because of simplified notification. The worst case scenario makes no real difference in terms of notification itself but prior checking could be very onerous and costly, resulting in many hidden and indirect costs. If this approach is adopted, the attitude and responsiveness of the Office of the Data Protection Registrar will be crucial.

Constraints - "Normal" Data

Processing non-sensitive data is allowed by Article 7 and paragraphs (b) and (f) are likely to be relevant, the latter where there is a contractual relationship between the data subject and the controller as will be the case in terms of private health care. Therefore, in the context of the normal provision of health care, there will be no significant constraints on the processing of ordinary data such as name, address, age, etc. However, even such mundane information may be commercially valuable. For example, travel companies offering exotic holidays will be very interested in a list of persons who have recently undergone private health care. Such persons may be interested in a holiday as part of their recuperation. With the advent of market forces in the provision of health care such list trading is not out of the question.

Commercial list trading of non-sensitive data by a controller in the health services area should be possible although it is likely to require the unambiguous consent of the data subjects under Article 7(a) unless such trading could be deemed to be within the legitimate interests of the controller within Article 7(f) which seems unlikely at the present time. The consent would be required to be obtained after collection of the data and after giving the data subject information as to the recipients or categories of recipients[1].

> Best case/ worst case - there is no significant latitude for derogation and there should be little constraint on processing activities except, perhaps in terms of processing not directly related to data subjects' own health care.

Constraints - "Sensitive" Data

Processing sensitive data (referred to in the Directive as special categories of data) is permitted under Article 8. Of particular concern here are data relating to health and, in some circumstances, sex life. Virtually any provider of health care will need to process such data[2]. In health care such processing is allowed where:

— the data subject gives explicit consent;

— it is necessary to protect the vital interests of the data subject or another where the data subject is physically or legally incapable of giving consent;

— it is required for medical purposes or the provision of care or treatment or the management of health-care services and where processed by a regulated health professional[3].

The second exception allowing processing will be appropriate in a number of circumstances, for example:

— where the data subject is injured, unconscious and needs urgent treatment;

— where the data subject is a minor or mentally incapable (surely, in this case, the data subject's parent or guardian must give consent although the Directive does not address this expressly);

— more controversially, where data relating to a data subject are processed to determine whether that data subject is a suitable organ donor for another person.

---

1 Article 10(c) - further information to guarantee fair processing.
2 Bear in mind the very wide definition of processing in Article 1.
3 The professional must be subject to an obligation of professional secrecy or processing may be by another person under an equivalent obligation, Article 8(3).

The exceptions allowing processing will apply in the vast majority of cases. However, it may not extend to processing of health data by other organisations such as schools, employers and insurance companies[1]. Therefore, Member States may, for reasons of substantial important public interest, further derogate from the general prohibition on processing sensitive data[2]. Recital 34 gives the areas of public health and social protection as examples, particularly so as to ensure the quality and cost-effectiveness of procedures used for settling claims for benefits and services in the health insurance system, scientific research and government statistics. Should Member States take advantage of this derogation, as the United Kingdom almost certainly will, they must provide specific and suitable safeguards to protect the fundamental rights and freedoms of individuals.

Returning again to the subject of list trading, it is not inconceivable that a health care provider might wish to improve its profitability by selling its data. Sensitive data legitimately may be of some value. For example, a private hospital may wish to sell a list of patients with walking difficulties to a company making stair lifts. It may sell details of patients with a weight problem to a company making exercise equipment or even details of impotent patients to a company making products designed to increase sex drive!

It is clear that such activities can only be permitted in relation to sensitive data where the data subject has given his or her explicit consent. Even then, it is possible that Member States may make provision preventing this by Article 8(2)(a). One possible manner in which this could be done is for the United Kingdom provisions implementing the Directive to give the Secretary of State power to make regulations limiting situations where the data subject's consent alone is sufficient to allow processing of sensitive data.

> Best case/ worst case - there should be no significant difference as the United Kingdom is certain to take advantage of the derogation allowing processing in the context of public health. Overall, the Directive is unlikely to significantly increase the constraints on processing sensitive data.

Extension to Paper Files

A great deal of health data are stored in paper files and manually processed. The costs of applying the data quality principles to such

---

1   Home Office, *Consultation Paper on the EC Data Protection Directive*, 1996 p28.
2   Article 8(4).

data as soon as the national legislation implementing the Directive comes into force would be horrendous. All manually processed personal data files would have to be inspected for compliance with the principles by that date. The work would be very time-consuming, costly and disruptive. Thankfully, the Directive contains the possibility of delaying the application of Articles 6 (principles relating to data quality), 7 and 8 (criteria for processing "normal" and special categories of data) by virtue of Article 32(2) for a period of up to 12 years from the date of adoption of the Directive[1].

It appears to be almost beyond doubt that the United Kingdom government will take advantage of this option. This means that, by ensuring that newly collected data comply and systematically and periodically destroying old data, by the year 2007, there will be little, if any manual processing that does not comply in all respects with Articles 6, 7 and 8. Hospitals, for example, may decide to retain data relating to past patients for a limited period only, say 5 years. Of course, general practitioners will need keep records for much longer but they should still ensure that new data complies and can take heart in the fact that the Council and Commission to the European Communities are aware of the difficulty. They jointly issued a statement to the effect that, at the end of the 12 year transitional period, controllers must take all reasonable steps to comply with Articles 6, 7 and 8 in respect of manual processing which do not prove impossible or involve a disproportionate effort in terms of cost, bearing in mind the importance of protecting the rights and freedoms of individuals[2].

The other provisions, such as informing data subjects and subject access will apply to manual files, though not for three years following the entry into force of the national provisions where the processing is already under way.

From the controller's point of view, one positive aspect is that the application of data protection law to manual processing should present the opportunity to critically examine present systems and processes. It could lead many to rationalise existing manual processing, improve quality and cost-effectiveness and, in some cases, have the data transferred to computer with resulting benefits.

---

1   The date of adoption is 24 October 1995.
2   Home Office, *Consultation Paper on the EC Data Protection Directive*, 1996 p48.

Links with Data Subjects

The entire population has some link or other with organisations involved directly or indirectly with the provision of health care. For this reason, the Directive's requirements controlling the relationship between data subjects and health care providers are critical both in their substance and in their manner of implementation. A worst case scenario would be where the Department of Health had to regularly inform the population of its processing and seek express consent and every health care provider would have to similarly inform all its patients or clients. On the other hand, there might be little difference in practice from the current regime as regards links with data subjects. Even the extension of data protection law to manually processed personal data files would have minimal effect because of current provisions giving such access.

Costs of administration and bureaucracy in the health service are already very high and it would be regrettable if the Directive resulted in significant increases in such costs. We all have an interest in having an efficient and value-for-money health service and, providing transparency of processing of health data can be maintained, there is nothing in this aim which directly conflicts with individuals' rights and freedoms.

Informing Data Subjects

The Department of Health was very concerned at the prospect of having to inform each and every member of the population that their data were being processed by the Department and the National Health Service. It estimated that the cost of doing this and obtaining each person's consent together with other costs associated with complying with the Directive would be in the region of £1bn[1]. Thankfully, this "nightmare scenario" is not a realistic outcome. All the basic information relating to a particular individual, such as name, address, age will be collected from that individual, for example, when registering with a doctor or dentist or on admission to a hospital. The relevant information required to be given under Article 10 can be given at that stage. It may be printed on a form which the individual reads and/or signs or it can be given orally.

A great deal of other personal data may be obtained as a result of observation, tests, X-rays and the like. The question is whether Article

---

1   Department of Health, *Draft EC Directive on Data Protection: Analysis of Costs* 1994.

11 applies to such data requiring information to be given to the data subject on recording or before disclosure to a third party. First, it is arguable that such data are indeed collected from the data subject, albeit indirectly. Consider a person who volunteers a sample of urine for testing. Surely, there should be no need to give any information to the data subject, apart perhaps from telling him or her what the sample is to tested for (the purpose of the processing). Anything further would be otiose except, of course, if some non-obvious use was intended in respect of the data.

Further information required by Articles 10 and 11 to guarantee fair processing should be unnecessary as regards all normal uses of individuals' data related to the health care. The same should apply with further uses for research or statistical purposes where individual data subjects cannot be identified from the data. In other cases, the data subject should be given the appropriate information.

Repeating the information given to data subjects given at the first contact, will not be required later unless there is a change to or extension of the purposes of processing or the identity of recipients. Both Articles 10 and 11 excuse the giving of information where the data subject already has it.

On the whole, informing data subjects on collection, recording or prior to disclosure should not be onerous and it should be possible to accommodate the duties easily within existing procedures. However, the provisions may require more explicit information to be given to patients undergoing tests. For example, it will no longer be appropriate to simply ask a patient to give a sample of urine or blood or to undergo an X-ray. The patient should be told why; for example, to check blood sugar levels, or to check whether a lump is benign. Where this may cause difficulty, for example, where a doctor suspects some fatal illness, the exception from providing information under Article 13(1)(g) being, *inter alia*, the protection of the data subject, should apply.

The requirement to give information as to the purposes of processing could help to reduce the cavalier attitude of some health professionals to their patients. This should improve the quality of health care or, at least, the patient's perception of health care. However, there is a danger in that giving more information about processing personal data could prompt patients to ask further questions, for example, as regards risks.

This could impact upon the concept of informed consent and could increase the professional's exposure to a negligence action[1].

Best case/ worst case - there should be no significant difference. Controllers in the health sector should be able to provide the necessary information at nominal additional cost by re-designing forms and procedures. There may be a small cost resulting from providing appropriate training to staff.

Subject Access

The Access to Health Records Act 1990 did not give rise to a stampede by patients to inspect their records held by health professionals. It is unlikely, therefore, that the Directive will have any significant effect on the volume of subject access requests. Nevertheless, those responsible for data protection in the health sector should be aware that further information must be given under the Directive than is presently the case and should modify their procedures for dealing with subject access accordingly.

Consent and Objections

In the context of the conventional provision of health care, there are no real issues relating to the data subject's consent or objection to processing on compelling legitimate grounds. It will only be in respect of unexpected or non-obvious uses of personal data that the questions of consent or objections might be raised. This would be so where personal data collected for health care were exploited commercially; a controversial issue in its own right. The Directive could, when implemented, severely prejudice such further uses of personal data.

Occasions when a data subject might object to the disclosure of his personal health could include where he or she has a highly contagious disease or severe mental disorder and has refused treatment. Another case could be where the data indicate paternity and, perhaps, disclosure to the Child Support Agency is envisaged[2]. Article 14 which provides for the right to object is not subject to the exemptions and restrictions in Article 13 but the right to object can be negated by national legislation. Where other public bodies anticipate disclosure of personal data to them from health care organisations, the right to object could be curtailed by statutory instrument.

---

1   *Sidaway v Bethlem Royal Hospital Governors* [1985] AC 871.
2   Of course, the objection must be justified on compelling legitimate grounds to be effective, Article 14(a).

Best case/worst case - there is no substantial difference. There will be, in the normal run of things, no requirement to obtain the data subject's consent nor to fear that the right to object will be used to any significant extent. However, uses of personal data other than those related to a data subject's health care or research in the public interest should require consent.

Transfers of Data to Third Countries

At the present time, there should be minimal transfer of personal data from the United Kingdom to third countries outside the EC in the context of health care. Transfer could be required where the data subject is in need of medical care in a third country and his or her health records are required urgently in that third country. Article 26 allows derogation from the prohibition on transfer to third countries not having an adequate level of protection, *inter alia*, where necessary to protect the vital interests of the data subject. However, this derogation needs legislative action.

As adequacy of protection is a qualitative measure (a third country may have adequate protection for certain forms of personal data only), it is expected that controllers will be able to seek guidance from the Data Protection Registrar. However, any obligation to seek prior authorisation is unlikely to be required[1].

With the growing privatisation of health care, foreign health care providers are likely to become involved in health care in the United Kingdom. For example, an American company might acquire a local private hospital in England. In such a case, there will be a wholly or partly owned English company running the hospital and which will be the controller for data processing activities. If the company then transfers its patient data to the parent company, apart from having to inform the data subject accordingly, consideration must be given to the provisions relating to transfer to third countries. In most cases, there will be no difficulty as the number of countries deemed to have inadequate levels of protection under any circumstances is likely to be small.

Even where the third country does not afford an adequate level of protection, transfer may still be possible where the controller adduces sufficient safeguards. It can be expected that the United Kingdom will take a pragmatic approach to cross-border flows of personal data and

---

1   Home Office, *Consultation Paper on the EC Data Protection Directive*, 1996 p45.

provide appropriate mechanisms for the transfer of data to third countries.

Best case/ worst case - there should be no significant difference as the United Kingdom is likely to put few barriers in place preventing transfer of personal data, taking advantage of the derogations in the Directive, with appropriate safeguards. Controllers will have to keep themselves informed as to which countries fail to provide adequate protection and put appropriate safeguards in place when transferring data to such countries[1].

Summary

It can be seen that providers of health care should be able to process health data with little constraint. Concerns about the application of data protection law to manual files has been met to a large extent by the possibility of delaying the application to manual files of some of the Directive's provisions until the year 2007. This should provide ample opportunity to rationalise paper files and destroy obsolete and unnecessary data by that time with little cost. If systems are put into place immediately so that all new data complies, the costs could easily be outweighed by the benefits of increased relevance and efficiency of processing. On the whole, with early consideration of the Directive's provisions and forward planning, health care providers have little to fear from the Directive as it is likely to be implemented in the United Kingdom.

---

1   It is likely that the Data Protection Registrar will issue guidance on this point.

Chapter 9 : Direct Sale Retailers

Introduction

A large number of people are employed in the retail sector and a large proportion of processing of personal data by retail organisations will be in relation to employees and issues relevant to employees are examined in Chapter 16. For many transactions, personal data is not processed. For example, an individual may walk into a store, ask for a particular article, pay for it with cash and walk out. However, some transactions will involve the use of credit cards or personal cheques or require the arrangement of a form of credit such as hire purchase.

Personal data relating to customers has the potential for being very valuable. Such data may help to predict what a particular customer is likely to be interested in buying in the future, what his or her likes and dislikes are, what spending power the customer is likely to have and so forth. In many cases, retailers like to develop an on-going relationship with customers to encourage customer loyalty.

Retailers also have links with wholesalers or suppliers and some of the data they process in respect of them will include a certain amount of personal data such as contact names and associated data. What has been said in relation to such data subjects in Chapter 4 applies just as much in this context and the remainder of this chapter concentrates on the processing of personal data relating to customers of retail outlets.

A large retail organisation will be made up of a head office (and/or a number of regional offices), one or more distribution centres and a number of retail outlets. For the purposes of this chapter, it is assumed that the organisation has a head office, a single distribution centre and a number of shops.

Personal Data Processing

Except in respect of the anonymous cash purchase[1], the retailer will process personal data. There are a number of ways in which this will be done, depending on the method of payment, as indicated below:

—   If the customer buys an article by credit card, the card details will be entered into the shop till/computer system. Typically, an authorisation slip will be printed out and signed by the customer, a copy of which is retained by the shop. During this process, the data may be transmitted to the head office and/or the credit card company.

—   The transaction may involve electronic funds transfer (for example, by "Switch") whereby details of the customer, transaction and retailer account are transmitted to the customer's bank for the transfer to be made.

—   In a hire purchase or similar credit transaction, the customer's personal details will be disclosed to a hire purchase company, usually following a check with a credit reference agency.

—   Even a purchase by cheque involves personal data. However, unless the details are entered into a computer, this is unlikely to be within the scope of the Directive as the cheque will not be held in a personal data filing system but simply forwarded with other cheques to the retailer's bank to be entered into the bank clearing system. Any long-term record kept by the shop is unlikely to identify the data subject.

Depending on the nature of the retail business, personal data may be collected from the data subject in other ways. For example, there may be a guarantee form to be completed and forwarded to a manufacturer. The retailer may offer an after sales or maintenance service in the case of goods such as motor vehicles, washing machines, electronic equipment. The retailer may offer its own credit cards or discount cards. There are numerous ways in which retailers can obtain personal data relating to their customers.

Apart from the sales transaction, retailers may use personal data for a number of purposes. For example, in the case of a car or washing machine personal data will be processed so as to give reminders as to servicing or, when the item reaches a certain age, to enquire whether

---

1   Even here personal data may be collected, for example, where a guarantee form is completed.

the customer is considering trading in his or her old machine for a new one. Retailers may also sell details of their customers to other retailers or service providers (or buy in data from third parties).

Most personal data processing carried out by or on behalf of controllers in the retail sector will be processed by computer. Only the smallest retailers will not make full use of information technology. Even many sole trader newsagents now have computer databases of their customers.

Data flows

Concentrating on personal data relating to customers, Figure 9.1 indicates the typical data flows that might be expected in a typical retail organisation. It will obtain personal data directly from the data subject via its shops or retail outlets. If the organisation goes in for direct marketing, it may also obtain personal data by buying in a database of potential customers. It may even sell personal data to other companies. Some personal data collected locally at a given retail outlet will be transferred or disclosed to the organisation's head office. The retail organisation will also have data flows with hire purchase companies and other credit providers and credit reference agencies. Data may be passed on to manufacturers of goods sold by the retailer, for example, on completed guarantee forms or as statistical returns.

Processing under the Directive

Almost all processing carried out in a retail environment is not of a sensitive nature falling within the special categories of processing in Article 8. It would be rare indeed that data of that type would be used in a retail environment. One exception might be where a retailer provides a special discount for members of a particular trade union and, in such cases, processing will be allowed if the individuals concerned have agreed to disclosure of their personal details to the retailer from the trade union. Alternatively, it may be that the data subject volunteers such information himself or herself to the retailer.

Even though processing of special categories of data may be rare, other processing could give rise for concern. Incorrect data relating to financial credit, debt or repayments could cause a data subject considerable inconvenience. Furthermore, individuals may not be happy to have information relating to their purchases divulged to third parties (or even relatives).

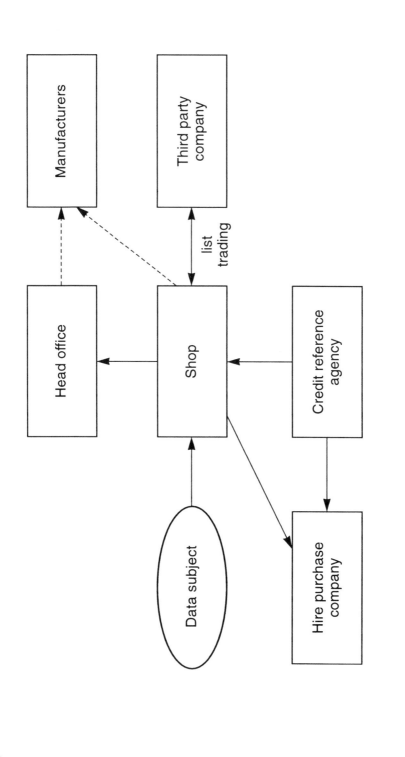

Figure 9.1 Data flows – Direct sales retailers

Notification

The government has expressed its intention to make full use of the scope offered by the Directive for easing the burden of formal registration[1]. Even so, the Directive allows exemption or simplification only for processing operations unlikely to adversely affect the rights and freedoms of data subjects[2]. It is difficult to predict to what extent formal notification will be required in the retail sector but, perhaps, notification will be required in the following circumstances:

— where the controller engages in list trading;

— where the controller processes data relating to data subjects' credit-worthiness;

— where the controller offers customers in-house credit facilities;

— in those rare cases where the controller processes sensitive data within Article 8[3].

However, in relation to disclosure, with the data subjects' consent, to third parties of personal data held by trade unions or charities, exemption from or simplification of notification is still possible under Article 18(4).

In practice, the need for notification will depend upon the scale and nature of the retailer's activities. Larger retailers, offering a range of credit facilities or engaging in direct marketing including buying in or selling databases of actual or potential customers are likely to be required to notify the supervisory authority formally. It may be that, for such activities, a simplified form of notification can be developed bearing in mind the present system is particularly cumbersome. Overall, however, the costs of notification whether formal or otherwise are unlikely to be significantly different from present costs.

> Best case - exemption from or simplification of notification for the vast majority of retailers. However, the relevant information should still be prepared to be available on request as required by Article 21(3).

---

1   Home Office, *Consultation Paper on the EC Data Protection Directive,* 1996, p33.
2   Article 18(2).
3   Being data revealing racial or ethnic origin, political opinions, religious or philosophical beliefs, trade-union membership and data concerning health or sex life.

Worst case - all retailers engaging in direct marketing, list trading credit provision will be required to notify. Notification procedures will remain much as they now are. Even bearing in mind the additional information required under the Directive, costs should not be significantly greater than at present.

Constraints - "Normal" Data

There should be few constraints over the processing of customer data for the purpose of contracting with the customer and keeping records of payments made and outstanding. Such processing is within Article 7(b), being necessary for the performance of a contract with the data subject. The consent of the data subjects will not be required for this[1]. Other processing, such as disclosing data to other credit providers or credit reference agencies about whether data subjects pay instalments promptly or not where the retailer has its own credit facilities could fall within Article 7(f) - being necessary for the purpose of the legitimate interests of the controller or third party to whom the data are disclosed. It is arguable that only disclosure of "black" or "grey" data could fall under this head and that it cannot justify the disclosure of "white" data, disclosing that the data subject has a good payment record and has never been in default[2].

Where personal data is used for marketing purposes either directly from the retailer or resulting from list trading where a copy of a customer database is sold to another retailer, the data subject's consent will be required. Although Article 14 gives a right to object to processing for the purposes of direct marketing, this may be provided for in two ways and it is likely that the United Kingdom will take the least onerous approach being simply that the right is publicised. Nevertheless, processing must be fair and, as the *Innovations* case has already demonstrated, it is preferable to give the data subject an opportunity to object to his or her data being used for direct marketing, whether by the retailer with whom the data subject has a contract or a retailer to which the data are intended to be disclosed. No doubt the "tick box" approach will prevail.

Best case/worst case: there is no significant latitude for derogation in respect of processing normal data in this context, except in relation to the mode of implementation of the data subject's right to object to direct marketing. It is almost certain that the United Kingdom will take

---

1   Consent could be implied because the data subject voluntarily enters into a contractual relationship with the controller.
2   The Data Protection Registrar has expressed concern at the disclosure of white data; see the *Tenth Report of the Data Protection Registrar*, HMSO, 1994, p19.

the least exigent option. Otherwise, the cost of informing data subjects before disclosure of personal data to third parties for direct marketing purposes could seriously undermine direct marketing.

Constraints - "Sensitive" Data

Apart from monitoring for discrimination amongst its own staff, retailers should not need to process sensitive data within Article 8 of the Directive. The exception mentioned above, where a retailer gives a discount for trade union membership, for example, is easily dealt with by seeking the consent of the data subject either through the union or by the data subject approaching the retailer offering the discount.

Best case/worst case - there is no significant processing of sensitive data by retailers in respect of customers.

Links with Data Subjects

In the vast majority of cases, links with data subjects will be direct and voluntary and set in a contractual context. That being so, providing data subjects with information as required under the Directive will be an easy matter, requiring some thought to be given to the design of forms and notices to accommodate the necessary information. In other cases, planning and co-operation between organisations should minimise the administrative burdens and costs associated with these provisions.

Informing Data Subjects

As the data subject will volunteer the personal data required by the retailer, informing on collection of the identity of the controller or representative and the purposes of the processing will be an easy matter. It is even questionable whether this information must be expressly given. Consider a newsagency operating a delivery service. An individual requiring newspapers and magazines to be delivered to his or her home will give the newsagent the following information: name and address, titles of newspapers and magazines to be delivered and commencement date. Surely, the newsagent is not expected then to announce:

"I am Mr Bloggs, manager of this store and representative of Crescent Newsagents Ltd and I will use the personal data you have just given me for the purpose of delivering newspapers and

---

1   Whatever one's personal views of direct marketing, it has a very important role in retailing in the United Kingdom and it is almost unthinkable that it would be seriously jeopardised.

magazines to your home address in accordance with your requirements and for submitting invoices to you at monthly intervals in respect of such deliveries."

Unless, of course, the newsagent is involved in list trading. Still worse if further information under Article 10 has to be given such as recipients or categories of recipients (the newspaper delivery boys and girls) and the right of access to the data. However, Article 10 does not require the information to be given where the data subject already has it and, in such a case, it is at least arguable that this is so because:

—   the newsagent's customer knows who he is dealing with - the name of the controller is probably writ large over the shop window (however, the name of the representative might not be);

—   the customer knows the purpose of processing - it is directly associated with his or her request to have newspapers delivered.

As some contracts between customers and retailers are oral this could make it difficult or impracticable to give the required information[1]. Unless the argument that the data subject already has the information is accepted, it may be sensible to formalise in writing such contracts as between customer and newsagent, thereby giving an opportunity to add appropriate wording to the form of agreement. For example:

By this agreement dated dd/mm/yy between

.... [customer]

and

.... [newsagent]

the newsagent agrees to deliver newspapers and/or magazines and/or other publications [the publications] as listed in the Schedule and as modified from time to time by agreement and the customer agrees to accept the same.

Clause 1. The customer agrees to pay the retail cost of the publications listed in the Schedule in addition to a delivery fee. A scale of delivery fees is displayed at the newsagent's premises.

---

1   Of course, this only applies where personal data are collected. In many cash transactions they are not collected.

Clause 2. The newsagent agrees to send to the customer invoices at the end of each calendar month and the customer agrees to pay such invoices within 14 days of receipt.

Clause 3. Modifications: a minimum of 1 week's notice is required for modifications to the Schedule.

Clause 4. Holidays, etc: a minimum of 1 week's notice is required to cease delivery during any period during which the customer is away or for temporary cessation of delivery for any other reason.

Clause 5. Data Protection: the customer agrees that the newsagent may enter details of the customer's name and address and publications into the newsagent's computer database and/or card index system. These details will be used for the purposes of delivering the publications and for billing and accounts. Under the Data Protection Act, the customer has a right of access to such data, for which the newsagent will charge a small fee.

Clause 6. The newsagent accepts no responsibility for late delivery howsoever caused ... etc.

Clause 7. This agreement is terminable by either party subject to a minimum of one calendar month's notice.

Signed etc.

The reader is left to ponder on how workable this is in practice - it all seems way over the top. Most people would be astonished to be asked to sign such an agreement. Perhaps the simplest way to conform would be to say: "Look Mr Smith, I will enter your name and address and details of papers you want on our computer so we can ensure prompt and reliable delivery to you. That's OK isn't it?"

Another situation where a retailer may ask for personal data is in relation to the issue of a discount card. For example, a retailer may offer a general "privilege" card available to any customer who chooses to take advantage of the scheme. Alternatively, a selected discount card might be offered to, for example, local government officers. In either case, it should be a simple task to add the necessary information to any form to be completed or, if the data is collected through a computer terminal, to display the relevant information on screen before the data is entered by the customer. As before, if it is envisaged that the data will be used for marketing, the data subject should be so informed and given the opportunity to object.

Best case/worst case - there should be no insurmountable hurdles to processing in the retail context. Any costs associated with informing data subjects can be minimised by adapting forms as appropriate or using other methods of supplying the required information to data subjects.

Subject Access

There are no particular difficulties flowing from subject access in the retail sector except the extension of subject access to manually processed personal data files. Thus, if the retailer keeps customer records on index cards of individual files, subject access will extend to these and not just computer records as at present. Retailers, in common with other controllers, should put appropriate mechanisms in place to deal with subject access to computer and manual files, taking into account that it will no longer be simply a matter of providing a copy of the personal data in question and information relating to purposes and recipients must be given together with knowledge of the logic involved in automated decisions.

The level of activity in terms of subject access in the retail sector is unlikely to be very great except where the retailer offers in-house credit. Where this is so, subject access requests can be expected from a significant proportion of persons refused credit facilities. Where the person concerned has no previous dealings with the retailer, it may simply be a matter of referring that person to the credit reference agency or other organisation which disclosed the relevant data as the retailer may not itself have recorded the fact of refusal of credit.

Best case/worst case - apart from extending subject access to manual files and providing additional information than is the present case a little planning should attain the objective of meeting these requirements at minimal cost.

Consent and Objections

The question of the data subject's consent should arise only in respect of non-obvious uses of the data. Marketing and list trading are examples where the data subject's consent ought to be sought. As mentioned above, the right to object to the use of personal data for direct marketing is unlikely to require that the specific consent of the data subject is obtained prior to marketing - this could increase the cost of such marketing prohibitively.

restriction

In all other cases, processing should be permitted within the Directive's spirit without seeking the data subject's consent. It is difficult to envisage a situation where the data subject would have compelling legitimate grounds to object to processing.

Best case/worst case - there is little here to interfere with the normal processing of personal data by retail organisations. As now, data subjects should be informed of non-obvious uses and given the opportunity to object.

Security

At first sight, security should not be a problem for the vast majority of controllers in all sectors. There are, however, a number of issues that are worthy of further consideration in respect of direct sales retailing. Of course, most retailers should have good security measures in place in terms of their computer systems. It is in their own interests to restrict access to data, personal or otherwise, to use appropriate and regularly changed passwords and to have back-up copies of programs and data which are updated regularly and stored in locked cabinets or, better still, a fireproof safe. Good security is important in so many respects, such as protecting against fraud or malicious damage to programs or data, that any reasonably efficient retail organisation will take it very seriously.

One area of concern is the possibility of other customers being able to read personal data relating to a particular customer displayed on a screen. This could happen where a customer of a newsagent wishes to pay his or her papers bill. The newsagent will retrieve the data on screen and this will include, typically, the customer's name and address and the current status of his or her account. There is a danger that a criminal could, in this way, find out the address of a vulnerable or frail person. Retailers should make sure that the screen display is not easily read by others and consider using the type of display used by banks which are impossible to read except from directly in front. It has to be said, however, that failure to take care that retailers screen displays are not visible to others will breach principle 8 of the current data protection principles.

As the Directive extends data protection law to manual processing of personal data files, retailers holding, for example, card index systems containing information about customers, must consider carefully how the Directive's obligations in respect of security affect processing paper databases. The following points must be taken into account:

— paper files and card indexes containing personal data must be kept securely and must not be left lying around so as to be accessible by persons not requiring to use them in the normal course of business; when not in use, they should be kept in locked cabinets or secure rooms;

— employees and others using such files and indexes must be informed of the importance of confidentiality and that they must process them only in accordance with the controller's instructions - it would be sensible to provide each employee with a written statement to this effect and make it a term of the contract of employment[1];

— there will be liability for accidental or unlawful destruction of personal data if the security measures taken are insufficient. Retail organisations should consider having duplicate copies of personal data in paper form;

— larger retail organisations are likely to use networks, local and wide area networks and security must be appropriate in respect of the transmission personal data over such networks.

Where processing is carried out on behalf of the controller by a processor, for example, where a retailer sends a copy of its customer database to a marketing firm for the purpose of analysing the buying profiles of the customers on behalf of the retailer, there must be formal contractual provisions relating to security.

As with processing generally, there is a three year transitional period during which processing already underway at implementation of the Directive in national law will be brought into compliance. Controllers will have some time to evaluate the security implications and implement appropriate measures where existing procedures are found wanting. However, security must be appropriate in respect of new personal data. Although further derogation from some of the provisions is possible in the case of manual records[2], this does not apply to security aspects.

Best case/worst case - there is no latitude for derogation from security aspects. Retailers should already have appropriate security measures in place in terms of computer data and there are other

---

1   Unauthorised access by an employee to his employer's computer systems can be a valid reason for summary dismissal; see *Denco Ltd v Joinson* [1991] IRLR 63, Employment Appeal Tribunal.
2   Article 32(2).

important reasons why they are likely to take security seriously and implement strong security measures. The same may not be true of manually processed data and there could be costs associated with improving security of such data. There could also be costs in terms of including appropriate terms in contracts with processors, educating employees and amending contracts of employment. The costs should not be large and there should be benefits from improved security and increased control over processing, whether automatic or manual.

Transfers of Data to Third Countries

Retailers may transfer personal data relating to their customers to third countries for processing for marketing or profiling purposes. Where the third country does not provide an adequate level of data protection, transfer will still be possible in most cases, either because the data subject has given his or her unambiguous consent or it is related to the performance of a contract with the data subject. In any case, the number of countries in which transfer would otherwise be prohibited is likely to be small[1].

Best case/worst case - it is unlikely that the provisions relating to transfer to third countries will result in any additional measures or costs. In rare cases where a third country does not afford an adequate level of data protection, retailers may have to adduce safeguards, typically contractual, and unless connected with the performance of a contract with the data subject, may have to seek data subjects' express consent.

Summary

Direct sales retailers are in a contractual relationship with their customers and processing associated with the performance and conclusion of such contracts should present no difficulties. Where retailers offer credit facilities, many of the comments made in respect of financial services in Chapter 7 will apply. Certainly, as far as the small retailer is concerned, the new law will have little impact and such retailers are likely to be saved the trouble and expense of registration. Leaflets, advertising literature and contract forms may all be used as a vehicle to inform the data subject and seek any necessary consents (or absence of objection).

---

1   Home Office, *Consultation Paper on the EC Data Protection Directive,* 1996 p43.

Providing direct sale retailers take account of the Directive's provisions, as implemented, in the manner in which they collect, use and disclose personal data relating to their customers, the new data protection law is unlikely to seriously interfere with their activities.

Particular issues requiring careful consideration are informing data subjects of non-obvious uses of their data and giving an opportunity to object to such uses. Arguably, the most significant impact of the Directive is the extension of data protection law to manual processing with the increased possibility of, and costs associated, with subject access and the need to evaluate and, in many cases, improve security to manual records.

Chapter 10 : Mail Order Retailers

Introduction

There are two forms of "mail order" selling. The traditional form involves distributing catalogues to "agents" who place orders for goods on behalf of themselves and, in some cases, for "clients" (typically friends and relatives), usually paying by instalments over a period of time. Essentially, this is a credit service. Some of the goods offered are usually obtainable elsewhere at lower cost for cash whilst other goods may otherwise be difficult to obtain, for example, fashionable clothing for men and women of ample proportions. Although somewhat old-fashioned by modern standards, this form of retail selling remains very popular.

The agents place their own orders and those of their "clients" and are responsible, in return for a commission, for collecting the periodic payments and forwarding them to the retail organisation.

The other form of mail order is where goods are advertised in brochures sent by post or advertised on television or other forms of direct marketing and the buyer orders the goods by forwarding a completed order form or by telephone. In most cases, the buyer will pay for the goods in full, usually by cheque or credit card.

Personal Data Processing

The nature of the personal data collected from individuals, whether agents or otherwise, is relatively innocuous. It may comprise little more than name and address and age[1]. Length of time at the present address may also be asked for as this may indicate stability. Where credit is involved, such as where the buyer pays by instalments, the mail order retailer is likely to check with a credit reference agency to verify that the customer, or agent, is a good credit risk. Where the relationship is ongoing, the retailer may build up confidence in the ability of the

---

1   Age may be important as regards the provision of credit or in terms of the nature of goods to be sold.

customer or agent to pay and allow greater credit limits. Similarly, details of late payment of instalments is likely to be kept. Particularly where agents are concerned, the retailer will get a feel for efficiency and timeliness in collecting and submitting repayments.

Where credit is involved, retailers might carry out limited automatic decision-making to determine whether or not to perform a contract with a new customer or agent. This may be simply no more than a check on postal codes to weed out applicants from areas notorious for bad-payers. Notwithstanding the efficacy of such processing from the retailer's point of view, it is arguable that it contravenes existing data protection law.

In *Equifax Europe Ltd v Data Protection Registrar*[1], Equifax, a credit reference agency, was using data relating to previous occupants of the applicant's home to determine credit-worthiness. The argument was that if a previous occupant was a bad credit risk, the present occupant was more likely to be a bad risk also. Equifax reckoned that this information was a good predictor of credit-worthiness even though the present occupant was unlikely to be related to, or even know, the previous occupant. The Data Protection Registrar served an enforcement notice claiming that this practice was in breach of the first data protection principle in that the data were not being processed fairly[2]. The Data Protection Tribunal agreed but modified the enforcement notice to allow the extraction and use of some information where it relates to a person with the same or a similar name to the applicant or to members of the applicant's family or household who are financially connected to the data subject. Otherwise, the use of such third party data was contrary to the first data protection principle. Basing decisions on postal code is only one step removed from this. We will see later whether the Directive will allow such processing.

Data flows
As mentioned earlier, only minimal information is likely to be collected from the data subject, either directly or through an agent with a catalogue. Further information will be obtained from a credit reference agency where credit is involved, as is the case usually. It is common for mail order companies to engage in list trading, both selling and buying lists of customers. For example, a mail order company offering its goods through catalogues distributed to agents may wish to send out literature advertising a new edition of its catalogue, buying in a list of persons who may be interested in becoming agents. It may sell a copy

---

1   (unreported) 28 February 1992, Data Protection Tribunal.
2   See also *CCN Systems Ltd v Data Protection Registrar* (unreported) 25 February 1991.

of a list of its agents or customers to another company which offers goods or services not offered by the mail order company. Figure 10.1 shows the data flows typical in relation to mail order retailing.

Customers buying through agents will have no direct contact with the mail order company and the agent will keep a record of each customer's details (name, address, goods ordered, date of order, payments made and balance outstanding). Some of this information may be passed on to the mail order company but this is not, strictly speaking, necessary as the agent remains responsible for the day to day running of the customer's account. If the customer fails to make payment, details may be passed to the mail order company for appropriate action.

Processing under the Directive

The role of the agent is central to the catalogue form of mail order trading. Therefore, it is vital to be able to classify that role in terms of the Directive. Is the agent simply a processor or a controller in his or her own right? To answer this, the definitions in Article 2 must be re-considered. The controller is the person who determines, alone or jointly, the purposes and means of processing whilst a processor is a person who processes the data on behalf of the controller. Three scenarios are possible and are shown in Figure 10.2.

First, in diagram (a), the mail order company collects information from the agent about himself or herself, for example, when the agent applies for a catalogue. In this case, the mail order company is the controller and the agent is a data subject. In diagrams (b) and (c), a customer has ordered goods through an agent. Either the agent is a processor and simply processes the relevant personal data relating to the customer on behalf of the mail order company or the agent is the controller with the mail order company being a recipient of the data. Whilst the agent will always be a data subject in respect of his or her own personal data, which of options (b) or (c) applies depends largely upon the degree of control exercised by the mail order company on the agent.

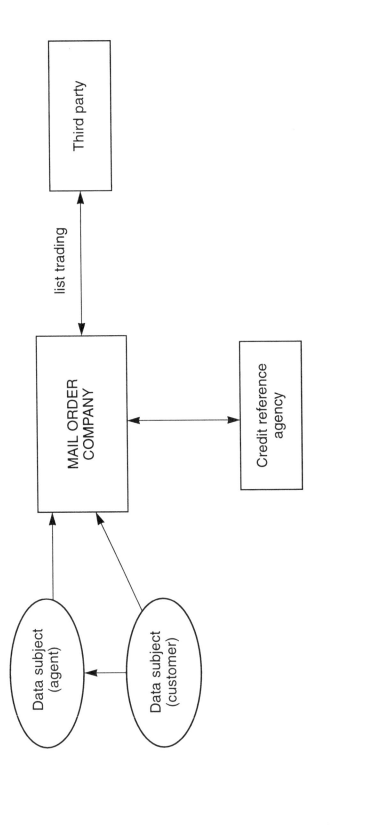

Figure 10.1 Personal data flows – mail order company

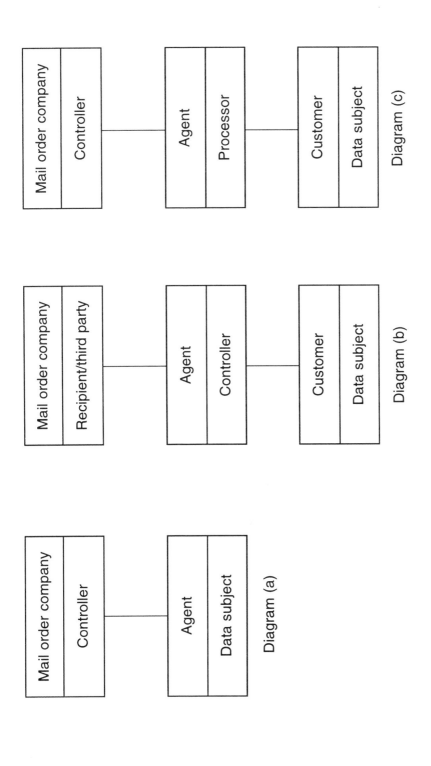

Figure 10.2 – The role of agents

Mail order companies, presently, are unlikely to rigorously control the content of and manner in which agents collect, record and process data relating to customers. Some agents may have card index systems, others may use simple computer databases or accounts programs[1] whilst others may keep scribbled notes on assorted scraps of paper. With such lack of control, it is easy to argue that the agent is the controller in respect of personal data relating to customers, as indicated in diagram (b) in Figure 10.2. If this is so, it brings the burden of all the responsibilities flowing from data protection law crashing down on them. They will have to notify their processing or, more likely, be prepared to provide equivalent information on request; they will have to comply with the data quality principles; they will have to provide information when collecting personal data from customers and, worse still, be prepared to comply with subject access requests.

In the context of the relatively informal nature of the agent-customer relationship as it now tends to be, the increase in bureaucracy may deter many from operating as agents. The alternative, in diagram (c), in which the mail order company is itself the controller, can be brought about by the company taking more control in respect of the processing. It can do this by providing agents with instructions as to what data are to be collected, how they are to be processed and what is to be done with the results of processing. There will also have to be a contractual guarantee as to security of processing. Even though this is less onerous for the agents, some could find it too much to cope with. Many agents who order goods on behalf of a small number of friends and relatives could be frightened off. Only those with high turnovers might be willing to continue.

Where there is no agent involved, the position is much simpler and many of the points discussed in the previous chapter in terms of direct sales retailers will apply. The remainder of this chapter will examine the main issues in the context of catalogue mail order which are the provisions as to notification and automated decisions.

Notification

As mentioned above, apart from the mail order retailer being a controller, individual agents could also be so classed, depending on the amount of control exercised over their processing of personal data by the retail organisation. Even if the mail order company has to notify its processing activity, it is most likely that individual agents will be exempt. The publicity requirements for the agents can easily be met by

---

1   The chances are that, of those who do use computers, very few have registered under the present Act.

preparation of a simple notice by the mail order company to be given to all its agents to show to any person who requests it, thereby satisfying the requirements of Article 21(3). There follows an example.

Data Protection

Notice of data processing operations as required to be made available to any person on request as required under data protection law[1].

Name of controller:	Mrs Audrey Thomas
Address:	123 Fosdyke Mews Newchester. NT5 9BF
Purposes of processing:	Customer/client administration. Typical activities being: recording and processing orders and payments; dealing with customer complaints or enquiries
Categories of data subject:	Customers of Acme Mail Order Ltd.
Categories of data:	Name, address, goods ordered, payments made and due and current balance
Recipients:	Acme Mail Order Ltd and associated companies.

In any event, it is unlikely in the extreme that any agent would be asked for sight of such information. Where the agent is deemed to be a processor, the mail order company would have, instead to insist on an appropriate contractual guarantee in respect of security of the data, backed up by an indemnity. That is the effect of Article 17(3). For example, the formal agreement between the mail order company and the agent would have to include a clause similar to that below.

6.1 Security of Processing

The Agent agrees to process personal data relating to customers of the Company only in accordance with the Company's instructions set out in leaflet No 97/4A, as amended. The Agent agrees to keep personal data confidential and fully secure from accidental or unlawful destruction or accidental loss, alteration, unauthorised disclosure or access. Furthermore, the Agent agrees to indemnify the Company in respect of any loss or damage resulting directly or indirectly from the Agent's failure to keep the data fully secure as aforesaid.

---

1   The precise statutory provision implementing Article 21(3) should be stated.

The formality of all this can be softened by the mail order company providing clear and easy to follow guidance on the type of security measures to be taken. Nevertheless, the traditional informal nature of mail order catalogue agencies could be compromised by this and it is not an easy matter to see how this result can be avoided. It is, however, worth bearing in mind that the security measures to be taken will not be onerous as, by Article 17(1), regard has to be had to costs and risks. The harm resulting from the loss or unauthorised disclosure of the type of personal data processed by agents is likely to be relatively small.

> Best case - agents will be classed as processors. Nevertheless, this will bring obligations in respect of security and confidentiality. The direct costs are small, being no more than the modification of or introduction of formal written contracts with the agents. However, the imposition of such obligations could frighten off some agents with a consequential downturn in turnover resulting from sales through agents

> Worst case - agents will be classed as controllers. They will have to comply with the Directive's provisions (for example, security, publicity, informing data subjects, subject access, data quality principles, etc.). Even if exempt from formal notification (most likely) this could deter many agents. However, direct costs should not be great.

Automated Decisions

The traditional form of mail order retailing using catalogues relies heavily on offering credit facilities. Customers may pay for the selected goods by instalments. Over a period of time, as more and more orders are placed and repayments made without default, the retailer will "get a feel" for the reliability of a person ordering goods, whether as an agent or in his or her own right. However, when a person first applies for a catalogue and submits his or her first order, the company have to be able to assess the creditworthiness of that person. Of course, a check may be carried out with a credit reference agency but this will not always provide the full picture. The person concerned may be unknown to the credit reference agency, having never previously used credit or banking services. How does the mail order company assess whether such a person is likely to repay the instalments? After all, he or she could be a fraudster who has changed name and/or address.

It is conceivable that some form of checking is carried out based on the simple information provided by new customer or agent. Such checking could be carried out automatically, as soon as the information is entered into the mail order company's computer by software specifically designed to give a preliminary assessment of likelihood of paying. That being so, the provisions in the Directive relating to automated decisions will apply.

To reiterate, Article 15(1) prohibits automated individual decisions by granting to a data subject a right not to be subject to a decision which produces legal effects or significantly affects him and which is based solely on automated processing of data intended to evaluate certain of his or her personal aspects, including creditworthiness. However, subject to the other provisions of the Directive[1], Article 15(2) allows such decisions in the course of entering into or performing a contract with the data subject providing any request by the data subject has been satisfied or there are suitable measures to safeguard his legitimate interests, such as by allowing him to stste his point of view.

On the face of it, automated decision making may be used in the context of determining whether a new customer or agent is to be given credit. It may be sensible for controllers using automated individual decisions to have some form of appeal procedure so that the applicant can have his or her say if turned down for credit in order to show compliance with the above proviso. But, even then, controllers must take account of the other provisions of the Directive, particularly the first principle relating to data quality, being that personal data must be processed fairly and lawfully. This is unlikely to be the case if the decision is made purely on the basis of some factor such as postal address. This may be a good predictor in an objective sense in that persons living within a particular postal district may be significantly more likely to fail to complete paying instalments. However, on a subjective level, *vis-à-vis* a particular individual this is not so. A particular person is not more likely to default on a credit arrangement simply because he or she happens to live in a district with above average levels of default. Something else is needed such as a previous history of default by that person.

Some inner cities areas are notorious for debt and crime. If a person is denied credit on the basis that he or she comes from the wrong part of town, that can hardly be deemed to be fair processing. It is analogous to the problem of processing third party data in *Equifax Europe Ltd v Data Protection Registrar*[2], discussed earlier and is, consequently, unlikely to be within the first principle.

---

1   Including, of course, the principles relating to data quality.
2   (unreported) 28 February 1992.

Taking the decision outside Article 15 by involving an employee in the decision making process is unlikely to help. Mail order retailers and other organisations using automated decision making must give due consideration to the principles and be prepared to modify their credit scoring systems accordingly. The inability to use accurate, though unfair predictors, such as postal address, could force mail order retailers to re-examine their credit policies. One possibility is that, until a good payment record is built up, the maximum amount of credit offered will have to be quite small - this can only harm turnover, at least for a period of time.

If mail order retailers and other credit-giving organisations can develop "fair" automated decision making, the amount of information concerning the logic involved to be given in response to data subject access requests need not be exhaustive as recital 41 shows that the right to such information must not adversely affect trade secrets and the like, providing at least some information is given.

Whether formal notification is required or not, details of the logic involved in automated decisions are not among the information to be given to the supervisory authority or any person on request. Therefore, in practice, what is likely to happen is that the controller will prepare a relatively bland and innocuous description of the logic to satisfy subject access requests. The controller, for fear of increasing its exposure to fraud, may be tempted to continue to use "unfair" factors. The controller may get away with that until such time as the Data Protection Registrar's suspicion is raised and she uses her powers of investigation to discover precisely the nature of the automated decision making. It may only be then that the controller is forced to implement "fairer" systems. This may be one aspect of the Directive where practical compliance with its spirit is not easy to achieve.

> Best case/worst case - because of the application of the principles, automated decision making, whilst theoretically possible in a contractual situation, may be severely curtailed with ensuing consequences. Unless they are able to make the decision making more fair as regards each individual, which may require far more information to be collected, mail order retailers may be forced to re-evaluate their credit giving arrangements.

---

1   For the purposes of Article 15, the decision must be based *solely* on automated decision-making.

Summary

There should be no real difficulties in respect of constraints on processing nor any special features about concerning links with data subjects. Of course, mail order retailers are likely to indulge in list trading by buying or selling lists of customers or both and what has been said in this context in relation to direct sales retailing in the previous chapter should apply here also.

It is clear that the main impact of the Directive of mail order retailing is on the role of agents. Whether classed as controllers in their own right or processors, this will affect the traditional relationships between mail order companies, their agents and their customers. It may result in companies in this form of retailing reconsidering how best to adapt their businesses. It may be that agents all but disappear and traditional customers buying through agents deal directly with the mail order company. This already happens to a significant extent. The majority of persons with mail order catalogues probably only buy goods for themselves and immediate family.

Automated individual decisions, if and to the extent that they are used by mail order retailers, could be severely constrained. Alternative approaches to determining credit-worthiness may have to be explored.

Chapter 11 : Manufacturing Company

Introduction

Generally, personal data processed by manufacturing companies is not of a sensitive nature but is mundane and ordinary. Primarily, the data processed will relate to employees, consultants and persons working for suppliers and sub-contractors. In the normal run of events, apart from the obligation of registration under the Data Protection Act 1984, data protection law has relatively little impact upon manufacturing companies. Of course, at the present time, data protection law only applies to automatically processed personal data and many smaller manufacturing companies will be in position to take advantage of the word processing exception[1] and under the payroll and accounts exception from registration and subject access[2]. Should registration be required, it should be a fairly simple matter for small manufacturing companies. The information to be submitted for registration purposes should be relatively straightforward. It may, for example, include personal data relating to employees which is used for purposes over and above normal payroll and accounts purposes and personal data contained in databases of suppliers and sub-contractors used by the manufacturing company.

Larger and more complex manufacturing companies have correspondingly more complex registrations under the Data Protection Act 1984. They are more likely to keep historical data and to disclose data to associated companies, such as a holding company or pensions company within a group of companies. Even then, the vast majority of data processing is not of a sensitive nature.

There are, however, some aspects of information handling in the manufacturing sector that could give rise for concern with the extension of data protection law to manual processing under the Directive and it is this form of processing together with the security

---

1   Any operation performed only for the purpose of preparing the text of documents is outside the definition of processing; section 1(8) of the Data Protection Act 1984.
2   Section 32(1) of the Data Protection Act 1984.

provisions that are of greatest significance in terms of the implementation of the Directive.

Personal Data Processing

The majority of personal data relating to employees are collected from them. Further data are collected from official bodies such as the Inland Revenue and DSS. Computer-held data concerning employees tends to be fairly mundane and includes information such as name, address, age, salary, qualifications, date of commencement, holiday entitlement, etc. Information about other data subjects such as consultants and employees of suppliers and sub-contractors is very sparse, comprising little more than name, job title, telephone, fax and email number.

More substantial information will be held in paper files. For example, in connection with employees, a file could contain information such as:

— details of periods of sickness and doctors' notes;

— results of staff appraisals;

— details of personal injuries sustained at work;

— details of any disabilities;

— courses attended;

— future prospects or plans in respect of the employee.

At the moment, this information is not within the scope of the Data Protection Act 1984 unless, having been converted out of the form in which they were processed automatically, it is intended to further so process them on a subsequent occasion[1].

Data flows
For a small manufacturing company, the data flows are simple and straightforward. Particular data flows associated with employees, such as to banks, potential mortgagees and in respect of references, are indicated but further discussion of these is postponed until Chapter 16 which concentrates on employees and consultants.

---

1   Section 1(5)(c) of the Data Protection Act 1984. For example, computer data may have been printed out on paper and the computer file erased but it is intended, in the future, to re-record the data on magnetic disk for processing by scanning the print-out with an optical character reader.

Figure 11.1 indicates the data flows that might be typical of a manufacturing company.

Apart from data flows to a parent company, to a bank paying salaries and to a pensions company, there will be flows of personal data to and from other organisations dealing with the manufacturing company such as suppliers and sub-contractors.

Factories are dangerous places and, inevitably, from time to time there will be accidents. There may be the possibility of diseases resulting from the use of a particular industrial process. Disclosures may be required in respect of personal injury claims resulting from accidents or diseases. Such disclosures may be required by an ex-employee and by bodies such as the DSS or Department of Health. Statistical returns will be made, to the DTI for example, both generally and in respect of accidents.

Processing under the Directive

Under present data protection law, there are no real constraints or significant issues. Manufacturing companies may find registering under the Act irksome but, even then, except for larger companies, this should not require substantial expense or bureaucracy. Arguably, the most significant impact of the Directive for manufacturing companies is the extension of data protection law to manual processing, for much personal data is kept by such companies in paper files.

Notification

As the government intends to take full advantage of the possibility of exemption from or simplification of the notification provisions[1], most small and medium-sized manufacturing companies will find that they are exempt from having to register. Even larger companies may be able to take advantage of exemption or a simplified notification where they appoint a data protection official if the United Kingdom decides to allow this possibility under implementing legislation. However, it should be noted that exemption from or simplification of notification are only possible where the rights and freedoms of data subjects are not adversely affected[2]. This should be the case in the context of conventional manufacturing companies providing they do not engage in creative use of personal data, such as list trading with employee data.

---

1   Home Office, *Consultation Paper on the EC Data Protection Directive,* 1996, p33. The Registrar also welcomes the opportunity to reduce the bureaucratic burden in respect of "non-risk" processing; Data Protection Registrar, *Response to the Consultation Paper,* 1996.

2   Article 18(2).

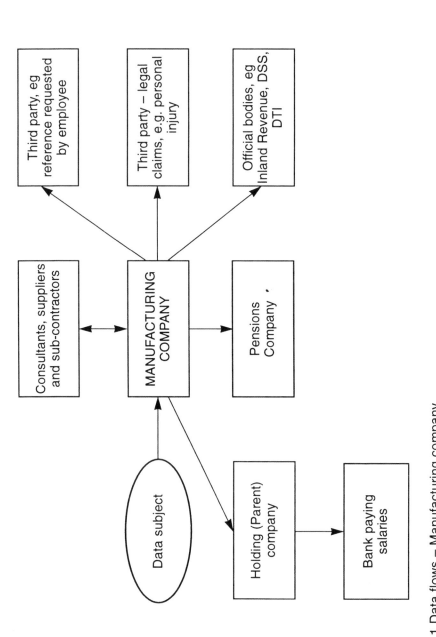

Figure 11.1 Data flows – Manufacturing company

Best case - almost all manufacturing companies will be exempt from formal notification. They will have to provide equivalent information on request, except in relation to security measures in accordance with Article 21.

Worst case - larger manufacturing companies with extensive personal data will be required to notify in simplified form and appoint a data protection official to oversee personal data processing and ensure that it complies with the Directive. This may involve prior checking by the official and may be subject to the sanction of the Data Protection Registrar.

Constraints - "Normal" Data

There should be no constraint over the use of personal data for the normal purposes of the manufacturing company. Processing should be allowed as being necessary for the legitimate purposes of the controller, for compliance with a legal obligation, for the performance of a contact with the data subject (for example, the contract of employment) or on the basis of public interest or the exercise of public authority vested in the controller or third party to whom the data are disclosed. In any event, as regards processing personal data concerning employees and consultants, express consent can easily be obtained although, this should not be necessary.

Best case/worst case - there will be no constraints over processing in the normal course of things.

Constraints - "Sensitive" Data

Special categories of data under Article 8 include health data. Personnel files (which may be on paper) may contain information about illness, diseases and disability. For example, the data subject may have a disability which requires the employer to take special measures as regards the working environment in which the individual is employed. Again, there should be no particular problems as consent can be easily obtained. Processing of such data may also be permitted because of the "vital interests of the data subject" exception in Article 8(2)(c) or employment law obligations under Article 8(2)(b). Additionally, statistical returns in relation to such data may be permitted under Article 8(3) - purposes of preventative medicine, etc or Article 8(4) public interest although, in the latter case, specific legislation would be required and the Commission notified accordingly[1].

---

1   Notification is required under Article 8(6).

Manufacturing companies are likely to keep historical records concerning employees, long after they have left the company. This may be very important in terms of defending claims in respect of personal injury, particularly where the individual's knowledge of the injury does not come for some time[1]. Article 8(2)(e) allows processing of, *inter alia*, special categories of data if necessary for the establishment, exercise or defence of legal claims.

Imagine that an employee in a factory, Bill Sykes, has a bad limp resulting from a road traffic accident some years ago. He is put in charge of a process involving the use of solvents. In the past he has complained of headaches and has had time off work occasionally, submitting doctor's notes accordingly. One day, Bill is injured as a result of a solvent spillage. He was unable to move out of the way quickly enough to avoid contact with the solvent. A medical examination shows that he will be scarred for life and, furthermore, he is in the early stages of a lung disease which could have been caused by the inhalation of fumes from the solvent. Two years after the accident, Bill has asked his solicitor to prepare a personal injury claim and counsel has been instructed to assess the potential liability of Bill's employer and the quantum of damages.

Bill's counsel has asked the solicitor to arrange for discovery of the following documents from the file concerning Bill held by the employer:

— records of Bill's past complaints about his headaches;

— two letters which Bill claims to have written concerning the headaches (Bill did not keep copies);

— the employer's information relating to Bill's limp.

Additionally, Bill's counsel would like the employer to disclose details of the wages and overtime earned by employees working in a similar capacity to Bill over the two years since Bill's accident. This information about "comparative earners" will be useful in assessing special damages up to the time of the court hearing.

Of course, such information may be useful to Bill's lawyers in preparation of his claim. Alternatively, it may be helpful to the employer. It may show, for example, that Bill admitted to having a drink problem which may have accounted for the headaches and that he willingly

---

1   The normal limitation period in respect of personal injury claims of three years does not start to run until the date of knowledge of the person injured if later than the date on which the cause of action accrued; section 11 of the Limitation Act 1980. The date of knowledge is further defined in section 14 of that Act.

volunteered to undertake the particular task. In either case, the exception in Article 8(2)(e) will apply - it is not limited to legal claims by the data subject or by the controller. A similar exception already exists under section 34(5) of the Data Protection Act 1984 which allows disclosure of personal data if required by or under any enactment, by any rule of law or court order or for purpose of obtaining legal advice or in the course of legal proceedings in which the person making the disclosure is a party or witness to the proceedings[1].

One difficulty facing companies keeping such historical data is how to comply with the principles relating to data quality, particularly in that the data must be adequate, relevant and not excessive, accurate and kept up to date and kept in a form identifying the data subject for no longer than necessary. It may be advisable when an employee leaves to examine the personal data and decide then, in accordance with well-considered policies, what to retain and what to destroy. Another factor is that data subjects may have a remedy if prejudiced later by destruction of data relating to them, at least on the basis of the law of negligence[2], where the controller is under a duty of care to retain the data and fails to do so.

Importantly, the derogation for manual processing is likely to be very helpful to manufacturing companies in respect of the considerable proportion of personal data which they hold in paper files and the like. Notwithstanding that the other provisions of the Directive will apply as usual (immediately for new processing after implementation and within three years of implementation for processing already under way) manually processed data may be exempt from Articles 6, 7 and 8 for up to 12 years from the date of adoption of the Directive[3]. Thus, the provisions relating to data quality principles and the criteria for processing normal and special categories of data will not apply until 24 October 2007, assuming the United Kingdom takes advantage of this option[4]. Even then, compliance will not be required for old files where it would prove impossible or involve a disproportionate effort[5].

---

1   For an example of this provision, see *Rowley v Liverpool City Council* (unreported) 26 October 1989, Court of Appeal, in which the appellant wanted data relating to comparative earners in order to prepare a personal injury claim against the respondent.
2   Under the Data Protection Act 1984, compensation may be available for loss or unauthorised (in terms of the data user) destruction of personal data; section 23. Article 22 requires Member States to provide remedies to data subjects for breach of the national provisions implementing the Directive. It is doubtful that this, *per se*, will give a remedy for deliberate destruction by the controller.
3   Article 32(2).
4   Home Office, *Consultation Paper on the EC Data Protection Directive*, 1996, pp48-49, implicitly accepts that it is beyond doubt that this derogation will be used in the United Kingdom. On the other hand, the Data Protection Registrar in her response

Best case/worst case - there will be no particular difficulties in respect of special categories of data, whether processed manually or automatically. Companies ought to consider how to take advantage of the derogation for manual processing of 12 years from some of the provisions of the Directive and develop procedures to ensure full compliance is achieved within that period of time. There should be some re-assessment of how long, to what extent and in what form, older data are retained.

Security

Most companies in the manufacturing sector probably take security relatively seriously though less so in comparison with organisations in the financial and banking sectors, where the fight against fraud is paramount. Nevertheless, most manufacturing companies will have good security in respect of their computer systems in terms of software and, because of the growing number of thefts of computer equipment, in terms of the physical security of their computers. Security in relation to manually processed data may not be as good, particularly as the type of personal data held by manufacturing companies is unlikely to have commercial value. This must be addressed and an objective evaluation of security should be undertaken with a view to proposing and implementing improvements. The following points are of particular interest:

—   in some cases, companies will engage the services of computer bureaux and other processors to process personal data on their behalf (bearing in mind the wide definition of processing). Particular measures must be taken to ensure the contract with any processor contains the required guarantees and indemnities;

—   security is important in terms of loss of personal data as well as unauthorised disclosure[1] and it is important that consideration is given to appropriate measures to recover from loss of data;

—   access to paper files must be limited and such files containing personal data should not be left lying around for anyone to see;

---

to the Consultation Paper sees only limited practical value in implementing the discretionary 12 years derogation for manual processing.

5   This is the effect of a joint statement by the European Council and Commission, see the Home Office, *Consultation Paper on the EC Data Protection Directive,* 1996, p49.

1   Under the Data Protection Act 1984, data subjects have a right to compensation for loss and unauthorised disclosure. This can be expected to continue and even be extended to other forms of "unlawful processing"; Article 22 of the Directive.

—   it may be advisable to have personal data in paper files scanned into computer files or otherwise duplicated as a backup copy.

Best case/worst case - there is no difference - appropriate security measures must be put into place in respect of all personal data, whether automatically processed or manually processed. This will require an appraisal study and, in many cases, improvement to be made to the physical security of paper files and the like. This will involve some costs, part of which may be recouped through reduced insurance premiums. There may also be the benefit of not being subjected to as many burglaries with the consequential disruption this causes.

Links with Data Subjects

There should be no particular problems relating to links with data subjects as the company will have an on-going relationship with the data subjects, whether its own employees or those working for other companies the manufacturing company comes into contact with. Providing information to data subjects should be easily catered for in most cases. Some re-design of forms and contracts of employment may be necessary.

The only issue of note is the fact that data subject access will be available in respect of manually processed personal data files. This could be quite onerous to comply with, particularly if the data is scattered through a number of files. However, the volume of subject access requests is not likely to be high and the possibility of charging a fee (at present up to £10) should be sufficient to deter those applying for subject access for no better reasons than curiosity or nuisance value.

Summary

Manufacturing companies will not be seriously affected by the Directive's provisions. However, that does not mean that they can ignore the new law altogether. As noted in this chapter, there are particular aspects that will need some thought and the putting in place of appropriate policies and measures. In particular, manufacturing companies will have to consider how they will:

—   inform data subjects on collection of data;

—   impose contractual guarantees on processors;

— improve security measures;

— deal with paper files and bring existing files to full compliance by 2007.

Further issues may be relevant, depending on the nature of processing of personal data, for example, if it transferred to a third country for processing, or if the company has further establishments in Europe and elsewhere.

Chapter 12 : Sole Trader

Introduction

In this chapter, we are concerned with sole traders such as shopkeepers, hairdressers, self-employed tradesmen or craftsmen (or women) such as bricklayers. Within this category, we can also include self-employed consultants and all forms of professionals operating as a "one-man" (or woman) business. Of course, the types of business operated by sole traders varies enormously but most of them will process the same basic categories of data. Consequently, there are some common themes in the nature of data processing carried out by sole traders and common data protection issues to be addressed by the bulk of them.

Personal Data Processing

The amount of personal data processing carried out by sole traders is relatively minimal. Typically, it will comprise little more than customer or client information together with data relating to suppliers and other persons the sole trader has contact with. Some examples follow.

Example 1
Gwen, a self-employed hairdresser, has a card index with names, addresses and telephone numbers of customers. On these cards, she also makes a note of any special requirements or characteristics affecting that person. This could be information relating to allergies of clients to particular hair dressing chemicals or preferences as to style. Gwen may have another card index with names, addresses and telephone numbers of suppliers of hairdressing equipment, shampoos and the like. These cards may include names of contact names but this will not be within the meaning of a personal data filing system as the cards will not be arranged so as to facilitate access to any data relating to these individuals[1]. Gwen will also keep an appointments book and accounts which may include names of customers, the dates of their appointments and payments

---

1   However, if the same information was stored on computer it would be within the scope of the Directive - personal data could then be retrieved by searching for a given individual's name.

made. Again these will not be classed as a personal data filing system and will be outside the scope of the Directive in terms of manual processing[1].

If appointments and accounts are stored on computer, it is more likely that processing will be within the Directive. The individuals are identifiable from that data and this is sufficient, however structured, to be classed as personal data within Article 2(a).

Example 2
Ronald is a self-employed bricklayer. He has a valid "tax exemption" certificate and is taxed on Schedule D[2]. The only personal data Ronald keeps relating to his work is an address book with names, addresses and telephone numbers of contractors and other clients he works for together with some information about builders' merchants. Ronald also has a mobile telephone which has a 100 number memory and he has stored the numbers of some of his most important clients and builders' merchants. Both the address book and telephone also have information about friends and relatives.

Recital 16 indicates that the Directive will apply to manual filing systems which are "structured according to specific criteria relating to individuals, so as to permit easy access to the personal data in question". Does this extend to address books? It is arguable that it does, being arranged alphabetically, it allows easy access to a particular person's personal data. On the other hand, under each letter of the alphabet, names, addresses and telephone numbers will not be structured in any particular way - they were probably recorded in the order that the information was collected. On balance, and considering the particular mischiefs the Directive is addressed at, it seems highly unlikely (and unnecessary) that such address books should be controlled by data protection law. Of course, data processed by individuals for personal or household activities is outside the scope of the Directive[3]. In many cases, address books kept by sole traders will contain a combination or private and business information.

If Ronald invests in an electronic organiser then it seems the Directive does apply, even though the information comprises no more than name, address and telephone number, because the definition of personal data in couched in terms of "any information relating to an identified or identifiable natural person".

If this is so and a paper address book is outside the scope of the Directive but an electronic address book is within the scope of the Directive, this runs counter to one of the stated principles underlying the Directive, being that there should be no difference in the applicability of the Directive depending on the techniques

---

1 Being unstructured in terms of the individuals and, hence, outside the scope of the Directive according to Recital 27.
2 In other words, the contractors he works for do not deduct tax from payments made to him. He pays his tax direct to the Inland Revenue.
3 Article 3(2).

used, "otherwise this would cause a serious risk of circumvention"[1]. Does this mean the Directive does apply to paper address books after all? Imagine Ronald's response when a stranger walks up to him and says "Please provide me with information about your processing of personal data in accordance with that required in Article 21(3) of the data protection Directive"!

The telephone storage of names and numbers is, incredibly, within the Directive, unless solely for personal or household activities.

Example 3
John has a full-time occupation in the accounts department of a large manufacturing company. However, in his own time, he occasionally does private work, preparing accounts for a small number of private clients. He uses a computer spreadsheet program to prepare these accounts and has a separate file for each client. Each file has a name made up of the first four letters of the client's surname followed by a dash and the first letter of the client's first name with a dot and the usual filename suffix, for example, "bain-d.wks".

John discloses details about his clients to the Inland Revenue.

It is clear that the personal data about clients is within the scope of the Directive. In respect of a similar scenario under present data protection law, it was held that a self-employed accountant using a spreadsheet to prepare client accounts was required to register under the Data Protection Act 1984[2].

In the light of such sole traders, some of the issues of data protection law under the Directive are discussed briefly.

Data flows
There will be little in the way of data flows, except from the data subject to the controller. Disclosures by the controller to third parties will take place in only a number of situations, such as disclosure to an authority such as the Inland Revenue. The simplicity of data flows in this area is indicated in Figure 12.1

Of course, other data flows may occur under particular circumstances such as disclosure for the prevention of or investigation of crime. This might apply where the data subject is being investigated for a criminal offence, such as money laundering, or income tax fraud. Alternatively, the sole trader may have personal data that can confirm a person's whereabouts at a given time.

---

1   Recital 27.
2   *Data Protection Registrar v Griffin* (unreported) 22 February 1993, Divisional Court of the Queen's Bench Division.

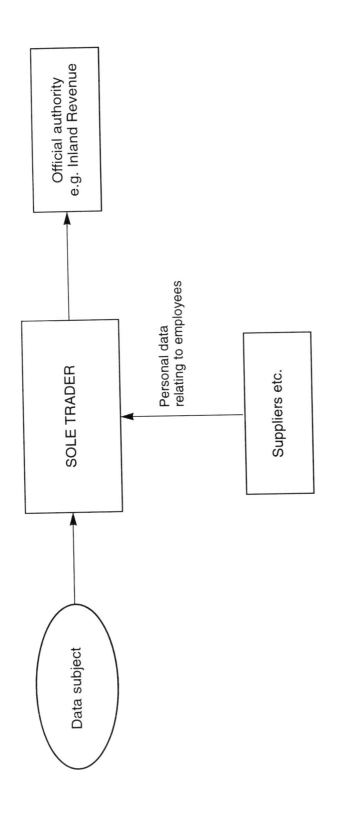

Figure 12.1 Data flows – Sole trader

Processing under the Directive

In the vast majority of cases, there will be little or no constraints over processing of personal data by sole traders. Except in rare cases, such as a sole trader providing health-related services (for example, a self-employed physiotherapist), personal data used by sole traders is not particularly sensitive and certainly not within the special categories of data within Article 8 of the Directive.

Notification
Given the nature of data processing carried out by sole traders and the government's stated desire to reduce the bureaucratic burden on business, most sole traders processing personal data will not be required to notify the supervisory authority formally. This should represent a welcome saving in bureaucracy for sole traders who, at the present time, must register under the Data Protection Act 1984 if they hold personal data and process it by automatic means. Given the growing use of computers by sole traders, this should result in a significant reduction in the size of the register[1].

It is unlikely that sole traders will pre-prepare information to satisfy the publicity requirements for exempt controllers and, so the costs of the notification and publicity provisions should be nil. Sole traders should, however, make themselves familiar with what information should be provided in the unlikely event of someone requesting that it be made available to them. Awareness should be achieved by the Office of the Data Protection Registrar producing appropriate literature outlining the provisions of the Directive as they affect small businesses and sole traders and offering appropriate guidance in an easy to understand fashion.

> Best case/worst case - there should be no difference - virtually all sole traders will be exempt from formal notification and should find compliance with the publicity requirements very easy, should they ever be asked for information as to their processing of personal data.

Constraints - "Normal" Data
There should be little to interfere with the processing of personal data by sole traders except in rare circumstances when the data are sensitive data.

---

1   However, there is probably a significant amount of "under-registration" by sole traders, Data Protection Registrar, *Eleventh Report of the Data Protection Registrar*, HMSO, 1995 p22. Although suspecting clear under-registration, the Registrar was unable to predict what the total size of the register should be.

Best case/worst case - there should be no constraints over the processing of normal data by sole traders. Either the data subject's consent will have been given (or can easily be obtained) and/or the processing is necessary for the legitimate purposes of the sole trader.

Constraints - "Sensitive" Data

In some cases, sole traders may process data that are within the special categories of data in Article 8. For example, a self-employed physiotherapist or acupuncturist will process health data relating to their clients. This should not be a problem as Article 8(3) allows processing in such circumstances providing it is by a health professional subject to some formal obligation of confidence, such as imposed by a professional body to which the professional belongs. In other cases, perhaps in relation to "fringe medicine" where there is no appropriate professional body, the data subject's consent can easily be obtained. As Article 8(2) requires explicit consent, it will be advisable to inform clients, at first contact, that their health data will be used to monitor their progress, etc.

Best case/worst case - there are no particular problems - the health care, etc. exception will apply in most cases and, if need be, the data subject's consent can easily be obtained.

Links with Data Subjects

The requirements in the Directive to inform data subjects on collection of their personal data should be very easy for sole traders to comply with. Simple statements such as the following will suffice:

"I agree to act as your tax adviser. To enable me to carry out my duties on your behalf, I need to have information about your receipts, payments out, expenses and the like. I will use this information to prepare your accounts and submit them to the Inland Revenue as and when required. Your information will be stored in a secure computer and will not be disclosed to anyone else other than the Inland Revenue, unless required by law, except with your prior approval."

"I am pleased that you have chosen me to style your hair. In order that I can contact you should I need to rearrange future

---

1   It is arguable that implied consent will suffice although Article 7(a) requires unambiguous consent. If, for example, a person engages an accountant to prepare his or her tax return, it is obvious that this will require some processing of his or her personal data.

appointments, with your permission, I will keep your name, address and telephone number in my card index system. I will not disclose this information to anyone else unless required by law to do so."

Providing information where the data have not been obtained from the data subject under Article 11 will be applicable only rarely as most sole traders will not pass their customer or client data on to anyone else. Even if personal data are obtained from a person other than the data subject or are disclosed to third parties, because there will usually be a continuing relationship between the sole trader and the client, this should be easy to achieve.

In the example of a tax adviser above who will disclose the data to the Inland Revenue (and Customs and Excise if the particular individual is registered for VAT), the information can usually be given at the outset. Alternatively, the controller could rely on the exemption in Article 13(1)(e) - important economic or financial interest of the Member State or European Union which includes taxation matters. Nevertheless, a guiding principle should be: if the information can be provided easily at no, or minimal, cost, then by all means provide it even if not required by the Directive. In this way the spirit of the Directive can be reinforced in terms of privacy of personal data and transparency of processing.

The subject access provisions, those relating to obtaining the data subject's consent and responding to objections to processing made by the data subject will not be onerous in terms of the vast majority of processing by sole traders. Subject access requests will be seldom made, if at all, and the fact that the sole trader and customer or client are in a contractual relationship will mean that the data subject is likely to give his or her consent in those rare cases when it may be required. Again, the contractual nature of the relationship makes the possibility of objecting to processing very remote. That is, of course, unless the sole trader decides to do something with the personal data which was not anticipated by the data subject at the time the data were collected.

Best case/worst case - there is no significant latitude in terms of implementation in the context of sole traders. The provisions requiring information to be given to data subjects, subject access, the obtaining of consent and responding to objections should be easy to address by the majority of sole traders processing personal data for conventional purposes. Costs will be nil or minimal only.

Summary

Sole traders should find little difficulty in complying with the Directive's provisions. In most cases, the data processed will not be sensitive and there should be no constraint over normal processing activities. Most sole traders will be exempt from notification and can expect little if any direct interference with their processing. Nevertheless, sole traders will be subject to the obligations contained in the Directive, as implemented, as much as any other controller and should make sure that they understand data protection law and process personal data in accordance with it.

Where sole traders are processing sensitive data, the obligations are greater and more extensive but still should be easy to comply with at little expense.

Sole traders who do not use computer technology will find the Directive has almost no impact on them, at least until the twenty-first century[1]. Even then, many manually processed files used by sole traders will not be sufficiently structured to be considered to be personal data filing systems and, as a result, are not within the scope of the Directive.

---

1   Until 24 October 2007 when, if the United Kingdom takes advantage of the manual processing derogation in Article 32(2), the full weight of the Directive's provisions will apply to personal data filing systems that are manually processed.

Chapter 13 : Professional Firm

Introduction

In many respects, the issues of the new data protection law for professional firms mirror those that apply in the cases of self-employed consultants, sole traders or manufacturing companies. This chapter will, therefore, concentrate only on those particular issues that are not covered in detail elsewhere. The application of data protection law as regards employees is covered in Chapter 16.

Some professional firms, such as architects, consulting engineers and planning consultants process data that are not particularly sensitive in nature. Others such as solicitors regularly handle sensitive data, particularly in respect of criminal convictions and civil judgments. Firms of management consultants process personal data that are sensitive in a commercial sense though not in terms of the meaning of special categories of data within Article 8 of the Directive. Generally, professional firms will owe an implied duty of confidence to their clients, for example, in the case of firms of solicitors, financial advisers or management consultants. In some respects this will represent the greatest constraint over their use of data, whether personal data or otherwise.

Personal Data Processing

Take a professional firm such as a firm of solicitors. It is likely to have a number of partners and employees. The firm's clients may range from large corporations to private individuals and its work may include both civil law such as company law, commercial law, contract, personal injury, family law, probate, wills, etc to criminal law. The work of the solicitor may be proactive, advising clients of measures to be taken to reach some goal, or reactive where a client is involved in litigation or being prosecuted for a criminal offence.

Contact with the clients will, typically, involve counselling and taking instructions and during these situations, personal data is likely to be obtained from the client, especially if the client is an individual.

Processing of personal data will be with the client's express or implied consent in almost all cases. The law of confidence, rules on self-incrimination and privilege will severely constraint the disclosure of personal data by a solicitor otherwise than with the client's consent, subject to the rules on discovery[1]. For solicitors and other types of firms such as accountants, the data flows will be relatively limited.

Processing of personal data is likely to be more diverse were the firm is, for example, a firm of architects or consulting engineers, as indicated below.

Data flows

Taking the example of a firm of architects, Figure 13.1 indicates some of the data flows that might be expected. The firm will collect data on its partners and employees, including *curricula vitae*. It may also collect personal data relating to individuals working for organisations the firm deals with, such as clients wanting buildings designed or their construction supervised and contractors, sub-contractors, manufacturers and suppliers of building materials. It will also process information concerning individuals workings for other firms carrying out related work such as consulting engineers and planning consultants. Minimal personal data may also be collected from local authorities and public utilities companies such as telecommunications companies and local electric and gas companies.

The firm is likely to disclose personal data to clients, who may wish to see *curricula vitae* of partners or employees to be directly concerned with the client's work. Local authorities, particularly planning departments, are likely to obtain some personal data relating to individuals within the firm of architects for the purpose of negotiations or discussions as regards planning approvals and for use by building inspectors so that they are able to contact the appropriate person within the firm to arrange for stage inspections of buildings under erection.

The firm will, from time to time, be asked to supply references on behalf of their past or present employees and will also invite references from other firms, local authorities and the like. Data will be recorded which concerns trainees at the firm for the purpose of satisfying training requirements for the Royal Institute of British Architects or other professional bodies.

---

1   Processing for the purposes of legal claims is specifically recognised in Article 8(2)(e) and disclosure as required by the rules of discovery can further be justified on the basis of Article 7(c) - necessary for compliance with a legal obligation to which the controller is subject.

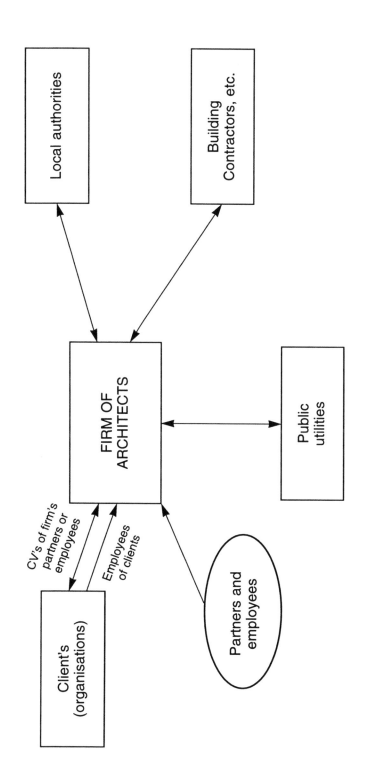

Figure 13.1 Data flows – Firm of architects

Processing under the Directive

There is little in the Directive to interfere with processing for purposes associated with the normal activities of most professional firms. The framework within which such firms have traditionally processed personal data means that processing is unlikely to adversely affect the rights and freedoms of individuals. This is so especially if the principles relating to data quality are adhered to as they must be by all controllers, unless exempt.

Notification

It is likely that most professional firms will be in a position to take advantage of the anticipated relaxation of the requirements to register. Preparing the information to be available to any person on demand should not, except for the largest of firms, be a particularly onerous task.

> Best case: there will be blanket exemption from registration for almost all types of professional firms except, possibly those processing sensitive personal data by automatic means, such as a solicitor's firm with client files stored electronically.

> Worst case: it is possible that large single-practice firms and multi-disciplinary practices handling a wide variety of data may, be required to appoint a data protection official and/or submit a simplified notification to the supervisory authority.

Constraints - "Normal" Data

For professional firms, most, if not all, processing will be permitted under Article 7(b) and (f). In exceptional circumstances, where the consent of the data subject is required, this should cause no insurmountable difficulties as the firm and the individual concerned will have an on-going relationship making the obtaining of consent an easy matter. It should be noted that where processing is carried on under Article 7(a), the consent must be unambiguous and it will not be satisfactory to rely on the concept of implied consent. However, it will be very rare when none of the other heads under Article 7 will apply. Where a present or ex-employee has applied for new employment and given the name of the firm or a partner of the firm as a reference it would be prudent to ensure that the individual has indeed given consent. As a matter of good practice and good manners, he or she should have informed the appropriate person accordingly.

Best case/worst case: there should be no significant difference and processing can proceed under the provisions of Article 7 without expense. Should the consent of the data subject be required, this can be easily and quickly obtained.

Constraints - "Sensitive" Data

Sensitive data within the special categories of data under Article 8 may be processed by professional firms for a number of purposes. For example, firms will need to keep records of partners or employees' disabilities to make satisfactory provision in terms of health, safety and welfare and to keep records of illnesses and other health problems. In some cases, the firm, as controller, will have the individual's explicit consent or the processing may be required to fulfil obligations under employment law[1].

In the context of lawyers processing personal data relating to their clients, Article 8(5) appears particularly restrictive. Unless derogation is made from the general prohibition of processing data relating to offences and criminal convictions except under official authority, it would appear the solicitors and barristers would not be able to obtain, record or use data which are vitally important in representing their clients[2]. This would be a nonsense, especially as there is no provision for processing such data with the data subject's consent. Legal representatives need to know data relating to an alleged offence and the circumstances surrounding it and details of previous convictions, if any, to be able to present their client's case to best advantage and, where a conviction ensues, make an appropriate speech in mitigation.

As regards administrative sanctions and civil judgments, processing is generally permitted unless Member States provide that such processing can only take place under the control of official authority. The government has already intimated that it does not intend to introduce any such requirement[3].

Best case/worst case: there should be no significant difference as processing of sensitive data will normally be with the data subject's consent or required by employment law. As regards criminal offences and convictions and civil judgments and the like, the United

---

1   For example, details of absences from work on account of illness may be required to be disclosed for purposes associated with payment of sickness benefit.

2   The phrase "exercise of official authority", though not without doubt, is likely to refer to processing in the exercise of a State function; Home Office, *Consultation Paper on the EC Data Protection Directive*, 1996, p20. It is likely that the government will enact an appropriate derogation, subject to satisfactory safeguards.

3   Home Office, *Consultation Paper on the EC Data Protection Directive*, 1996, p28.

Kingdom is expected to provide a sensible mechanism allowing such processing in appropriate circumstances.

Links with Data Subjects

Maintaining links with data subjects should not present any major difficulties for professional firms, except perhaps in terms of past employees, for which see Chapter 16. Certainly as far as clients who are individuals and persons working for clients, local authorities and other bodies and companies the professional firm has contact with, there should be little difficulty providing the necessary information under Articles 10 and 11. It would be sensible for the firm to consider to whom it intends to disclose data collected from individuals, whether employees or otherwise, and make sure that the individual is informed accordingly at the time the data are collected from him or her.

There are unlikely to be any significant issues flowing from the requirements as to the data subject's consent and the possibility of data subjects objecting to processing on legitimate grounds is remote. That is not to say that such consents and objections will never occur but they will be so rare that it impossible to lay down appropriate procedures apart from what has been said in these respects in other chapters.

Subject access is likely to be infrequent and, where it does occur, it is likely to come from employees (or disgruntled partners!) of the firm.

> Best case/worst case: links with data subjects should not unduly trouble professional firms, providing that they consider the relevant provisions of the Directive and how they may be addressed. Associated costs are likely to be very small.

Summary

As has been seen above, there are few significant impacts for professional firms over and above those that apply in the context of employees. Savings may accrue from removal of the need to register which most firms are likely to be able to take advantage of. Nevertheless, professional firms would do well to evaluate their present information handling activities (automatic and manual) in the context of the Directive's provisions and take the necessary measures and adapt their policies and strategies in respect of information to ensure compliance with the new law. Particular regard should be had to manual files and to potential disclosures of personal data. The opportunity to rationalise and streamline data processing operations should not be missed.

In some cases, professional firms may find that the new law will hardly affect them at all. Even so, they should educate all the partners and managers as to the implications of data protection law and, importantly, the importance of the principles relating to data quality and the need to take appropriate security measures. For example, a professional firm using a third party disaster recovery company should make sure that the contract contains the appropriate contractual warranties and indemnities.

Chapter 14 : Insurance Services

Introduction

Insurance companies have long since been in a special position as regards their contracts with insured persons. Insurance companies were vulnerable to fraud, particularly because they traditionally relied on the proposer for the relevant information. Consequently, insurance contracts are *uberrimae fidei*. There is a positive duty of disclosure placed upon the proposer which may be extended by the terms of the contract itself as in *Dawsons Ltd v Bonnin*[1]. Furthermore, sections 2 to 4 of the Unfair Contract Terms Act 1977 do not apply to insurance contracts.

There are two basic forms of insurance being *indemnity insurance* whereby the insurer will be reimbursed for loss to the insured property[2] and *contingency insurance* where the insured sum is payable upon the occurrence of a pre-determined event, such as the death of the insured person[3]. For the most part, the issues discussed below are similar whichever form of insurance is concerned. Both types require the collection and use of considerable personal data[4]. Another aspect of insurance is the role of the insurance broker, if there is one. In some circumstances, the broker will be deemed to be acting as the agent of the insurance company whilst in other circumstances, the broker will be deemed to be the agent of the proposer or insurer.

The insurance sector has undergone a number of developments in recent years. In particular, there is more marketing of services, there has been an increase in the range of services offered and more shared use of data by insurance companies. These particular issues were highlighted in the Registrar's Tenth Report[5].

---

1   [1922] 2 AC 413.
2   For example, insurance in respect of a motor vehicle or the contents of a house.
3   Normally referred to as life assurance.
4   Unless, of course, the insurer is a corporation. Even here, information as to the directors may be required to be given.
5   Data Protection Registrar, *Tenth Report of the Data Protection Registrar*, HMSO, 1994, p21.

Personal Data Processing

Insurance companies require considerable information from proposers (persons applying to take out insurance). For example, a proposal form to be completed by an individual for insurance for a motor vehicle will include such information as:

—   name, address, age, sex;

—   type of licence held and for how long, driving experience;

—   details of any accidents, previous claims and convictions;

—   details of other named drivers, as above;

—   details of the vehicle and uses to which the proposer intends to put it to;

—   whether the proposer has been refused insurance;

—   type of cover required, excess, etc.

For life assurance, the proposer will be required to give information including:

—   name, address, age, sex, marital status;

—   "lifestyle" (whether a smoker, drinker, dangerous sports undertaken, etc);

—   details of serious accidents, illnesses, diseases and operations;

—   name and address of family doctor;

—   details of the beneficiary under the policy.

Additionally, the proposer may be required to undergo a medical examination. As can be seen, in both cases, the amount of information can be substantial and much of it could be sensitive within Article 8 of the Directive. It is vitally important, therefore, that processing such data is carefully controlled and disclosures are restricted.

Though there may be some areas of concern, on the whole the insurance industry takes data protection law very seriously. In 1993, the Association of British Insurers published a code of practice for complying with the data protection principles. The Office of the Data

Protection Registrar was involved in discussion when the code was being formulated[1].

Insurance companies share data relating to claims through the Comprehensive Loss Underwriting Exchange. The purposes are twofold: to prevent fraud and for underwriting purposes. The Registrar expressed concern and changes to proposal forms and other forms were made although there was still an issue that placing details as to past claims might involve a breach of confidence unless done with the insurer's express consent.

Another, potentially more sinister, use of personal data is the "impaired lives register" which contains details of persons who have been refused life assurance cover or, because of health reasons, offered such cover only on the basis of increased premiums. Notwithstanding the implications of the Directive, there are significant issues here under existing data protection law.

Data flows

Some typical data flows to and from insurance companies are indicated in Figure 14.1. Of course, data will be collected directly from the data subject but, in some cases, the proposer or insured person will be asked to give information relating to another data subject. This might include, for example, a named driver for car insurance purposes or a spouse or other beneficiary of a life assurance policy. Where life assurance or medical insurance is involved, the data subject may be asked if his or her family doctor can be approached or the individual may be asked to submit to a medical examination with a nominated doctor or consultant.

Personal data is likely to be shared with other insurance companies, either directly or through a third party holding, for example, a register of claims. The insurance company may become involve in list trading, in the future if not at present, and data may be disclosed to statutory bodies or public authorities.

---

1   Where considered appropriate the Registrar has, under section 36(4) of the Data Protection Act 1984, a duty to encourage trade associations and other bodies representing data users to prepare and disseminate such codes of practice.

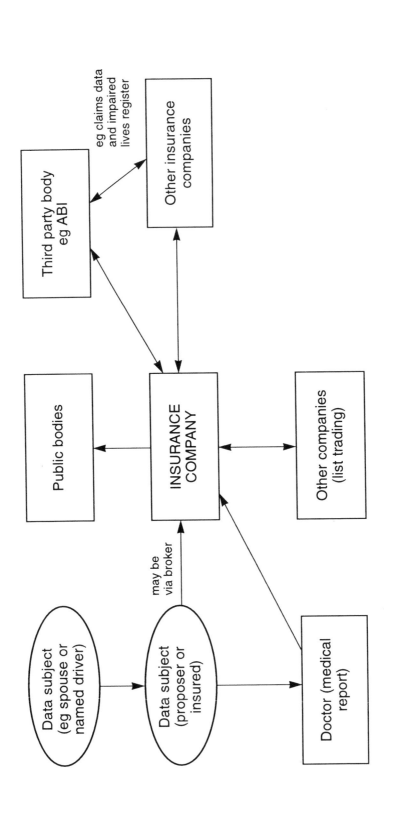

Figure 14.1 – Insurance company

Processing under the Directive

Insurance companies hold immense amounts of personal data. It is reckoned that the industry holds some 195 million personal files, most of which are on paper[1]. The data held will, inevitably, include some sensitive data but it has to be accepted that insurance companies have a genuine need to have at least some sensitive data, in order to accurately assess whether to accept a proposal, to calculate insurance premiums and to protect themselves against fraud. The effects of the Directive could have significant effects on the insurance sector, especially as many of its personal data files are on paper at the present time.

Notification

It is likely that insurance companies will have to formally notify the supervisory authority unless the option of appointing an in-house data protection official is permitted in the United Kingdom. Apart from public bodies, the health service and banking, this could be another sector where such an approach might be workable. However, even with the appointment of an in-house data protection official, a simplified notification would seem most appropriate rather than complete exemption from notification. For a simplified notification the Data Protection Registrar recommends that the following information be given:

— name and address of controller or representative, if any;

— name and address of the data protection official;

— the purposes for which processing is taking place[2].

The in-house official would have to maintain a register of processing activities; perhaps including the same sort of details that would be required under full notification.

> Best case: simplified notification subject to the appointment of an in-house data protection official is a plausible scenario. It is unlikely that all processing of personal data by insurance companies, because of the nature of the data and/or the nature of the processing will be exempt from notification altogether. There may be some limited prior checking carried out by the data protection official in conjunction with or in accordance with guidance from the supervisory authority.

---

1   House of Lords, *Protection of Personal Data*, HL Paper 75, 1993, p62.
2   Data Protection Registrar, *Consultation Paper on the EC Data Protection Directive: Response of the Data Protection Registrar*, 1996, para 7.12.

Worst case: full notification required and prior checking by the supervisory authority of processing of data such as that in the impaired lives register. However, prior checking will not be widespread, it will only apply where there are significant risks to rights and freedoms of individuals[1].

Constraints - "Normal" Data

Non-sensitive data will be processed under Article 7(a), (b) or (f); that is, with the data subject's consent, necessary for the performance of a contract to which the data subject is a party, etc or necessary for the legitimate interests of the controller or third party to whom the data are disclosed.

The contractual justification will apply where an individual is applying for insurance or has an insurance policy with the controller and the processing is directly associated with either. The legitimate interests of insurance companies will include their normal day to day operations and assessing personal data so as to decide whether or not to insure a particular individual and, if so, to determine the premium. Disclosure to third parties under Article 7(f) could cover disclosure to third party insurance companies of information relating to claims or a refusal to insure a particular person. It is at least arguable that such disclosure is necessary to the legitimate interests of the third party insurers to allow them to assess risk and to check whether a proposer has fully disclosed details of past claims and the like. It could also be necessary to prevent and detect fraud.

Collecting personal data relating to a relative of a person proposing insurance could be deemed to be by consent, for example, where one spouse gives details of the other spouse who will be a named driver on a car insurance policy. However, it may be safer to obtain the positive assent of that other person, bearing in mind the general nature of consent required in the Directive.

Processing personal data for marketing activities by the insurance company should be permissible by the usual tick box approach on any form that the data subject signs and this could allow disclosure to other *identifiable* companies either within the same group of companies or otherwise[2].

---

1   The government intends to restrict prior checking to situations where there is a "clear and real risk"; Home Office, *Consultation Paper on the EC Data Protection Directive,* 1996, p36.
2   As the data subject's consent must be unambiguous, it might be better to seek the positive consent of the data subject.

Best case/worst case: there should be no significant difference. Under normal circumstances, there should be no real constraint over processing normal data. Where marketing activities are envisaged, the data subject's consent, which should be unambiguous, should be obtained.

Constraints - "Sensitive" Data

Where life assurance or health or medical insurance is concerned, the data are likely to include a significant proportion of sensitive data within Article 8. Other forms of insurance could also involve sensitive data. For example, proposal forms usually ask for details of convictions and, in some cases, ask for information concerning general health and physical impairment[1].

In most cases, processing of such data will be permitted under Article 8(2)(a), that is, where the data subject has given explicit consent. Processing of data relating to criminal convictions is likely to be allowed in the United Kingdom for insurance purposes, providing organisations like the Association of British Insurers (ABI) do not contemplate keeping a complete register of criminal convictions. This would be highly unlikely as the ABI will not be interested in parking convictions or other trivial offences.

The impaired lives register may cause some concern and there is obviously a conflict of interests in the processing of such data. On the one hand insurance companies suffer the usual commercial pressures and they need such information to assess risk and premiums. On the other hand, it seems regrettable that particular individuals are singled out as being bad risks, probably through no fault of their own. It is likely that such processing will be subject to prior checking and, possibly, separate regulation in addition to the new or modified Data Protection Act, before it can proceed.

Collection of health data from an individual's general practitioner or from a consultant engaged by the insurance company should not present a problem because it will be with the data subject's consent. However, disclosure of health data and data relating to criminal offences, except to other insurance companies either directly or through the ABI[2], is more problematic. A prudent insurance company will obtain express consent unless there is a specific provision enacted to allow this[3]. The data subject must be made fully aware of

---

1   This is not limited to life assurance. Such information is asked for in proposal forms for car insurance.
2   In which case the data subject's consent should be obtained.
3   On the basis of substantial public interest; Article 8(4).

subsequent disclosures, unless covered by exceptions provided for under Article 13.

Whilst the data subject's consent will be the main reason why sensitive data can be processed, it should not be forgotten that Member States, under Article 8(2)(a), may lay down situations where even the data subject's consent will not permit processing to take place. This might be so where an insurance company insists on consent to some use of the data for purposes not directly associated with insuring the data subject as a condition of providing the insurance cover requested.

> Best case: processing of sensitive data for purposes connected with the provision of insurance services should be able to proceed on the basis of the data subject's consent. Processing for other purposes will be permitted provided the data subject has been informed and has given his or her consent.

> Worst case: As above except there may be some restrictions on insurance companies sharing sensitive data. This may be allowed only after prior checking and then within a constrained regulatory framework. There may be specific legislation preventing the data subject to consent to uses not connected with insurance services where consent is required as a condition of entering into a contract of insurance[1].

Links with Data Subjects

In the majority of cases, the insurance company processing personal data will have direct contact with the data subject to whom the data relate. Providing the necessary information to data subjects and obtaining consents should, in such cases, be an easy matter, requiring at most a simple redesign of leaflets and proposal or renewal forms to be completed by the data subject.

Informing Data Subjects

By modifying proposal forms and accompanying leaflets, insurers should easily be able to provide the necessary information under Article 10 - informing data subjects on collection of data from the data subject. There is no specific requirement that the information must be given at the time of collection and, in the case of insurance arranged over the telephone[2] it may be acceptable to provide the information along with the certificate of insurance or the cover note. This would

---

1   This prohibition could be applied in other sectors such as banking and health care.
2   Now a very common way to arrange car insurance and house contents insurance.

certainly be so where the intended processing is "obvious"; that is, it is for the purposes of providing a quotation or arranging the insurance cover. However, as we have already seen, where the intended processing is non-obvious, such as where it will be used for marketing purposes, the present law requires that the data subject is informed about this at the outset[1]. If such processing is envisaged at the time the data are collected, it would seem that the data subject is informed at that time, however inconvenient it may be.

If the data are used for non-obvious purposes at a later date, or disclosed to another organisation for marketing purposes, the data subject must be informed under Article 11, unless he already has the information[2]. It is unlikely that the specific option of informing the data subject before disclosure for marketing purposes coupled with the right to object under Article 14(b) will be taken up in the United Kingdom[3].

Best case: informing data subjects will not be difficult, requiring an appropriate notice on forms coupled with a "tick box".

Worst case: providing quotes and arranging insurance over the telephone could be made more difficult, requiring an appropriate statement of non-obvious uses and eliciting the data subject's approval. Alternatively, seeking positive consent later may suffice[4].

Subject Access

The fact that the insurance industry has a great many paper files containing personal data raises the spectre of mass subject access. However, the reality is unlikely to be very dramatic. The volume of subject access requests will be low thanks, in some part, to the possibility of charging a fee. In any case, most persons have a good idea of the information that their insurance company has concerning them. Where subject access is more likely is where there is a problem, such as a refusal to insure or a sudden and unexpected request for a large increase in premium. Nevertheless, insurance companies should consider evaluating the accuracy of their personal data files as should the ABI in respect of registers held by it.

---

1   *Innovations (Mail Order) Ltd v Data Protection Registrar*, 29 September 1993, Data Protection Tribunal.
2   Subject to the limited exception where the provision of information would prove impossible or involve a disproportionate effort.
3   However, the government seems fairly neutral about whether to use this option or the other which is simply to give a right to object which could, for example, be exercised by virtue of the Mailing Preference Scheme; Home Office, *Consultation Paper on the EC Data Protection Directive*, 1996, p31.
4   That is, the personal data will not be processed for the non-obvious purposes (typically marketing) unless the data subject gives positive consent at a later date. Some form of prize draw may encourage the data subject to respond accordingly.

It may be timely for insurance companies to investigate making further use of computer technology and placing far more personal data on computers than is presently the case.

> Best case/worst case: no significant difference. Subject access requests are unlikely to be made in large numbers. They can be expected in particular circumstances such as following a refusal to insure. Responding to a single request could prove expensive unless mechanisms for dealing with subject access have been put in place.

Consent and Objections

In terms of processing for normal insurance purposes, there should be no significant issues in connection with the data subject's consent. Objecting to processing on "compelling legitimate grounds" could provide more difficult. A particular area of concern could be in relation to the disclosure of sensitive data relating to criminal convictions or illnesses or diseases which may reduce life expectancy. Article 14(a) gives the data subject a right to object, at least where the processing is taking place under Article 7(e) or (f). However, it seems that the right to object will not be extended beyond those forms of processing[1]. The question then arises: is processing under Article 7 and Article 8 mutually exclusive or is there some overlap? Can processing of sensitive data also be necessary for the legitimate interests of the controller? As the data user's consent is a separate criteria allowing processing under Article 7 and Article 8 is couched in terms of a general prohibition on processing sensitive data, it seems unlikely. We will have to wait for implementing legislation to see how the right to object under Article 14(a) will operate in the insurance sector.

If data subjects can object to processing data indicating that they have a reduced life expectancy or criminal convictions, this would have a serious impact on the provision of insurance services. Of course, the objection has to be justified, though by whom it is not clear. Even if it is exercised successfully, the same outcome can result from deleting the data and replacing it with a statement to the effect that that particular individual has exercised the right[2].

> Best case/worst case: obtaining consent should be relatively easy and seldom withheld, except where required for marketing purposes. The data subject's right to object will not be exercised in

---

1   Or so the government intimate; Home Office, *Consultation Paper on the EC Data Protection Directive,* 1996, p30.
2   That is, it will be apparent that there was some data indicating a problem, in terms of insurable risk, with or associated with the individual concerned.

many cases and the fact of its exercise may lead insurance companies simply to refuse to insure the individual in the future[1].

Brokers

Usually, insurance brokers will be deemed to be the agent of the insurance company. This will be the case where the broker gives a quotation for insurance, issues a cover note, forwards the proposal form and payment to the company. The broker may make representations to the proposer about the scope and nature of the insurance offered. However, where a broker assists a person to complete an insurance proposal form, it would seem that the broker is acting as the proposer's agent.

The main significance of a broker, in most situations, being the agent of the insurance company is in relation to the security aspects of the Directive[2]. The broker is a processor on behalf of the insurance company as controller and must carry out the processing under a written contract with the controller which stipulates:

— the broker may only process as the controller instructs; and

— the broker must take appropriate security measures as set out in Article 17(1).

The broker will probably be asked to indemnify the controller against breaches of security and, as a result, brokers may wish to evaluate and improve, if necessary, their security measures in respect of personal data. Of course, it will also be important for insurance companies to insist that brokers acting on their behalf abide by the principles relating to data quality and this may be backed up by an appropriate warranty. Conversely, brokers may require a warranty from insurance companies they act for that the data they are required to collect are not excessive, etc.

Summary

The insurance industry processes vast amounts of personal data, much of which is of a sensitive nature. It is clear that the model of data protection law as set out in the Directive could have a significant impact on how and to what extent insurance companies obtain and disclose personal data.

---

1   There is little if anything in present discrimination laws that could force an insurance company to insure someone it did not want to on such grounds.
2   Articles 16 and 17. Notwithstanding rights and obligations under the law of agency.

With this in mind, insurance companies should review their existing computer processing activities and closely examine their manual processing. Existing methods are likely to require at least some modification. The application of data protection law to manual processing is of particular importance to the insurance sector which should, in spite of the limited derogation until 2007 for manual files, reflect on how the principles relating to data quality affect manual files with a view to putting appropriate systems in place sooner rather than later. Subject access to manual files will be a possibility soon and, although unlikely to be at high levels, insurance companies would do well to be in a position to accede to such requests with minimum delay, fuss and expense.

The expansion of interest in the insurance industry into modern marketing techniques will need careful planning to ensure that the requirements to inform data subjects and obtain their consent are complied with in a fair and efficient manner.

Continuing dialogue between the insurance industry and the Data Protection Registrar is likely to prove fruitful in developing codes of practice allowing processing that meets the needs of the industry and yet remains faithful to the principal objective of protecting the rights and freedoms of individuals with particular reference to their right to privacy under the Directive, as required by Article 1 of the Directive.

Chapter 15 : Local Authority

Introduction

Local authorities process massive amounts of personal data. The data processed range from the simple and innocuous, such as normal employee records, to data of a very sensitive nature, such as data relating to adoption records, criminal charges and offences and health data. The nature of the processing varies from processing within a local authority department in-house to disclosure to a wide variety of third parties.

The diversity of local authority data processing is a measure of the variety of different functions carried out by each local authority department. A typical local authority will have a number of departments with appropriate responsibilities, such as:

— chief executive's (town clerk) department;

— social services and welfare;

— education;

— housing;

— engineer's department;

— architect's department;

— planning;

— treasurer's department;

— libraries;

— parks and allotments.

There may be others. In some cases, individual departments may be grouped together. Some local authorities operate on a single tier basis whilst others operate on a two-tier basis, such as individual borough councils within a county council area. Functions and responsibilities will be divided between the county and borough though there may be some overlap.

Personal Data Processing

The picture becomes more complex when the functions of an individual department are considered. For example, a social services department[1] may have responsibilities including:

— social work, dealing with disadvantaged and problem families;

— helping the homeless;

— adoption and fostering;

— day care centres for the elderly, disabled and children;

— homes for the elderly, disabled and children;

— home care, including for example, meals on wheels and home help;

— child offenders.

A social services department, apart from processing personal data associated with the above responsibilities, will also disclose them to a number of other departments, bodies and agencies and will receive equivalent data from third parties[2].

Data flows
Consideration of the diversity of work carried out by a social services department gives some indication of the scale and complexity of processing. The department will deal with children who may be in care, appearing before a youth court, up for adoption or being fostered. The department will have responsibilities with respect to the elderly (for example, residential homes, day centres or meals on wheels), for the

---

1   Most of this chapter concentrates on data processing in the context of a social services department. For a description of current practice in this context, see Pearce P, Parslowe P, Francis H, Macara A and Watson D *Personal Data Protection in Health and Social Services*, Croom Helm 1988.

2   Social services have an obligation of confidence which restricts disclosure of personal data; see *Gaskin v Liverpool City Council* [1980] 1 WLR 1549 and *Birmingham City Council v O* [1983] 1 All ER 497.

disabled and persons with learning difficulties. Further social work will involve "at risk" families and the vulnerable of society.

Typical data flows to and from a social services department are shown in Figure 15.1 which gives some indication of the complexity of data flows for many local authority departments. There may be other data flows. In the example shown, data is collected from "clients", being persons making use of social services facilities, such as general social work, long term and day care facilities for the elderly, disabled and children at risk, adoption and fostering services, etc.

Processing under the Directive

Some of the data processed by social services departments will be of a sensitive nature within Article 8 of the Directive. In many cases it will include health data, data concerning racial and ethnic origin and data relating to criminal convictions and charges. Other data that could be classed as sensitive in a wider sense may include information about income and means including financial commitments, learning difficulties, special needs and details of parents and other relatives.

Not only will such sensitive data be used by the department, internally, it is likely also to be disclosed to a number of other persons connected directly or indirectly with the department as well as other bodies and agencies. It can be seen that the principles relating to data quality are of the utmost importance in this context.

Notification
Local authority departments are just the sort of controller for which the appointment of an in-house personal data protection official could be most appropriate. This could be one way in which local authorities could be exempt from formal notification or be subject to a simplified procedure. The duties of a personal data protection official are, in particular:

— ensuring the internal application of data protection law in an independent manner; and

— keeping a register of processing operations carried out by the controller which would contain the information otherwise required to be submitted to the supervisory authority, apart from details of security measures, and which would be available to be inspected by any person requesting sight of it[1].

---

1   Article 18(2).

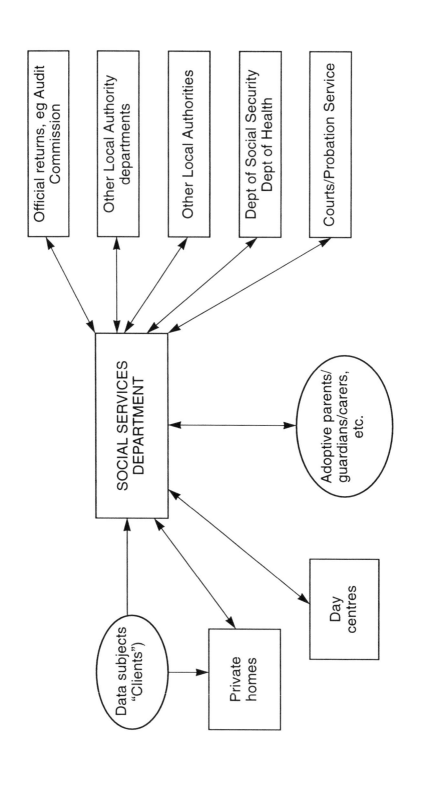

Figure 15.1 – Data flows, local authority, social services

The Home Office, in its consultation paper on the Directive[1], recognises that there could be some interest in such an approach, particularly amongst organisations already having specialist data protection officers, as is the case in respect of local authorities[2]. For personal data protection officials appointed by local authorities there would not be the difficulty of potential conflicts of interests as there might be in commercial organisations.

Exemption from notification is also possible in respect of publicly available registers, whether open to the public in general or to persons demonstrating a legitimate interest[3]. Examples being the electoral roll and registers of planning applications and such like.

Exemption from or simplification of notification does not appear to apply in relation to sensitive data within Article 8[4]. Exemption or simplification under Article 18(2) is only possible for categories of processing which, taking account of the data to be processed, are unlikely to adversely affect the rights and freedoms of data subjects. It is not clear whether this means the special categories of data within Article 8, but the recitals suggest that it is. For example, recital 33, which supports and relates to Article 8, is written in terms of data which are capable by their nature of infringing fundamental freedoms or privacy. Although the language is different, it seems that the intention is to require full notification in respect of processing within Article 8 with the sole exception of processing by voluntary organisations and the like under Article 8(2)(d).

If this is so, then local authorities would still be required to comply with the formal notification requirements in respect of sensitive data. A significant proportion of personal data processed by a social services department is sensitive data. For all other processing, exemption from or simplification of the notification requirements could be possible if the local authority appoints a personal data protection official, or more likely, a number of such officials, perhaps at least one or more for each department. Of course, such officials would also prepare and submit applications for notification to the supervisory authority.

The result of the notification requirements as implemented could be a mixture of notification for some processing operations and exemption from others subject to appointing a personal data protection official. This seems to be the worst of both worlds. However, local authorities

---

1   Home Office, *Consultation Paper on the EC Data Protection Directive,* 1996.
2   Ibid at p34.
3   Article 18(3).
4   Except for certain processing by voluntary organisations, trade unions and the like within Article 8(2)(d).

already have officers responsible for data protection and it is possible that they will be able to cope with the additional requirements without having to significantly increase staffing.

Prior checking of processing operations likely to present specific risks to the rights and freedoms of data subject is provided for by Article 20. This would be carried out by the supervisory authority or, if there is one, the in-house personal data protection official. Prior checking should be required for a very limited number of processing operations and this is made clear by recital 54. The government is unsure as to what type of processing operations will be subject to prior checking or how the prior checking procedures will operate in practice[1]. Clearly from a local authority perspective, prior checking by an in-house personal data protection official is preferable to having to seek the opinion or approval of the supervisory authority as the latter could take some time and processing must not proceed until after checking.

> Best case - the appointment of in-house personal data protection officials will result in substantial exemption from the notification requirements. Such officials would also be responsible for prior checking, perhaps in liaison with the supervisory authority. Staffing increases will be minimal because there are officers with data protection responsibilities already in place.

> Worst case - the mixture of formal notification for some processing and exemption for other processing subject to the appointment of personal data protection officials could prove cumbersome and require a significant increase in staffing. Extensive prior checking by the supervisory authority would, if required to any great extent, detrimentally affect the efficiency of data processing and result in undesirable delays. However, if prior checking by the supervisory authority is required, the government intends to impose time limits.

Constraints - "Normal" Data
There should be no difficulty in terms of processing non-sensitive personal data. A great deal of processing carried out by local authorities falls within one or more of the criteria in Article 7. For example, processing might be necessary to comply with a legal requirement, or in order to protect the vital interests of the data subject or necessary for the performance of official authority. Many of the obligations placed on local authorities in respect of care provision, education and housing fall within these categories.

---

1   Home Office, *Consultation Paper on the EC Data Protection Directive,* 1996 pp36-37.

As local authorities operate within a legislative framework the most apt category is that in Article 7(e) being "processing necessary ... in the exercise of official authority vested in the controller or in a third party to whom the data are disclosed". Not only does this permit processing by the local authority in question in the majority of cases, it also covers appropriate disclosures to local authorities, either from other local authorities, between local authority departments and from other organisations. Consequently, the data subject's unambiguous consent to processing of non-sensitive personal data will be required in rare cases only.

Of course, local authorities are subject to the data protection principles and past experience has shown that, as much as any other form of organisation processing personal data, they can contravene the principles. A number of problems were found with the amount of information being collected by local authorities in connection with the community charge ("poll tax"). In *Rhondda BC v Data Protection Registrar*[1], the Data Protection Tribunal upheld the Registrar's interpretation of the fourth data protection principle (that personal data held for any purpose or purposes shall be adequate, relevant and not excessive in relation to that purpose or those purposes) and confirmed his enforcement notice issued against the officers in charge of collecting information. They had been asking for individuals' dates of birth which, except to the extent that a person was over or under 18 years of age, was irrelevant. In *CCRO of Runneymede BC v Data Protection Registrar*[2], information relating to the type of property in which the poll tax payer resided was considered excessive and contrary to the fourth principle.

> Best case/worst case - there is no significant difference. Local authorities will be able to process non-sensitive data without constraint, except in exceptional circumstances. However, they will have to ensure that their processing is in accordance with the principles relating to data quality.

Constraints - "Sensitive" Data
Some local authority departments could process substantial amounts of sensitive personal data relating to health and, possibly also, racial and ethnic origin. The special categories of personal data listed in Article 8(1), being personal data "revealing racial or ethnic origin, political opinions, religious or philosophical beliefs, trade union membership and data concerning health or sex life" are not exhaustive. The remainder of the Article makes that clear and the acid test is given in recital 33, being

---

1   (unreported) 11 October 1991, Data Protection Tribunal.
2   (unreported) 1990, Data Protection Tribunal.

data which are capable by their nature of infringing fundamental freedoms or privacy. For example, details of relatives, adoption and fostering and whether a person has been in local authority care could also be included in sensitive data.

Social services departments will process some data relating to health, for example, in relation to disabled persons attending training centres of day care centres run by the local authority. Information concerning racial origin may also be processed because this may be important as to the type of service offered or for monitoring to detect and prevent discrimination.

There are a number of provisions in Article 8 which will allow processing of sensitive data by local authorities without having to rely on obtaining the data subject's consent. Processing may be performed where authorised by law, to protect the vital interests of the data subject and in respect of the provision of health care services. Otherwise, Member States may lay down further exemptions from the general prohibition on processing sensitive personal data on the grounds of substantial public interest. Processing data relating to offences and convictions is permitted if carried out under the control of "official authority". This will be useful, for example, where a social services department is preparing a report on a young person who is being prosecuted for a criminal offence.

The recitals give further indication of the scope of the above provisions allowing processing. For example, recital 34 mentions derogation from the prohibition on processing sensitive data where justified in the public interest in areas such as public health and social protection. Recital 35 is in terms of processing by official authorities for achieving aims laid down in constitutional law[1].

As is the case with non-sensitive data, the fact that local authorities act within a legislative framework suggests that most of their processing is authorised by law, whether expressly or impliedly. Adequate safeguards are required by Article 8(2)(b) in respect of such processing and it is at least arguable that the publicity requirements together with the provisions for informing data subjects and data subjects' rights of access and rectification, etc will provide adequate safeguards. However, recital 34 talks of "specific and suitable" safeguards. It is not clear whether something further is required and, if so, what it should be. Perhaps a local authority board may be required to be set up to hear objections and complaints made by data subjects. The board

---

1   Presumably this includes public law.

could be chaired by the in-house personal data protection official, if there is one, and would be charged with making recommendations to the local authority.

Best case/worst case - there should be no significant constraints on the processing of sensitive data within the scope of local authorities' normal obligations. Specific provision over and above the usual safeguards for data subjects may be required.

Links with Data Subjects

Local authorities have links with almost every citizen, in one way or another. Apart from local authority maintained registers, such as the electoral roll, a very high proportion of persons living within an authority's boundaries make use of the facilities and services afforded by the authority, or authorities where a two-tier system is in place. Education, libraries, housing, local taxation and social services are just some of the areas where there are links with individuals which will involve the processing of their personal data. Therefore, the provisions in the Directive relating to the links between the controller and the data subject are of some significance. Fortunately, there will usually be an ongoing relationship between the local authority and the data subjects which will alleviate, to some extent, the costs associated with the obligations to inform data subjects, respond to data subject access requests and deal with consents and objections to processing.

Informing Data Subjects
Most local authority departments, in common with a social services department, will have a continuing relationship with the data subjects it provides services for. Therefore, notifying data subjects on collection as to the identity of the controller and the purposes of processing, plus any other information necessary to guarantee fair processing in accordance with Article 10 of the Directive, should be any easy matter. This may entail adding an appropriate notice on a form signed by or on behalf of the data subject or by requiring the officer collecting the information to provide the data subject with an appropriate explanation.

Where the data have not been collected directly from the data subject, notification under Article 11 is required on recording or before first "unanticipated"[1] disclosure to a third party unless, in certain cases, it proves impossible or requires a disproportionate effort (subject to

---

1   Unanticipated at the time the data were collected; recital 39.

safeguards)[1]. There are likely to be numerous disclosures to third parties in respect of data processed by most local authority departments, especially social services. However, the vast majority of these will be known at the time the data are initially collected and if appropriate information is given to the data subject at that time, this will excuse the department providing subsequent information. A little thought and forward planning can considerably reduce the burden of providing information required under Article 11.

Although the Directive does not specifically so provide, it is submitted that appropriate notification given to a parent, guardian or next of kin will suffice to satisfy the notification requirements. This could be particularly important in terms of minors and adults without the mental capacity to understand.

> Best case - local authority departments have continuing links with data subjects and they can provide the required information by placing an appropriate notice on forms or by giving the information orally.

> Worst case - unless subsequent disclosures to third parties can be anticipated at the time the personal data are collected from the data subject, further information may have to be given, possibly by post. This could prove expensive but should be necessary only if the local authority is unable to predict all future disclosures.

Subject Access

The Access to Personal Files Act 1987 already gives a right of access to personal data files, including those processed manually, held by local authority housing and social services departments. These are two of the main areas where sensitive data may be processed and for which subject access is, arguably, most important. The Directive will extend subject access to all manual files processed by all local authority departments, subject to the exceptions permitted under Article 13.

At the present time, local authorities have to respond to subject access for all automatically processed personal data and manually processed data in the two areas mentioned above. Systems should be in place already to deal with this and the increased costs in extending subject access to all manually processed personal data files is unlikely to be high. A significant increase in the present level of subject access, which is relatively low, is not anticipated.

---

1   Recital 40 indicates factors to be taken into account as to whether the provision of information would involve a disproportionate effort. These are the number of data subjects, the age of the data and any compensatory measures adopted.

It should be noted that the Directive requires that more information is furnished than is presently the case. Nevertheless, this should be easy to comply with by providing a simple statement outlining:

— the purposes of processing;

— the categories of data concerned;

— the recipients or categories of recipients to whom the data are to be disclosed; and

— a generalised description in broad terms of any logic involved in any automated decisions.

Such information could be contained in a leaflet handed over with a copy of the data subject's personal data. It might usefully also include a statement setting out the data subject's right to rectification and might also be used to provide the necessary information to data subjects on collection of their personal data.

> Best case/worst case - no significant difference - increases in subject access requests are likely to be small and furnishing the additional information may require a simple pre-printed statement to be given to the data subject along with a copy of his or her personal data.

Consent and Objections
As noted above, providing local authorities restrict their processing of personal data to that required in the pursuit of their usual objectives within the legislative framework establishing and maintaining their duties and responsibilities, there should be little need to specifically obtain the consent of the data subjects. In some cases, processing will be required by express legal provision, in other cases it will be necessarily associated with the normal exercise of local authority functions.

If a local authority strays outside its usual range of duties and provides services over and above those which it is obliged to provide, there may be an issue of data subjects' consent. It is not inconceivable that local authorities will offer further services as a means of increasing income. If this is so, consideration must be given to obtaining consent although, in many cases, processing may be within Article 7(f), being necessary for the legitimate interests of the controller.

The data subject's right to object to processing on compelling legitimate grounds, as provided for by Article 14(a), is likely to be relevant only in very rare cases[1]. Even then, this will only tend to relate to particular processing operations rather than in terms of a complete prohibition on processing a particular data subject's personal data. A data subject may object to disclosure of personal data relating to him or her to a relative or an employer. For example, a person may have applied for a council flat but does not want his or her parents to be told this for fear of upsetting them. A person may not want an employer to know that he or she was in care as a child or was adopted or fostered.

Local authority departments probably already are sensitive to such requests[2] and the right to object will not involve them with much extra work. They may wish to set up a panel to deal with objections. The local authority ombudsman may also be involved if a data subject is not happy about the local authority's decision in this and other areas of application of data protection law.

> Best case/worst case - there is no significant difference - consent will be required only rarely unless the authority is acting outside its traditional role. Objections to processing are also likely to be rare.

Summary

On the whole, local authorities have little to fear from the Directive which has a number of provisions aimed at processing by such bodies. However, this does not mean that it can be ignored and there are some important changes ahead. With foresight the changes can be implemented relatively easily.

The possibility of an in-house personal data protection official is of some interest and the appointment of such persons may be useful in terms of the development and effecting of suitable and effective policies for compliance with the Directive as implemented in the United Kingdom.

Local authorities have massive amounts of personal data stored in paper files including substantial amounts of archived information. The postponement of the full rigours of the Directive for such data files already in existence until 2007 will be welcomed. However, local authorities, in common with other organisations holding large amounts of personal data in paper files, should consider putting procedures in place now to vet the information for compliance over a reasonable

---

1   It is likely to be limited to processing under Articles 7(e) and (f), the former including processing carried out in the exercise of official authority. The government has expressed its intention to so limit it; Home Office, *Consultation Paper on the EC Data Protection Directive*, 1996 p30.
2   In some cases, there could be a duty of confidence.

period of time. Consideration should also be given to all data processing carried out with a view to increasing its utility and effectiveness, taking greater advantage of information technology and getting rid of obsolete and irrelevant data. Greater streamlining and efficiency should ensue, resulting in potential savings that could far outweigh the costs of complying with the new data protection law.

Chapter 16 : Employees and Consultants

Introduction

Employers need a certain amount of information about their employees so that they can pay them, deduct tax and national insurance contributions and make payments into a pension fund or for private health care. Basic information required for these purposes, such as name, address, bank account and bank sort number, salary, PAYE code, etc, is usually stored on computer and falls within the scope of existing data protection law. A major exception to registration under the Data Protection Act 1984 is where the data are processed for payroll or accounts[1]. In particular, the payroll exception is important and covers both remuneration and pensions.

The majority of employers keep much more extensive data about their employees than is simply required for payroll purposes. In many cases, each employee will have a discrete paper file containing his or her basic details such as name, address, date of birth, sex, marital status, starting salary, PAYE code and bank details. Other information will be kept in the file and this could include the following:

— salary increases;

— details of promotions;

— holiday entitlement and leave taken;

— period of sick and doctors' notes or self certification records;

— training record;

— health and safety record;

— authorisations including level of access to the employer's information;

---

1   Section 32 of the Data Protection Act 1984.

— completed staff appraisal forms;

— statements about the employer's future plans[1];

— outcomes of disciplinary hearings and appeals therefrom.

Much of this information will be collected and created over a period of time, during the employment. Existing data protection law does not apply to such data unless they are processed by computer[2] and the application of data protection law to manual files of this sort is very significant.

The implications of data protection law as between employer and employee are similar to some of the issues as between a client and self-employed consultant. In many cases, it may be difficult to determine on which side of the line a person is. Essentially, it is a matter of distinguishing between a contract of service (employees) and a contract for services (consultants). This is important in the context of employment law[3] and the ownership of intellectual property rights[4].

To classify a person as an employee or self-employed person, questions such as who controls the work, whether the person is entitled to sick pay, who provides a pension, the method of payment, whether tax is deducted at source and financial responsibility may provide an overall test[5]. In *Beloff v Pressdram Ltd*[6] the question of ownership of the copyright subsisting in a memorandum written for the editor of *The Observer* newspaper fell to be determined. This required deciding whether the person who had written the memorandum was an employee or not[7].

---

1 Unlike statements of opinion, statements of intentions as regards the data subject are excluded from the meaning of personal data under the present law; section 1(3) of the Data Protection Act 1984.

2 That is, automatically processed. Other areas of law may be applicable in some circumstances, such as the law of breach of confidence and the law of defamation.

3 For example, in relation to unfair dismissal and redundancy.

4 The basic rule as to first ownership of copyright is that the author is the first owner except, *inter alia*, when the author is an employee and creates the work in the course of employment, subject to any agreement to the contrary; section 11(2) of the Copyright, Designs and Patents Act 1988. The copyright subsisting in a commissioned work created by a self-employed consultant will belong to the consultant unless provision has been made to assign the copyright to the person commissioning the creation of the work.

5 *Market Investigations Ltd v Minister of Social Security* [1969] 2 QB 173 per Cooke J at 185.

6 [1973] 1 All ER 241.

7 Ungoed-Thomas J referred to a number of indicia which could be used to decide whether the contract was a contract of service (the person being an employee) or a contract for services. He decided that the former was the case.

As far as data protection law is concerned, the distinction is of less significance. However, an organisation is likely to hold far less data relating to consultants than it will in respect of its employees. For consultants, the type of data held will include name and address, invoices submitted and payments made, VAT registration number (if applicable) and details of work undertaken.

For consultants, tax is unlikely to be stopped by the organisation and the consultant will generally pay tax on the basis of Schedule D Class II. The organisation for whom the consultant is working will pay on invoices without deduction for tax. Payment may be made by cheque or direct to the consultant's nominated bank account through the BACS system. Where there is an on-going relationship between the organisation and the consultant, more data will be collected but even then it is unlikely to be anywhere near as extensive as that kept about employees.

Personal Data Processing

The majority of data processing carried out by employers in respect of their employees and by persons or organisations using the services of self-employed consultants will be for internal purposes only. Nevertheless, there will some occasions when the data are disclosed to others. The nature of data processing by employers and persons engaging consultants does not usually give rise to particular concerns. Relatively little, if any, sensitive data within the meaning of Article 8 of the Directive will be processed and even then it should fall within the parameters contained therein allowing processing as provided for in the Directive.

An important aspect for employers and the like is that there is a continuing relationship with the employee or consultant. Therefore, providing information is likely to be an easy matter. So too, for that matter, should be obtaining consent if it is required.

Typically, an employer will hold a separate file for each employee. Most of these files will be in paper form. Potentially, the extension of data protection law to manual files could well prove to be the most onerous for employers were it not for the possibility of derogating from some of the provisions in the Directive for some time.

One point to bear in mind is that employees appear to fall within the definition of "recipient", being "... a natural or legal person, public authority, agency or other body to whom data are disclosed, whether a third party or not ..."[1]. If employees processing data on behalf of their employers are to be so regarded, statements as to recipients for the purposes of notification and providing information to data subject should include employees within the description. For example, "We disclose personal data to employees, agents and other companies within our group".

Data flows

Employers will collect a large proportion of personal data concerning their employees direct from the employees themselves. They will also obtain data from other sources, such as the Inland Revenue (PAYE), civil courts (attachment of earnings orders), other companies within a group or departments in a public authority. Personal data will be disclosed to government departments (official returns), other companies within a group or departments in a public authority, banks paying salaries, the Inland Revenue, third party companies or authorities requiring job references[2] and clients requiring *curricula vitae* of employees to be engaged upon a particular scheme or project. Further data flows may take place where the employee needs a reference such as for a potential mortgagee of an employee intending to buy a house or potential insurer. Figure 16.1 shows these data flows.

Processing under the Directive

For many employers, as regards processing of their employees' personal data, present data protection law does not hold any terrors. Some smaller companies may be able to rely on the payroll exception, but most employers will (or should) have a registration covering, *inter alia*, the processing of employee data. The bureaucracy involved is relatively slight and the standard descriptions published by the Data Protection Registrar will prove helpful[3]. For example, standard purpose P001 covers personnel and employee administration. This includes "contract personnel", presumably meaning persons working under a contract for services, that is, self employed persons. Standard data classes include a number relevant to employees such as details of current employment, recruitment, termination, career history, work and health and safety record, trade union membership, payment and deductions, employer's property issued to employee, work management details, performance assessment, training record and security details, such as passwords and levels of authorisation.

---

1   The definitions of recipient and third party are not without ambiguity; Home Office, *Consultation Paper on the EC Data Protection Directive,* 1996, pp14 -15. It is not clear what is meant by the last part of the definition which states that "... authorities which may receive data in the framework of a particular inquiry shall not be regarded as recipients".
2   Particularly in relation to references, the laws of defamation and negligent misstatement may also be important.
3   The Data Protection Registrar, *Notes to help you to apply for Registration, including Standard Descriptions of Purposes and Data Classes,* 1985.

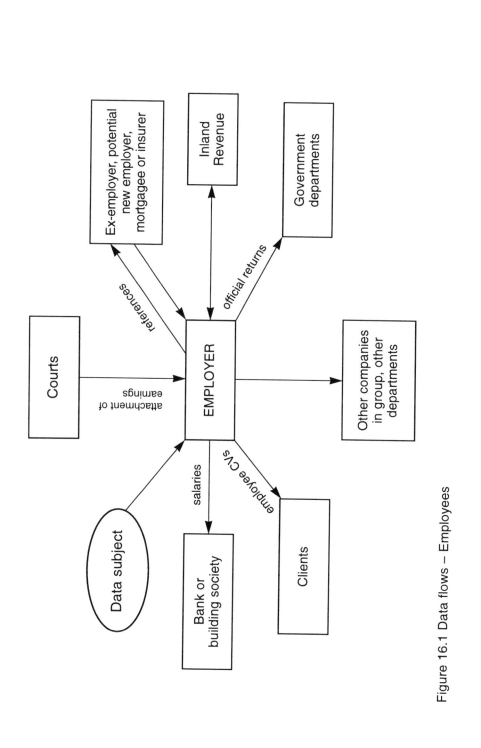

Figure 16.1 Data flows – Employees

Apart from the extension of data protection law to manual files, it would be reasonable to expect that the new law should not unduly affect or constrain the employer's day to day processing of personal data relating to employees and self-employed consultants. Notification should be simpler and, in the vast majority of cases, the employer will be able to process for purposes associated with the employer's normal and legitimate business activity or the performance of authority vested in the employer in the case of a public body.

Notification

Exemption from notification should be widely available for processing employee data in view of the stated intention of the government to that effect[1]. If there is a change of government between the time of writing and implementation of the Directive by national law, it would be reasonable to expect the new government to take a similar approach. The yardstick for exemption from notification is that the rights and freedoms of data subjects are unlikely to be affected adversely[2]. In view of the fact that employees can exercise their right to subject access and have rights to have incorrect data rectified, etc, employees rights and freedoms will not be prejudiced by any exemption from notification. Part of the rationale underlying notification is that individuals can find out about a particular controller's processing activity. This could be important where an individual wants to find out whether a particular controller is likely to be processing data about him before making a subject access request. Employees already know that their employer is processing his or her personal data. ·

Another justification for notification is that it gives the supervisory authority an opportunity to examine the controller's intended processing activities and to determine whether it is likely to comply with the principles relating to data quality. Again, with employee data, there should be no particular need to do this in most cases providing the employer is processing data in the normal course of running a business or public authority department. It might be different if the employer processes data for different purposes, for example, if the employer sells details of employees to marketing companies, or is deliberately flouting data protection law. In the latter case, it can be expected that employees would soon complain to the supervisory authority which would exercise its powers of investigation and enforcement.

Best case/worst case - exemption from notification should be widespread in terms of employee data and data relating to self-

---

1   Home Office, *Consultation Paper on the EC Data Protection Directive,* 1996, p33.
2   Article 18(2).

employed consultants[1]. Manually processed files are almost certain to be exempt anyway. Employers should still prepare a statement complying with the publicity requirements in Article 21(3) - this information could be given to existing employees and included in materials normally given to new employees. Costs are likely to be low and there may be some minor savings because of the exemption from notification.

Constraints - "Normal" Data

There should be no difficulty in processing non-sensitive data about employees in ways associated with normal business purposes such as employee administration, payment of salaries, etc. Clearly, this will fall within Article 7(f), being processing "... necessary for the purposes of the legitimate interests pursued by the controller or by the third party or parties to whom the data are disclosed ...". This would cover processing in-house and disclosures to the tax authorities, other companies within a group or departments within a public body. It should also cover disclosures to government bodies collecting statistical information or for the purposes of other official returns.

Job references are within Article 7(a) as the data subject will have given his or her unambiguous consent because, the employee or potential employee will have requested that some other person write and submit a reference. Sometimes, an existing employee may apply for a position with another employer and give the name of a senior manager or director at his present employer without informing or asking that person. Even then, there is implicit consent; the very act of writing the name on the application form should be enough. Where care should be taken is where a potential employer asks the current employer for information about the employee when the employee has not volunteered the name of a person at his present employer who will supply a reference. In those circumstance, the employee has not given consent, expressly or impliedly, and none of the other provisions in Article 7 seem to apply. Such disclosure could fall within the second limb of Article 7(f) which is in terms of the interests of the controller or third party to whom the data are disclosed are overridden by the fundamental rights and freedoms of the data subject, requiring protection under Article 1(1). If such an "unsolicited" reference is asked for, it would be better to inform the data subject first and ask whether he or she consents to a reference being given.

---

1   It is reasonable to assume that, if the controller has to notify in respect of other data, such as that relating to customers, he will not be required to notify in respect of employee data simply as a result of that fact.

Where an employee wants to buy a house or take out life assurance, the bank, building society or insurance company may wish to check some details with the employer, such as income, length of time in post, etc. Disclosure will be permitted under Article 7(a) providing the individual is informed that his or her employer will be approached and does not object. It may be simply a matter of placing an appropriate notice on the application form or proposal form.

Where the employer is a public body such as a local authority or government department, processing of non-sensitive data will be covered, *mutatis mutandis*, by Article 7(e). The same provisos as regards references will apply in a similar way.

> Best case/worst case - there should be very little constraint in the course of processing for the usual purposes associated with employee administration and management. Some consideration should be given to situations where the data subject's consent will be required. Even where this is so, it should not be onerous.

Constraints - "Sensitive" Data

Sensitive data within Article 8 will include, in the context of employees, data signifying trade union membership and relating to health, the latter for purposes associated with obligations under the Health and Safety at Work etc Act 1974 and similar provisions. Processing will be allowed where the data subject has given explicit consent. Where the data are required to be processed for employment law purposes, Article 8(b) is applicable. If the employer has in-house medical staff, processing may proceed under Article 8(3) for purposes of preventative medicine and health care. Data concerning trade union membership may be disclosed to third parties if the employee consents.

It is not an easy matter to think of any examples where an employer might want to process sensitive data in such a way that the employee's consent is not obtained or given and the other provisions of Article 8 allowing processing do not apply. Even then, there is always the possibility of further derogation by virtue of Article 8(4) on the grounds of substantial public interest.

> Best case/worst case - there is no significant latitude for derogation except on public interest grounds. In any case, there should be little constraint over processing as, where processing of sensitive data is envisaged, it should be an easy matter to obtain the employee's consent.

Links with Data Subjects

Employers have continuing links with present employees and there should be little difficulty or expense in providing information as required under the Directive to them or of complying with other aspects involving links with data subjects. Employers also have data relating to past employees and, at least for a limited time, applicants for employment. It is in respect of these data subjects that more difficulties may present themselves though, again and providing some thought is given to methods of compliance, the administrative and financial burdens should not be high.

Informing Data Subjects

Present employees and applicants for employment can be easily informed in accordance with Article 10 when their data are collected from them. Where job application forms are used, an appropriate notice can be printed on it. As regards present employees, there is an obligation to provide a written contract of employment and a statement may be incorporated into this. Many employers also provide handbooks to employees giving basic information about the organisation, disciplinary procedures, health and safety policy, etc and an appropriate statement can be included here. By making use of these various methods of informing data subjects under Article 10, there should be little need to provide information under Article 11[1].

The minimum information to be provided under Article 10 must identify the controller (and his representative, if any) and describe the purposes of processing for which the data are intended. Typically this will identify purposes associated with employee administration generally, the payment of remuneration, pensions, health and safety, work planning, employee assessment and promotions in addition to keeping records of duties, career, accidents, training, trade union membership, etc for various purposes such as the welfare of the employee and purposes required by law.

Further information may be required under Article 10 to guarantee fair processing. Although probably not required at this stage, it may be sensible and less costly in the long run, to give details about recipients, such as employees and agents, other companies within a group, banks for the payment of salaries, pension companies, etc. If not given at the time the data are collected, this information must be given before disclosure to the third party.

---

1   Which deals with the situation where the data being recorded or disclosed to a third party have not been collected directly from the data subject.

It may be advisable to add a note stating that failure to provide the information in a timely fashion may result in delay in payment of salary or wages or the availability of some other benefit as appropriate together with a reminder as to the data subject's right of access and rectification of inaccurate data concerning him or her. Such information is amongst the further information that may be required under Article 10. It is difficult to predict when it must be provided[1] and, as it should be relatively easy to provide and unlikely to be controversial, there is little to be gained from withholding it.

Where a disclosure to a third party is to take place that was not envisaged at the time the data were collected and the data subject does not already have it, the data subject must be given information at least identifying the controller and the purposes. Further information may be required in order to guarantee fair processing. The controller is excused if, subject to safeguards being laid down, it would prove impossible or require a disproportionate effort. This is unlikely to be the case as regards present employees. In the unlikely event that the employer has to provide information under Article 11[2], it should not prove difficult to do because of the day to day contact with the employee. Of course, if the disclosure is at the employee's request, for example, it is to a building society at which the employee has applied for a mortgage, there will be no need to give information - the data subject should already know because the building society should have made it clear that it would ask his or her employer for information about salary, length of time in post, etc.

Some data will not have been collected directly from the data subject. It may be information from a doctor who has undertaken a medical examination of the data subject prior to commencement of employment or information from a previous employer. There should be ample opportunity to give the required information; for example, in the letter of appointment. However, it is sensible for employers to review the information that is given and the timing of giving that information to make sure the Directive's provisions are complied with. For example, with respect to a medical examination prior to taking up the appointment, the letter offering employment could state:

---

1   It is required if necessary to guarantee fair processing but Article 6(1)(a) requires data to be processed fairly and lawfully. Perhaps there will be circumstances when processing can only be fair if the data subject is told at the outset about intended recipients rather than leaving it until disclosure is imminent; cf *Innovations (Mail Order) Ltd v Data Protection Registrar* (unreported) 29 September 1993, Data Protection Tribunal, discussed in Chapter 3.
2   Either because the employer genuinely did not envisage the disclosure or failed to take an earlier opportunity to inform the employee.

Before commencing your duties, you are required to undergo a medical examination at [name of doctor or practice]. The results of the examination will be forwarded to the company's personnel department where it will be reviewed and stored for future consultation. The purpose of the medical examination is to ensure that you are not given duties you are unable to perform safely or without risk to your health and well-being and that the company may make provision for your health, safety and welfare as appropriate. The contents of the medical report will not be used for any other purpose without your permission and will be kept confidential. The report will not be disclosed to a third party except when required by law or to protect the vital interests of yourself or another person.

The statement should have appropriate savings, typically, in accordance with the Directive. Another point to consider in terms of informing data subjects is the possibility of exceptions from the application of the provisions in Articles 10 and 11 which are laid out in Article 13.

Employers are likely to retain information concerning past employees for some time. This may be for reasons associated with health and safety, such as monitoring industrial injuries or diseases or for statistical research. Other reasons why it is important to retain information is connected with legal claims in the future by a previous employee, for example, in respect of an injury sustained at work. Bearing in mind that the limitation time for personal injury claims does not start to run until the injured person has knowledge of information indicating that he or she may have a claim, it is important to retain records for some time. Some industrial diseases may not show any symptoms for a considerable time. Further, the ex-employee may have been under a legal disability.

In the normal run of events, past employee data will not be used or disclosed in such a way that will trigger an obligation to provide information under Article 11. The ex-employee should already have the necessary information, for example, "Following termination of your appointment, we will retain some of your personal data for the purposes of monitoring health and safety, providing references at your request, in connection with legal claims or as required by law". Otherwise, the ex-employee will have to be informed under Article 11. This could be difficult if he or she has moved - in which case, the provision of information may well prove impossible or require a disproportionate effort and, hence, the employer may be excused.

Best case/worst case - employers who consider the requirements on informing data subjects and make appropriate provision, as discussed above, will be able to comply relatively easily and at minimal cost. Providing information to ex-employees may be difficult if they were not previously informed about disclosures. In many such cases, the employer will be able to claim that providing the information is impossible or requires a disproportionate effort[1].

Subject Access

Relatively few employees are likely to exercise their right of subject access. In many cases, they will have a pretty good idea of what data the employer has concerning them. The possibility of having to pay a fee, at present a maximum of £10, should deter many who have no better reason than satisfying idle curiosity. It is different where an employee thinks that his or her employer has incorrect data concerning him or her or has some data of a highly sensitive nature. At present, subject access is limited to automatically processed data and, as regards such data, the new law should make little difference, except that more information is given to the data subject in addition to a copy of the data, being:

— the purposes of processing;

— the categories of data concerned;

— the recipients or categories of recipients to whom the data are disclosed; and

— knowledge of the logic involved in any automated decisions[2].

Granting subject access to personal data filing systems could increase the number of subject access requests. Except for those files where processing was already underway prior to commencement of the new provisions, and which do not have to comply for up to three years by Article 32(2), subject access to manually processed files falling within the definition of personal filing systems[3] will be available to employees. The further derogation for manual filing systems[4] for up to 12 years from the date of adoption of the Directive does not extend to subject

---

1 The scope of this provision is difficult to predict. Article 11(2) excuses provision of information where "... in particular for statistical purposes or for the purposes of historical or scientific research ..." or where expressly laid down by law. Member States must provide appropriate safeguards.
2 Automated decisions will be very rare in the context of employees; at least at the present time. Who knows what the future may bring.
3 Article 2(c). Recital 27 indicates that an important aspect is that the system allows easy access to personal data relating to a particular individual.
4 Article 32(2).

access so, even though manual files will not have to comply to Article 6, 7 or 8 until 24 October 2007, subject access will be available not more than three years following implementation of the Directive in the case of pre-existing files. Of course, for new processing activities commencing after the new law comes in to force, the full impact of that new law will be felt immediately. It is important to note that manually processed personnel files are almost certain to be structured in such a way as to be within the scope of the Directive.

It is not clear from the wording of Article 12(a) whether the data subject must be given access to the actual personal data or whether a copy of those data will suffice. Recital 41 indicates that one of the main purposes of granting rights of subject access is so the data subject may verify the accuracy of the data and the lawfulness of processing. If this is so, there seems no reason why the data subject should be given a copy of the personal data to take away and simply letting the data subject examine his or her file for a reasonable period of time should suffice. This is particularly so in the context of employees. If this is so, it marks a departure from the present law which requires that the data subject exercising his or her right of access be given a copy of the data[1].

A further difficulty in terms of subject access is where the file contains personal data concerning other persons. This could cause considerable difficulty in blocking out such data and, certainly, it would have to be blocked out[2]. One way might be to give the data subject a photocopy of the file with the personal data of other persons blacked out. With computers it is not such a problem because it should be easy to suppress the other information in any print-out. Employers should consider how to comply with subject access requests in respect of paper files.

One reason why employees may want to see their files is to see any references written concerning them. For example, an employee may have been unable to gain employment elsewhere and now wants to see references written by his manager because he suspects they are not very good. If subject access is provided to references, this could expose an employer to claims for defamation or negligent misstatement. Article 13 allows Member States to derogate from subject access in a number of circumstances. One is the protection of the data subject or

---

1   Section 21(1) of the Data Protection Act 1984. Of course, implementing legislation may insist that a copy is given - this may be justified as a way of ensuring fair processing.
2   If it is not suppressed there is likely to be a breach of the principles relating to data quality. Under the Data Protection Act 1984, the data user must be satisfied that the other person has consented to the disclosure or must block any data identifying that other person.

of the rights and freedoms of others[1]. Is it a right or freedom to be able to give one's views about an employee's work performance and personality in confidence to a third party contemplating offering employment to that employee?

If subject access extends to job references it could reduce their value significantly. Persons writing references would tend only to include positive aspects. This could leave them open to claims for negligent misstatement from the new employer, for example, if the employee turns out to be totally hopeless and inept and the reference contained no warning to that effect. The use of disclaimers on references, a feature that is becoming more common, will not necessarily be effective because of the Unfair Contract Terms Act 1977 and the application of the "reasonableness test" to such disclaimers.

The Data Protection Registrar has, in the past, expressed concern about enforced subject access. This is where an employer requires a prospective employee to carry out a subject access request in respect of any personal data stored on the police national computer system and to hand over the details to the employer. The employer's intention is to confirm whether the person concerned has a criminal record. Whilst this might be appropriate in terms of certain types of employees, such as persons working in children's homes, and others, such as taxi drivers applying for local authority licences, it could be seen to be an invasion of privacy in many situations.

The government is proposing specific legislation to allow potential employees access to criminal records of job applicants in sensitive areas such as child-care and education. It is proposed that a "Criminal Conviction Certificate" costing up to £20 will have to be obtained by job applicants from the new criminal records agency which should be operational by 1998[2]. There are fears that such provisions, if implemented, could eventually be extended to less sensitive areas of employment.

Although the Registrar has called for controls to prevent or restrict enforced subject access[3], it continues and the Directive contains no specific provision to prohibit it, unless the words "without constraint" in Article 12(a) are interpreted to mean without duress[4]. One difficulty

---

1   Article 12(g).
2   Anon, *Computing*, 27 June 1996, p3.
3   Data Protection Registrar, T*enth Report of the Data Protection Registrar June 1994,* HMSO, 1995 p24 and Appendix 2.
4   The French version text is "sans constrainte" which, according the Registrar, means "without duress". The Registrar continues to hold the view that enforced subject access is an abuse of the right of subject access; Data Protection Registrar,

is that the copy of the personal data so obtained by the data subject is shown to the employer ostensibly with the data subject's consent. Also, the police authority making the disclosure will not know the purpose of the subject access request unless the person making the request volunteers it. Article 1(1) of the Directive talks about protecting the fundamental rights and freedoms of natural persons, particularly their right to privacy with respect to processing their personal data. The conflict is apparent where the type of employment is such that the safety or well-being of persons could be severely compromised by appointing an employee with a particular type of criminal record.

Some bodies and authorities may keep and share other forms of personal data which could indicate that a particular individual, although he or she does not have a conviction because of an acquittal or because the case was withdrawn, has been charged with or prosecuted with an offence of a relevant type. For example, bodies running children's homes and homes for the mentally ill might wish to keep data about persons who have been prosecuted for, but not convicted, of sexual or violent offences against children and others. Such information may be even more extensive and cover situations were a person has been suspected of such an offence but there has been insufficient evidence on which to charge that person.

In respect of holding such data and enforced subject access, it is clear that the vagueness of the existing law is unsatisfactory. Article 8(5) allows derogation from the prohibition of processing data relating to convictions, etc except under official authority. It is clear that the opportunity ought to be taken in the legislation implementing the Directive to define precisely when enforced subject access is permissible and when processing other sensitive information is permissible. It is possible that, in the context of bodies and authorities charged with the care of children and vulnerable persons be allowed to keep relevant information on the basis of important public interest[1].

> Best case - numbers of subject access requests will remain low but will be more costly to satisfy because information about processing, etc has to be given in addition to giving access to the data and because of the extension of subject access to manually processed personal data filing systems. There may be a modest increase in demand for subject access because of this latter factor. Enforced subject access will continue to be possible.

Response of the Data Protection Registrar to the Consultation Paper on the EC Data Protection Directive, 1996 para 9.12.

1   Possible under Article 8(4) subject to suitable safeguards.

Worst case - as above but there may be a greater increase in subject access requests prompting employers to trawl through existing paper files to check for accuracy of personal data because of the compensation provisions. Enforced subject access will be severely restricted.

Consent and Objections

In most cases, there will be no issues of the data subject's consent and objections to processing by employees and self-employed consultants. Of course, consent may be an issue in terms of enforced subject access as mentioned above. The consent is not necessarily freely given as required by Article 2(h). It is arguable that, simply by reading the data the employer is processing it as the definition of processing includes use[1]. If so, there would appear to be no express justification for processing by the prospective employer in the Directive.

Generally, consent will not be required as processing can proceed on the basis of the provisions in Article 7 other than the data subject's consent or, where appropriate, under the exceptions in Article 8 as discussed above.

Objecting to processing on compelling legitimate grounds should not be relevant in terms of the usual type of personal data relating to employees processed by employers for normal and usual activities. There may be an issue, however, where the employer wishes to make some other use of the data, such as by selling a copy of an employee database to a marketing company. Another situation may be where the employer has information to the effect that the employee has a previous criminal conviction and intends to pass this information on to a new employer but the conviction is a spent conviction under the Rehabilitation of Offenders Act 1974.

Best case/worst case - there should be few occasions when obtaining the consent of data subjects or data subjects objecting to processing should be issues. These are only likely to be required if an employer wishes to process the data in a manner not normally associated with the employer's business or if the employer wishes to disclose some particularly sensitive data to other employers or, internally, to a number of its own employees.

---

1   However, in *R v Brown* [1996] AC 543, the House of Lords, by a three to two majority, held that simply viewing personal data on a screen did not amount to use - something further had to be done in respect of the data.

Summary

Much of what has been said in this chapter also applies to organisations using the services of self-employed consultants. The issues and implications are generally less extensive because far less personal data will be collected and processed. The data may comprise little more than name, address, VAT registration number, and records of work done and payments made.

Providing they take appropriate and timely action, employers have little to fear about the impact of the Directive on their processing of personal data relating to their employees. For usual processing activities there should be little in the way of constraints and providing information to employees and consultants engaged by an organisation should present little difficulty and additional expense if planned for.

Informing employees and consultants as required in Articles 10 and 11 should be a relatively simple matter and may require little more than the insertion of an additional notice on forms, employment contracts and the like. There may be more difficulty in respect of ex-employees because the relationship is no longer a continuing one with frequent and ongoing contact. But here, providing information under Article 11 may be excused on the grounds of impossibility or disproportionate effort.

"Grey areas" in the Directive, and indeed under existing data protection law, concern job references, enforced subject access and the holding of particular forms of sensitive data including that relating to unsubstantiated claims of criminal conduct. It is to be hoped that the opportunity will be taken to clarify these areas in the legislation implementing the Directive.

APPENDIX

DIRECTIVE 95/46/EC OF THE EUROPEAN PARLIAMENT AND OF THE COUNCIL

of 24 October 1995

on the protection of individuals with regard to the processing of personal data and on the free movement of such data

THE EUROPEAN PARLIAMENT AND THE COUNCIL OF THE EUROPEAN UNION,

Having regard to the Treaty establishing the European Community, and in particular Article 100a thereof,

Having regard to the proposal from the Commission[1],

Having regard to the opinion of the Economic and Social Committee[2],

Acting in accordance with the procedure referred to in Article 189b of the Treaty[3],

(1)   Whereas the objectives of the Community, as laid down in the Treaty, as amended by the Treaty on European Union, include creating an ever closer union among the peoples of Europe, fostering closer relations between the States belonging to the Community, ensuring economic and social progress by common action to eliminate the barriers which divide Europe, encouraging the constant improvement of the living conditions of its peoples, preserving and strengthening peace and liberty and promoting democracy on the basis of the fundamental rights recognised in the constitution and laws of the Member States and in the European Convention for the Protection of Human Rights and Fundamental Freedoms;

(2)   Whereas data-processing systems are designed to serve man; whereas they must, whatever the nationality or residence of natural persons, respect their fundamental rights and freedoms, notably the right to privacy, and contribute to economic and social progress, trade expansion and the well-being of individuals;

(3)   Whereas the establishment and functioning of an internal market in which, in accordance with Article 7a of the Treaty, the free

---

1   OJ C 277, 5.11.90, p. 3 and OJ C 311, 27.11.92, p30.
2   OJ C 159, 17.6.91, p38.
3   Opinion of the European Parliament of 11 March 1992 (OJ C 94, 13.4.92, p198), confirmed on 2 December 1993 (OJ C 342, 20.12.93, p30); Council common position of 20 February 1995 (OJ C 93, 13.4.95, p1) and Decision of the European Parliament of 15 June 1995 (OJ C 166, 3.7.95).

movement of goods, persons, services and capital is ensured require not only that personal data should be able to flow freely from one Member State to another, but also that the fundamental rights of individuals should be safeguarded;

(4)   Whereas increasingly frequent recourse is being had in the Community to the processing of personal data in the various spheres of economic and social activity; whereas the progress made in information technology is making the processing and exchange of such data considerably easier;

(5)   Whereas the economic and social integration resulting from the establishment and functioning of the internal market within the meaning of Article 7a of the Treaty will necessarily lead to a substantial increase in cross-border flows of personal data between all those involved in a private or public capacity in economic and social activity in the Member States; whereas the exchange of personal data between undertakings in different Member States is set to increase; whereas the national authorities in the various Member States are being called upon by virtue of Community law to collaborate and exchange personal data so as to be able to perform their duties or carry out tasks on behalf of an authority in another Member State within the context of the area without internal frontiers as constituted by the internal market;

(6)   Whereas, furthermore, the increase in scientific and technical co-operation and the co-ordinated introduction of new telecommunications networks in the Community necessitate and facilitate cross-border flows of personal data;

(7)   Whereas the difference in levels of protection of the rights and freedoms of individuals, notably the right to privacy, with regard to the processing of personal data afforded in the Member States may prevent the transmission of such data from the territory of one Member State to that of another Member State; whereas this difference may therefore constitute an obstacle to the pursuit of a number of economic activities at Community level, distort competition and impede authorities in the discharge of their responsibilities under Community law; whereas this difference in levels of protection is due to the existence of a wide variety of national laws, regulations and administrative provisions;

(8)   Whereas, in order to remove the obstacles to flows of personal data, the level of protection of the rights and freedoms of individuals with regard to the processing of such data must be equivalent in all Member States; whereas this objective is vital to the internal market but cannot be achieved by the Member States alone, especially in view of the scale of the divergences which currently exist between the relevant laws in the Member States and the need to co-ordinate the laws of the Member States so as to ensure that the cross-border flow of personal data is regulated in a consistent manner that is in keeping with the objective of the internal market as provided for in Article 7a of the

Treaty; whereas Community action to approximate those laws is therefore needed;

(9)   Whereas, given the equivalent protection resulting from the approximation of national laws, the Member States will no longer be able to inhibit the free movement between them of personal data on grounds relating to protection of the rights and freedoms of individuals, and in particular the right to privacy; whereas Member States will be left a margin for manoeuvre, which may, in the context of implementation of the Directive, also be exercised by the business and social partners; whereas Member States will therefore be able to specify in their national law the general conditions governing the lawfulness of data processing; whereas in doing so the Member States shall strive to improve the protection currently provided by their legislation; whereas, within the limits of this margin for manoeuvre and in accordance with Community law, disparities could arise in the implementation of the Directive, and this could have an effect on the movement of data within a Member State as well as within the Community;

(10)   Whereas the object of the national laws on the processing of personal data is to protect fundamental rights and freedoms, notably the right to privacy, which is recognised both in Article 8 of the European Convention for the Protection of Human Rights and Fundamental Freedoms and in the general principles of Community law; whereas, for that reason, the approximation of those laws must not result in any lessening of the protection they afford but must, on the contrary, seek to ensure a high level of protection in the Community;

(11)   Whereas the principles of the protection of the rights and freedoms of individuals, notably the right to privacy, which are contained in this Directive, give substance to and amplify those contained in the Council of Europe Convention of 28 January 1981 for the Protection of Individuals with regard to Automatic Processing of Personal Data;

(12)   Whereas the protection principles must apply to all processing of personal data by any person whose activities are governed by Community law; whereas there should be excluded the processing of data carried out by a natural person in the exercise of activities which are exclusively personal or domestic, such as correspondence and the holding of records of addresses;

(13)   Whereas the activities referred to in Titles V and VI of the Treaty on European Union regarding public safety, defence, State security or the activities of the State in the area of criminal laws fall outside the scope of Community law, without prejudice to the obligations incumbent upon Member States under Article 56 (2), Article 57 or Article 100a of the Treaty establishing the European Community; whereas the processing of personal data that is necessary to safeguard

the economic well-being of the State does not fall within the scope of this Directive where such processing relates to State security matters;

(14)   Whereas, given the importance of the developments under way, in the framework of the information society, of the techniques used to capture, transmit, manipulate, record, store or communicate sound and image data relating to natural persons, this Directive should be applicable to processing involving such data;

(15)   Whereas the processing of such data is covered by this Directive only if it is automated or if the data processed are contained or are intended to be contained in a filing system structured according to specific criteria relating to individuals, so as to permit easy access to the personal data in question;

(16)   Whereas the processing of sound and image data, such as in cases of video surveillance, does not come within the scope of this Directive if it is carried out for the purposes of public security, defence, national security or in the course of State activities relating to the area of criminal law or of other activities which do not come within the scope of Community law;

(17)   Whereas, as far as the processing of sound and image data carried out for purposes of journalism or the purposes of literary or artistic expression is concerned, in particular in the audiovisual field, the principles of the Directive are to apply in a restricted manner according to the provisions laid down in Article 9;

(18)   Whereas, in order to ensure that individuals are not deprived of the protection to which they are entitled under this Directive, any processing of personal data in the Community must be carried out in accordance with the law of one of the Member States; whereas, in this connection, processing carried out under the responsibility of a controller who is established in a Member State should be governed by the law of that State;

(19)   Whereas establishment on the territory of a Member State implies the effective and real exercise of activity through stable arrangements; whereas the legal form of such an establishment, whether simply branch or a subsidiary with a legal personality, is not the determining factor in this respect; whereas, when a single controller is established on the territory of several Member States, particularly by means of subsidiaries, he must ensure, in order to avoid any circumvention of national rules, that each of the establishments fulfils the obligations imposed by the national law applicable to its activities;

(20)   Whereas the fact that the processing of data is carried out by a person established in a third country must not stand in the way of the protection of individuals provided for in this Directive; whereas in these

cases, the processing should be governed by the law of the Member State in which the means used are located, and there should be guarantees to ensure that the rights and obligations provided for in this Directive are respected in practice;

(21)   Whereas this Directive is without prejudice to the rules of territoriality applicable in criminal matters;

(22)   Whereas Member States shall more precisely define in the laws they enact or when bringing into force the measures taken under this Directive the general circumstances in which processing is lawful; whereas in particular Article 5, in conjunction with Articles 7 and 8, allows Member States, independently of general rules, to provide for special processing conditions for specific sectors and for the various categories of data covered by Article 8;

(23)   Whereas Member States are empowered to ensure the implementation of the protection of individuals both by means of a general law on the protection of individuals as regards the processing of personal data and by sectorial laws such as those relating, for example, to statistical institutes;

(24)   Whereas the legislation concerning the protection of legal persons with regard to the processing data which concerns them is not affected by this Directive;

(25)   Whereas the principles of protection must be reflected, on the one hand, in the obligations imposed on persons, public authorities, enterprises, agencies or other bodies responsible for processing, in particular regarding data quality, technical security, notification to the supervisory authority, and the circumstances under which processing can be carried out, and, on the other hand, in the right conferred on individuals, the data on whom are the subject of processing, to be informed that processing is taking place, to consult the data, to request corrections and even to object to processing in certain circumstances;

(26)   Whereas the principles of protection must apply to any information concerning an identified or identifiable person; whereas, to determine whether a person is identifiable, account should be taken of all the means likely reasonably to be used either by the controller or by any other person to identify the said person; whereas the principles of protection shall not apply to data rendered anonymous in such a way that the data subject is no longer identifiable; whereas codes of conduct within the meaning of Article 27 may be a useful instrument for providing guidance as to the ways in which data may be rendered anonymous and retained in a form in which identification of the data subject is no longer possible;

(27)   Whereas the protection of individuals must apply as much to automatic processing of data as to manual processing; whereas the scope of this protection must not in effect depend on the techniques used, otherwise this would create a serious risk of circumvention; whereas, nonetheless, as regards manual processing, this Directive covers only filing systems, not unstructured files; whereas, in particular, the content of a filing system must be structured according to specific criteria relating to individuals allowing easy access to the personal data; whereas, in line with the definition in Article 2 (c), the different criteria for determining the constituents of a structured set of personal data, and the different criteria governing access to such a set, may be laid down by each Member State; whereas files or sets of files as well as their cover pages, which are not structured according to specific criteria, shall under no circumstances fall within the scope of this Directive;

(28)   Whereas any processing of personal data must be lawful and fair to the individuals concerned; whereas, in particular, the data must be adequate, relevant and not excessive in relation to the purposes for which they are processed; whereas such purposes must be explicit and legitimate and must be determined at the time of collection of the data; whereas the purposes of processing further to collection shall not be incompatible with the purposes as they were originally specified;

(29)   Whereas the further processing of personal data for historical, statistical or scientific purposes is not generally to be considered incompatible with the purposes for which the data have previously been collected provided that Member States furnish suitable safeguards; whereas these safeguards must in particular rule out the use of the data in support of measures or decisions regarding any particular individual;

(30)   Whereas, in order to be lawful, the processing of personal data must in addition be carried out with the consent of the data subject or be necessary for the conclusion or performance of a contract binding on the data subject, or as a legal requirement, or for the performance of a task carried out in the public interest or in the exercise of official authority, or in the legitimate interests of a natural or legal person, provided that the interests or the rights and freedoms of the data subject are not overriding; whereas, in particular, in order to maintain a balance between the interests involved while guaranteeing effective competition, Member States may determine the circumstances in which personal data may be used or disclosed to a third party in the context of the legitimate ordinary business activities of companies and other bodies; whereas Member States may similarly specify the conditions under which personal data may be disclosed to a third party for the purposes of marketing whether carried out commercially or by a charitable organisation or by any other association or foundation, of a political nature for example, subject to the provisions allowing a data subject to object to the processing of data regarding him, at no cost and without having to state his reasons;

(31)   Whereas the processing of personal data must equally be regarded as lawful where it is carried out in order to protect an interest which is essential for the data subject's life;

(32)   Whereas it is for national legislation to determine whether the controller performing a task carried out in the public interest or in the exercise of official authority should be a public administration or another natural or legal person governed by public law, or by private law such as a professional association;

(33)   Whereas data which are capable by their nature of infringing fundamental freedoms or privacy should not be processed unless the data subject gives his explicit consent; whereas, however, derogations from this prohibition must be explicitly provided for in respect of specific needs, in particular where the processing of these data is carried out for certain health-related purposes by persons subject to a legal obligation of professional secrecy or in the course of legitimate activities by certain associations or foundations the purpose of which is to permit the exercise of fundamental freedoms;

(34)   Whereas Member States must also be authorised, when justified by grounds of important public interest, to derogate from the prohibition on processing sensitive categories of data where important reasons of public interest so justify in areas such as public health and social protection - especially in order to ensure the quality and cost-effectiveness of the procedures used for settling claims for benefits and services in the health insurance system - scientific research and government statistics; whereas it is incumbent on them, however, to provide specific and suitable safeguards so as to protect the fundamental rights and the privacy of individuals;

(35)   Whereas, moreover, the processing of personal data by official authorities for achieving aims, laid down in constitutional law or international public law, of officially recognised religious associations is carried out on important grounds of public interest;

(36)   Whereas where, in the course of electoral activities, the operation of the democratic system requires in certain Member States that political parties compile data on people's political opinion, the processing of such data may be permitted for reasons of important public interest, provided that appropriate safeguards are established;

(37)   Whereas the processing of personal data for purposes of journalism or for purposes of literary or artistic expression, in particular in the audiovisual field, should qualify for exemption from the requirements of certain provisions of this Directive in so far as this is necessary to reconcile the fundamental rights of individuals with freedom of information and notably the right to receive and impart information, as guaranteed in particular in Article 10 of the European

Convention for the Protection of Human Rights and Fundamental Freedoms; whereas Member States should therefore lay down exemptions and derogations necessary for the purpose of balance between fundamental rights as regards general measures on the legitimacy of data processing, measures on the transfer of data to third countries and the power of the supervisory authority; whereas this should not, however, lead Member States to lay down exemptions from the measures to ensure security of processing; whereas at least the supervisory authority responsible for this sector should also be provided with certain ex-post powers, e.g. to publish a regular report or to refer matters to the judicial authorities;

(38)   Whereas, if the processing of data is to be fair, the data subject must be in a position to learn of the existence of a processing operation and, where data are collected from him, must be given accurate and full information, bearing in mind the circumstances of the collection;

(39)   Whereas certain processing operations involve data which the controller has not collected directly from the data subject; whereas, furthermore, data can be legitimately disclosed to a third party, even if the disclosure was not anticipated at the time the data were collected from the data subject; whereas, in all these cases, the data subject should be informed when the data are recorded or at the latest when the data are first disclosed to a third party;

(40)   Whereas, however, it is not necessary to impose this obligation if the data subject already has the information; whereas, moreover, there will be no such obligation if the recording or disclosure are expressly provided for by law or if the provision of information to the data subject proves impossible or would involve disproportionate efforts, which could be the case where processing is for historical, statistical or scientific purposes; whereas, in this regard, the number of data subjects, the age of the data, and any compensatory measures adopted may be taken into consideration;

(41)   Whereas any person must be able to exercise the right of access to data relating to him which are being processed, in order to verify in particular the accuracy of the data and the lawfulness of the processing; whereas, for the same reasons, every data subject must also have the right to know the logic involved in the automatic processing of data concerning him, at least in the case of the automated decisions referred to in Article 15 (1); whereas this right must not adversely affect trade secrets or intellectual property and in particular the copyright protecting the software; whereas these considerations must not, however, result in the data subject being refused all information;

(42)   Whereas Member States may, in the interest of the data subject or so as to protect the rights and freedoms of others, restrict rights of access and information; whereas they may, for example, specify that

access to medical data may be obtained only through a health professional;

(43)　Whereas restrictions on the rights of access and information and on certain obligations of the controller may similarly be imposed by Member States in so far as they are necessary to safeguard, for example, national security, defence, public safety, or important economic or financial interests of a Member State or the Union, as well as criminal investigations and prosecutions and action in respect of breaches of ethics in the regulated professions; whereas the list of exceptions and limitations should include the tasks of monitoring, inspection or regulation necessary in the three last-mentioned areas concerning public security, economic or financial interests and crime prevention; whereas the listing of tasks in these three areas does not affect the legitimacy of exceptions or restrictions for reasons of State security or defence;

(44)　Whereas Member States may also be led, by virtue of the provisions of Community law, to derogate from the provisions of this Directive concerning the right of access, the obligation to inform individuals, and the quality of data, in order to secure certain of the purposes referred to above;

(45)　Whereas, in cases where data might lawfully be processed on grounds of public interest, official authority or the legitimate interests of a natural or legal person, any data subject should nevertheless be entitled, on legitimate and compelling grounds relating to his particular situation, to object to the processing of any data relating to himself; whereas Member States may nevertheless lay down national provisions to the contrary;

(46)　Whereas the protection of the rights and freedoms of data subjects with regard to the processing of personal data requires that appropriate technical and organisational measures be taken, both at the time of the design of the processing system and at the time of the processing itself, particularly in order to maintain security and thereby to prevent any unauthorised processing; whereas it is incumbent on the Member States to ensure that controllers comply with these measures; whereas these measures must ensure an appropriate level of security, taking into account the state of the art and the costs of their implementation in relation to the risks inherent in the processing and the nature of the data to be protected;

(47)　Whereas where a message containing personal data is transmitted by means of a telecommunications or electronic mail service, the sole purpose of which is the transmission of such messages, the controller in respect of the personal data contained in the message will normally be considered to be the person from whom the message originates, rather than the person offering the transmission services; whereas, nevertheless, those offering such services will normally be considered controllers in respect of the processing of the additional personal data necessary for the operation of the service;

(48) Whereas the procedures for notifying the supervisory authority are designed to ensure disclosure of the purposes and main features of any processing operation for the purpose of verification that the operation is in accordance with the national measures taken under this Directive;

(49) Whereas, in order to avoid unsuitable administrative formalities, exemptions from the obligation to notify and simplification of the notification required may be provided for by Member States in cases where processing is unlikely adversely to affect the rights and freedoms of data subjects, provided that it is in accordance with a measure taken by a Member State specifying its limits; whereas exemption or simplification may similarly be provided for by Member States where a person appointed by the controller ensures that the processing carried out is not likely adversely to affect the rights and freedoms of data subjects; whereas such a data protection official, whether or not an employee of the controller, must be in a position to exercise his functions in complete independence;

(50) Whereas exemption or simplification could be provided for in cases of processing operations whose sole purpose is the keeping of a register intended, according to national law, to provide information to the public and open to consultation by the public or by any person demonstrating a legitimate interest;

(51) Whereas, nevertheless, simplification or exemption from the obligation to notify shall not release the controller from any of the other obligations resulting from this Directive;

(52) Whereas, in this context, *ex post facto* verification by the competent authorities must in general be considered a sufficient measure;

(53) Whereas, however, certain processing operations are likely to pose specific risks to the rights and freedoms of data subjects by virtue of their nature, their scope or their purposes, such as that of excluding individuals from a right, benefit or a contract, or by virtue of the specific use of new technologies; whereas it is for Member States, if they so wish, to specify such risks in their legislation;

(54) Whereas with regard to all the processing undertaken in society, the amount posing such specific risks should be very limited; whereas Member States must provide that the supervisory authority, or the data protection official in co-operation with the authority, check such processing prior to it being carried out; whereas following this prior check, the supervisory authority may, according to its national

law, give an opinion or an authorisation regarding the processing; whereas such checking may equally take place in the course of the preparation either of a measure of the national parliament or of a measure based on such a legislative measure, which defines the nature of the processing and lays down appropriate safeguards;

(55)   Whereas, if the controller fails to respect the rights of data subjects, national legislation must provide for a judicial remedy; whereas any damage which a person may suffer as a result of unlawful processing must be compensated for by the controller, who may be exempted from liability if he proves that he is not responsible for the damage, in particular in cases where he establishes fault on the part of the data subject or in case of *force majeure*; whereas sanctions must be imposed on any person, whether governed by private or public law, who fails to comply with the national measures taken under this Directive;

(56)   Whereas cross-border flows of personal data are necessary to the expansion of international trade; whereas the protection of individuals guaranteed in the Community by this Directive does not stand in the way of transfers of personal data to third countries which ensure an adequate level of protection; whereas the adequacy of the level of protection afforded by a third country must be assessed in the light of all the circumstances surrounding the transfer operation or set of transfer operations;

(57)   Whereas, on the other hand, the transfer of personal data to a third country which does not ensure an adequate level of protection must be prohibited;

(58)   Whereas provisions should be made for exemptions from this prohibition in certain circumstances where the data subject has given his consent, where the transfer is necessary in relation to a contract or a legal claim, where protection of an important public interest so requires, for example in cases of international transfers of data between tax or customs administrations or between services competent for social security matters, or where the transfer is made from a register established by law and intended for consultation by the public or persons having a legitimate interest; whereas in this case such a transfer should not involve the entirety of the data or entire categories of the data contained in the register and, when the register is intended for consultation by persons having a legitimate interest, the transfer should be made only at the request of those persons or if they are to be the recipients;

(59)   Whereas particular measures may be taken to compensate for the lack of protection in a third country in cases where the controller offers appropriate safeguards; whereas, moreover, provision must be made for procedures for negotiations between the Community and such third countries;

(60)   Whereas, in any event, transfers to third countries may be effected only in full compliance with the provisions adopted by the Member States pursuant to this Directive, and in particular Article 8 thereof;

(61)   Whereas Member States and the Commission, in their respective spheres of competence, must encourage the trade associations and other representative organisations concerned to draw up codes of conduct so as to facilitate the application of this Directive, taking account of the specific characteristics of the processing carried out in certain sectors, and respecting the national provisions adopted for its implementation;

(62)   Whereas the establishment in Member States of supervisory authorities, exercising their functions with complete independence, is an essential component of the protection of individuals with regard to the processing of personal data;

(63)   Whereas such authorities must have the necessary means to perform their duties, including powers of investigation and intervention, particularly in cases of complaints from individuals, and powers to engage in legal proceedings; whereas such authorities must help to ensure transparency of processing in the Member States within whose jurisdiction they fall;

(64)   Whereas the authorities in the different Member States will need to assist one another in performing their duties so as to ensure that the rules of protection are properly respected throughout the European Union;

(65)   Whereas, at Community level, a Working Party on the Protection of Individuals with regard to the Processing of Personal Data must be set up and be completely independent in the performance of its functions; whereas, having regard to its specific nature, it must advise the Commission and, in particular, contribute to the uniform application of the national rules adopted pursuant to this Directive;

(66)   Whereas, with regard to the transfer of data to third countries, the application of this Directive calls for the conferment of powers of implementation on the Commission and the establishment of a procedure as laid down in Council Decision 87/373/EEC[1];

(67)   Whereas an agreement on a *modus vivendi* between the European Parliament, the Council and the Commission concerning the implementing measures for acts adopted in accordance with the procedure laid down in Article 189b of the EC Treaty was reached on 20 December 1994;

---

1   OJ L197, 18.7.87, p33.

(68)   Whereas the principles set out in this Directive regarding the protection of the rights and freedoms of individuals, notably their right to privacy, with regard to the processing of personal data may be supplemented or clarified, in particular as far as certain sectors are concerned, by specific rules based on those principles;

(69)   Whereas Member States should be allowed a period of not more than three years from the entry into force of the national measures transposing this Directive in which to apply such new national rules progressively to all processing operations already under way; whereas, in order to facilitate their cost-effective implementation, a further period expiring 12 years after the date on which this Directive is adopted will be allowed to Member States to ensure the conformity of existing manual filing systems with certain of the Directive's provisions; whereas, where data contained in such filing systems are manually processed during this extended transition period, those systems must be brought into conformity with these provisions at the time of such processing;

(70)   Whereas it is not necessary for the data subject to give his consent again so as to allow the controller to continue to process, after the national provisions taken pursuant to this Directive enter into force, any sensitive data necessary for the performance of a contract concluded on the basis of free and informed consent before the entry into force of these provisions;

(71)   Whereas this Directive does not stand in the way of a Member State's regulating marketing activities aimed at consumers residing in territory in so far as such regulation does not concern the protection of individuals with regard to the processing of personal data;

(72)   Whereas this Directive allows the principle of public access to official documents to be taken into account when implementing the principles set out in this Directive,

HAVE ADOPTED THIS DIRECTIVE:

CHAPTER I

GENERAL PROVISIONS

Article 1

Object of the Directive

1.   In accordance with this Directive, Member States shall protect the fundamental rights and freedoms of natural persons, and in

particular their right to privacy with respect to the processing of personal data.

2.   Member States shall neither restrict nor prohibit the free flow of personal data between Member States for reasons connected with the protection afforded under paragraph 1.

Article 2

Definitions

For the purposes of this Directive:

(a)   'personal data' shall mean any information relating to an identified or identifiable natural person ('data subject'); an identifiable person is one who can be identified, directly or indirectly, in particular by reference to an identification number or to one or more factors specific to his physical, physiological, mental, economic, cultural or social identity;

(b)   'processing of personal data' ('processing') shall mean any operation or set of operations which is performed upon personal data, whether or not by automatic means, such as collection, recording, organisation, storage, adaptation or alteration, retrieval, consultation, use, disclosure by transmission, dissemination or otherwise making available, alignment or combination, blocking, erasure or destruction;

(c)   'personal data filing system' ('filing system') shall mean any structured set of personal data which are accessible according to specific criteria, whether centralised, decentralised or dispersed on a functional or geographical basis;

(d)   'controller' shall mean the natural or legal person, public authority, agency or any other body which alone or jointly with others determines the purposes and means of the processing of personal data; where the purposes and means of processing are determined by national or Community laws or regulations, the controller or the specific criteria for his nomination may be designated by national or Community law;

(e)   'processor' shall mean a natural or legal person, public authority, agency or any other body which processes personal data on behalf of the controller;

(f)   'third party' shall mean any natural or legal person, public authority, agency or any other body other than the data subject, the controller, the processor and the persons who, under the direct authority of the controller or the processor, are authorised to process the data;

(g) 'recipient' shall mean a natural or legal person, public authority, agency or any other body to whom data are disclosed, whether a third party or not; however, authorities which may receive data in the framework of a particular inquiry shall not be regarded as recipients;

(h) 'the data subject's consent' shall mean any freely given specific and informed indication of his wishes by which the data subject signifies his agreement to personal data relating to him being processed.

Article 3

Scope

1. This Directive shall apply to the processing of personal data wholly or partly by automatic means, and to the processing otherwise than by automatic means of personal data which form part of a filing system or are intended to form part of a filing system.

2. This Directive shall not apply to the processing of personal data:

— in the course of an activity which falls outside the scope of Community law, such as those provided for by Titles V and VI of the Treaty on European Union and in any case to processing operations concerning public security, defence, State security (including the economic well-being of the State when the processing operation relates to State security matters) and the activities of the State in areas of criminal law,

— by a natural person in the course of a purely personal or household activity.

Article 4

National law applicable

1. Each Member State shall apply the national provisions it adopts pursuant to this Directive to the processing of personal data where:

(a) the processing is carried out in the context of the activities of an establishment of the controller on the territory of the Member State; when the same controller is established on the territory of several Member States, he must take the necessary measures to ensure that each of these establishments complies with the obligations laid down by the national law applicable;

(b)   the controller is not established on the Member State's territory, but in a place where its national law applies by virtue of international public law;

(c)   the controller is not established on Community territory and, for purposes of processing personal data makes use of equipment, automated or otherwise, situated on the territory of the said Member State, unless such equipment is used only for purposes of transit through the territory of the Community.

2.   In the circumstances referred to in paragraph 1 (c), the controller must designate a representative established in the territory of that Member State, without prejudice to legal actions which could be initiated against the controller himself.

CHAPTER II

GENERAL RULES ON THE LAWFULNESS OF THE PROCESSING OF PERSONAL DATA

Article 5

Member States shall, within the limits of the provisions of this Chapter, determine more precisely the conditions under which the processing of personal data is lawful.

SECTION I

PRINCIPLES RELATING TO DATA QUALITY

Article 6

1.   Member States shall provide that personal data must be:

(a)   processed fairly and lawfully;

(b)   collected for specified, explicit and legitimate purposes and not further processed in a way incompatible with those purposes. Further processing of data for historical, statistical or scientific purposes shall not be considered as incompatible provided that Member States provide appropriate safeguards;

(c)   adequate, relevant and not excessive in relation to the purposes for which they are collected and/or further processed;

(d)   accurate and, where necessary, kept up to date; every reasonable step must be taken to ensure that data which are inaccurate or incomplete, having regard to the purposes for which they were collected or for which they are further processed, are erased or rectified;

(e)   kept in a form which permits identification of data subjects for no longer than is necessary for the purposes for which the data were collected or for which they are further processed. Member States shall lay down appropriate safeguards for personal data stored for longer periods for historical, statistical or scientific use.

2.   It shall be for the controller to ensure that paragraph 1 is complied with.

SECTION II

CRITERIA FOR MAKING DATA PROCESSING LEGITIMATE

Article 7

Member States shall provide that personal data may be processed only if:

(a)   the data subject has unambiguously given his consent; or

(b)   processing is necessary for the performance of a contract to which the data subject is party or in order to take steps at the request of the data subject prior to entering into a contract; or

(c)   processing is necessary for compliance with a legal obligation to which the controller is subject; or

(d)   processing is necessary in order to protect the vital interests of the data subject; or

(e)   processing is necessary for the performance of a task carried out in the public interest or in the exercise of official authority vested in the controller or in a third party to whom the data are disclosed; or

(f)   processing is necessary for the purposes of the legitimate interests pursued by the controller or by the third party or parties to whom the data are disclosed, except where such interests are overridden by the interests for fundamental rights and freedoms of the data subject which require protection under Article 1 (1).

SECTION III

SPECIAL CATEGORIES OF PROCESSING

Article 8

The processing of special categories of data

1   Member States shall prohibit the processing of personal data revealing racial or ethnic origin, political opinions, religious or philosophical beliefs, trade-union membership, and the processing of data concerning health or sex life.

2.   Paragraph 1 shall not apply where:

(a)   the data subject has given his explicit consent to the processing of those data, except where the laws of the Member State provide that the prohibition referred to in paragraph 1 may not be lifted by the data subject's giving his consent; or

(b)   processing is necessary for the purposes of carrying out the obligations and specific rights of the controller in the field of employment law in so far as it is authorised by national law providing for adequate safeguards; or

(c)   processing is necessary to protect the vital interests of the data subject or of another person where the data subject is physically or legally incapable of giving his consent; or

(d)   processing is carried out in the course of its legitimate activities with appropriate guarantees by a foundation, association or any other non-profit-seeking body with a political, philosophical, religious or trade-union aim and on condition that the processing relates solely to the members of the body or to persons who have regular contact with it in connection with its purposes and that the data are not disclosed to a third party without the consent of the data subjects; or

(e)   the processing relates to data which are manifestly made public by the data subject or is necessary for the establishment, exercise or defence of legal claims.

3.   Paragraph 1 shall not apply where processing of the data is required for the purposes of preventive medicine, medical diagnosis, the provision of care or treatment or the management of health-care services, and where those data are processed by a health professional subject under national law or rules established by national competent bodies to the obligation of professional secrecy or by another person also subject to an equivalent obligation of secrecy.

4.   Subject to the provision of suitable safeguards, Member States may, for reasons of substantial public interest, lay down exemptions in addition to those laid down in paragraph 2 either by national law or by decision of the supervisory authority.

5.   Processing of data relating to offences, criminal convictions or security measures may be carried out only under the control of official authority, or if suitable specific safeguards are provided under national law, subject to derogations which may be granted by the Member State under national provisions providing suitable specific safeguards. However, a complete register of criminal convictions may be kept only under the control of official authority.

Member States may provide that data relating to administrative sanctions or judgements in civil cases shall also be processed under the control of official authority.

6.   Derogations from paragraph 1 provided for in paragraphs 4 and 5 shall be notified to the Commission.

7.   Member States shall determine the conditions under which a national identification number or any other identifier of general application may be processed.

Article 9

Processing of personal data and freedom of expression

Member States shall provide for exemptions or derogations from the provisions of this Chapter, Chapter IV and Chapter VI for the processing of personal data carried out solely for journalistic purposes or the purpose of artistic or literary expression only if they are necessary to reconcile the right to privacy with the rules governing freedom of expression.

SECTION IV

INFORMATION TO BE GIVEN TO THE DATA SUBJECT

Article 10

Information in cases of collection of data from the data subject

Member States shall provide that the controller or his representative must provide a data subject from whom data relating to himself are collected with at least the following information, except where he already has it:

(a)   the identity of the controller and of his representative, if any;

(b)   the purposes of the processing for which the data are intended;

(c)   any further information such as

—   the recipients or categories of recipients of the data,

—   whether replies to the questions are obligatory or voluntary, as well as the possible consequences of failure to reply,

—   the existence of the right of access to and the right to rectify the data concerning him

in so far as such further information is necessary, having regard to the specific circumstances in which the data are collected, to guarantee fair processing in respect of the data subject.

Article 11

Information where the data have not been obtained from the data subject

1.   Where the data have not been obtained from the data subject, Member States shall provide that the controller or his representative must at the time of undertaking the recording of personal data or if a disclosure to a third party is envisaged, no later than the time when the data are first disclosed provide the data subject with at least the following information, except where he already has it:

(a)   the identity of the controller and of his representative, if any;

(b)   the purpose of the processing

(c)   any further information such as

—   the categories of data concerned,

—   the recipients or categories of recipients,

—   the existence of the right of access to and the right to rectify the data concerning him

in so far as such further information is necessary, having regard to the specific circumstances in which the data are processed, to guarantee fair processing in respect of the data subject.

2.   Paragraph 1 shall not apply where, in particular for processing for statistical purposes or for the purposes of historical or scientific research, the provision of such information proves impossible or would involve a disproportionate effort or if recording or disclosure is expressly laid down by law. In these cases Member States shall provide appropriate safeguards.

SECTION V

THE DATA SUBJECT'S RIGHT OF ACCESS TO DATA

Article 12

Right of access

Member States shall guarantee every data subject the right to obtain from the controller:

(a)   without constraint at reasonable intervals and without excessive delay or expense:

—   confirmation as to whether or not data relating to him are being processed and information at least as to the purposes of the processing, the categories of data concerned, and the recipients or categories of recipients to whom the data are disclosed,

—   communication to him in an intelligible form of the data undergoing processing and of any available information as to their source,

—   knowledge of the logic involved in any automatic processing of data concerning him at least in the case of the automated decisions referred to in Article 15 (1);

(b)   as appropriate the rectification, erasure or blocking of data the processing of which does not comply with the provisions of this Directive, in particular because of the incomplete or inaccurate nature of the data;

(c)   notification to third parties to whom the data have been disclosed of any rectification, erasure or blocking carried out in compliance with (b), unless this proves impossible or involves a disproportionate effort.

SECTION VI

EXEMPTIONS AND RESTRICTIONS

Article 13

Exemptions and restrictions

1.   Member States may adopt legislative measures to restrict the scope of the obligations and rights provided for in Articles 6 (1), 10, 11 (1), 12 and 21 when such a restriction constitutes a necessary measures to safeguard:

(a)   national security;

(b)   defence;

(c)   public security;

(d)   the prevention, investigation, detection and prosecution of criminal offences, or of breaches of ethics for regulated professions;

(e)   an important economic or financial interest of a Member State or of the European Union, including monetary, budgetary and taxation matters;

(f)   a monitoring, inspection or regulatory function connected, even occasionally, with the exercise of official authority in cases referred to in (c), (d) and (e);

(g)   the protection of the data subject or of the rights and freedoms of others.

2.   Subject to adequate legal safeguards, in particular that the data are not used for taking measures or decisions regarding any particular individual, Member States may, where there is clearly no risk of breaching the privacy of the data subject, restrict by a legislative measure the rights provided for in Article 12 when data are processed solely for purposes of scientific research or are kept in personal form for a period which does not exceed the period necessary for the sole purpose of creating statistics.

SECTION VII

THE DATA SUBJECT'S RIGHT TO OBJECT

Article 14

The data subject's right to object

Member States shall grant the data subject the right:

(a)   at least in the cases referred to in Article 7 (e) and (f), to object at any time on compelling legitimate grounds relating to his particular situation to the processing of data relating to him, save where otherwise provided by national legislation. Where there is a justified objection, the processing instigated by the controller may no longer involve those data;

(b)   to object, on request and free of charge, to the processing of personal data relating to him which the controller anticipates being processed for the purposes of direct marketing, or to be informed before personal data are disclosed for the first time to third parties or used on their behalf for the purposes of direct marketing, and to be expressly offered the right to object free of charge to such disclosures or uses.

Member States shall take the necessary measures to ensure that data subjects are aware of the existence of the right referred to in the first subparagraph of (b).

Article 15

Automated individual decisions

1.   Member States shall grant the right to every person not to be subject to a decision which produces legal effects concerning him or significantly affects him and which is based solely on automated processing of data intended to evaluate certain personal aspects relating to him, such as his performance at work, creditworthiness, reliability, conduct, etc.

2.   Subject to the other Articles of this Directive, Member States shall provide that a person may be subjected to a decision of the kind referred to in paragraph 1 if that decision:

(a)   is taken in the course of the entering into or performance of a contract, provided the request for the entering into or the performance of the contract, lodged by the data subject, has been satisfied or that there are suitable measures to safeguard his legitimate interests, such as arrangements allowing him to put his point of view; or

(b)   is authorised by a law which also lays down measures to safeguard the data subject's legitimate interests.

SECTION VIII

CONFIDENTIALITY AND SECURITY OF PROCESSING

Article 16

Confidentiality of processing

Any person acting under the authority of the controller or of the processor, including the processor himself, who has access to personal data must not process them except on instructions from the controller, unless he is required to do so by law.

Article 17

Security of processing

1.   Member States shall provide that the controller must implement appropriate technical and organisational measures to protect personal data against accidental or unlawful destruction or accidental loss, alteration, unauthorised disclosure or access, in particular where the

processing involves the transmission of data over a network, and against all other unlawful forms of processing.

Having regard to the state of the art and the cost of their implementation, such measures shall ensure a level of security appropriate to the risks represented by the processing and the nature of the data to be protected.

2.   The Member States shall provide that the controller must, where processing is carried out on his behalf, choose a processor providing sufficient guarantees in respect of the technical security measures and organisational measures governing the processing to be carried out, and must ensure compliance with those measures.

3.   The carrying out of processing by way of a processor must be governed by a contract or legal act binding the processor to the controller and stipulating in particular that:

—   the processor shall act only on instructions from the controller,

—   the obligations set out in paragraph 1, as defined by the law of the Member State in which the processor is established, shall also be incumbent on the processor.

4.   For the purposes of keeping proof, the parts of the contract or the legal act relating to data protection and the requirements relating to the measures referred to in paragraph 1 shall be in writing or in another equivalent form.

SECTION IX

NOTIFICATION

Article 18

Obligation to notify the supervisory authority

1.   Member States shall provide that the controller or his representative, if any, must notify the supervisory authority referred to in Article 28 before carrying out any wholly or partly automatic processing operation or set of such operations intended to serve a single purpose or several related purposes.

2.   Member States may provide for the simplification of or exemption from notification only in the following cases and under the following conditions:

—   where, for categories of processing operations which are unlikely, taking account of the data to be processed, to affect adversely the rights and freedoms of data subjects, they specify the purposes of the processing, the data or categories of data undergoing processing, the category or categories of data subject, the recipients or categories of recipient to whom the data are to be disclosed and the length of time the data are to be stored, and/or

—   where the controller, in compliance with the national law which governs him, appoints a personal data protection official, responsible in particular:

—   for ensuring in an independent manner the internal application of the national provisions taken pursuant to this Directive

—   for keeping the register of processing operations carried out by the controller, containing the items of information referred to in Article 21 (2),

thereby ensuring that the rights and freedoms of the data subjects are unlikely to be adversely affected by the processing operations.

3.   Member States may provide that paragraph 1 does not apply to processing whose sole purpose is the keeping of a register which according to laws or regulations is intended to provide information to the public and which is open to consultation either by the public in general or by any person demonstrating a legitimate interest.

4.   Member States may provide for an exemption from the obligation to notify or a simplification of the notification in the case of processing operations referred to in Article 8 (2) (d).

5.   Member States may stipulate that certain or all non-automatic processing operations involving personal data shall be notified, or provide for these processing operations to be subject to simplified notification.

Article 19

Contents of notification

1.   Member States shall specify the information to be given in the notification. It shall include at least:

(a)   the name and address of the controller and of his representative, if any;

(b)   the purpose or purposes of the processing;

(c)   a description of the category or categories of data subject and of the data or categories of data relating to them;

(d)   the recipients or categories of recipient to whom the data might be disclosed;

(e)   proposed transfers of data to third countries;

(f)   a general description allowing a preliminary assessment to be made of the appropriateness of the measures taken pursuant to Article 17 to ensure security of processing.

2.   Member States shall specify the procedures under which any change affecting the information referred to in paragraph 1 must be notified to the supervisory authority.

Article 20

Prior checking

1.   Member States shall determine the processing operations likely to present specific risks to the rights and freedoms of data subjects and shall check that these processing operations are examined prior to the start thereof.

2.   Such prior checks shall be carried out by the supervisory authority following receipt of a notification from the controller or by the data protection official, who, in cases of doubt, must consult the supervisory authority.

3.   Member States may also carry out such checks in the context of preparation either of a measure of the national parliament or of a measure based on such a legislative measure, which define the nature of the processing and lay down appropriate safeguards.

Article 21

Publicising of processing operations

1. Member States shall take measures to-ensure that processing operations are publicised.

2.   Member States shall provide that a register of processing operations notified in accordance with Article 18 shall be kept by the supervisory authority.

The register shall contain at least the information listed in Article 19 (1) (a) to (e).

The register may be inspected by any person.

3.   Member States shall provide, in relation to processing operations not subject to notification, that controllers or another body appointed by the Member States make available at least the information referred to in Article 19 (1) (a) to (e) in an appropriate form to any person on request.

Member States may provide that this provision does not apply to processing whose sole purpose is the keeping of a register which according to laws or regulations is intended to provide information to the public and which is open to consultation either by the public in general or by any person who can provide proof of a legitimate interest.

CHAPTER III

JUDICIAL REMEDIES, LIABILITY AND SANCTIONS

Article 22

Remedies

Without prejudice to any administrative remedy for which provision may be made, *inter alia* before the supervisory authority referred to in Article 28, prior to referral to the judicial authority, Member States shall provide for the right of every person to a judicial remedy for any breach of the rights guaranteed him by the national law applicable to the processing in question.

Article 23

Liability

1.   Member States shall provide that any person who has suffered damage as a result of an unlawful processing operation or of any act incompatible with the national provisions adopted pursuant to this Directive is entitled to receive compensation from the controller for the damage suffered.

2.   The controller may be exempted from this liability, in whole or in part, if he proves that he is not responsible for the event giving rise to the damage.

Article 24

Sanctions

The Member States shall adopt suitable measures to ensure the full implementation of the provisions of this Directive and shall in particular lay down the sanctions to be imposed in case of infringement of the provisions adopted pursuant to this Directive.

CHAPTER VI

TRANSFER OF PERSONAL DATA TO THIRD COUNTRIES

Article 25

Principles

1.   The Member States shall provide that the transfer to a third country of personal data which are undergoing processing or are intended for processing after transfer may take place only if, without prejudice to compliance with the national provisions adopted pursuant to the other provisions of this Directive, the third country in question ensures an adequate level of protection.

2.   The adequacy of the level of protection afforded by a third country shall be assessed in the light of all the circumstances surrounding a data transfer operation or set of data transfer operations; particular consideration shall be given to the nature of the data, the purpose and duration of the proposed processing operation or operations, the country of origin and country of final destination, the rules of law, both general and sectoral, in force in the third country in question and the professional rules and security measures which are complied with in that country.

3.   The Member States and the Commission shall inform each other of cases where they consider that a third country does not ensure an adequate level of protection within the meaning of paragraph 2.

4.   Where the Commission finds, under the procedure provided for in Article 31 (2), that a third country does not ensure an adequate level of protection within the meaning of paragraph 2 of this Article,

309

Member States shall take the measures necessary to prevent any transfer of data of the same type to the third country in question.

5.   At the appropriate time, the Commission shall enter into negotiations with a view to remedying the situation resulting from the finding made pursuant to paragraph 4.

6.   The Commission may find, in accordance with the procedure referred to in Article 31 (2), that a third country ensures an adequate level of protection within the meaning of paragraph 2 of this Article, by reason of its domestic law or of the international commitments it has entered into, particularly upon conclusion of the negotiations referred to in paragraph 5, for the protection of the private lives and basic freedoms and rights of individuals.

Member States shall take the measures necessary to comply with the Commission's decision.

Article 26

Derogations

1.   By way of derogation from Article 25 and save where otherwise provided by domestic law governing particular cases, Member States shall provide that a transfer or a set of transfers of personal data to a third country which does not ensure an adequate level of protection within the meaning of Article 25 (2) may take place on condition that:

(a)   the data subject has given his consent unambiguously to the proposed transfer; or

(b)   the transfer is necessary for the performance of a contract between the data subject and the controller or the implementation of precontractual measures taken in response to the data subject's request; or

(c)   the transfer is necessary for the conclusion or performance of a contract concluded in the interest of the data subject between the controller and a third party; or

(d)   the transfer is necessary or legally required on important public interest grounds, or for the establishment, exercise or defence of legal claims; or

(e)   the transfer is necessary in order to protect the vital interests of the data subject; or

(f)   the transfer is made from a register which according to laws or regulations is intended to provide information to the public and which is open to consultation either by the public in general or by any person who can demonstrate legitimate interest, to the extent that the conditions laid down in law for consultation are fulfilled in the particular case.

2.   Without prejudice to paragraph 1, a Member State may authorise a transfer or a set of transfers of personal data to a third country which does not ensure an adequate level of protection within the meaning of Article 25 (2), where the controller adduces adequate safeguards with respect to the protection of the privacy and fundamental rights and freedoms of individuals and as regards the exercise of the corresponding rights; such safeguards may in particular result from appropriate contractual clauses.

3.   The Member State shall inform the Commission and the other Member States of the authorisations it grants pursuant to paragraph 2.

If a Member State or the Commission objects on justified grounds involving the protection of the privacy and fundamental rights and freedoms of individuals, the Commission shall take appropriate measures in accordance with the procedure laid down in Article 31 (2).

Member States shall take the necessary measures to comply with the Commission's decision.

4.   Where the Commission decides, in accordance with the procedure referred to in Article 31 (2), that certain standard contractual clauses offer sufficient safeguards as required by paragraph 2, Member States shall take the necessary measures to comply with the Commission's decision.

CHAPTER V

CODES OF CONDUCT

Article 27

1.   The Member States and the Commission shall encourage the drawing up of codes of conduct intended to contribute to the proper implementation of the national provisions adopted by the Member States pursuant to this Directive, taking account of the specific features of the various sectors.

2.   Member States shall make provision for trade associations and other bodies representing other categories of controllers which have drawn up draft national codes or which have the intention of amending or extending existing national codes to be able to submit them to the opinion of the national authority.

Member States shall make provision for this authority to ascertain, among other things, whether the drafts submitted to it are in accordance with the national provisions adopted pursuant to this Directive. If it sees fit, the authority shall seek the views of data subjects or their representatives.

3.   Draft Community codes, and amendments or extensions to existing Community codes, may be submitted to the Working Party referred to in Article 29. This Working Party shall determine, among other things, whether the drafts submitted to it are in accordance with the national provisions adopted pursuant to this Directive. If it sees fit, the authority shall seek the views of data subjects or their representatives. The Commission may ensure appropriate publicity for the codes which have been approved by the Working Party.

CHAPTER VI

SUPERVISORY AUTHORITY AND WORKING PARTY ON THE PROTECTION OF INDIVIDUALS WITH REGARD TO THE PROCESSING OF PERSONAL DATA

Article 28

Supervisory authority

1.   Each Member State shall provide that one or more public authorities are responsible for monitoring the application within its territory of the provisions adopted by the Member States pursuant to this Directive.

These authorities shall act with complete independence in exercising the functions entrusted to them.

2.   Each Member State shall provide that the supervisory authorities are consulted when drawing up administrative measures or regulations relating to the protection of individuals' rights and freedoms with regard to the processing of personal data.

3.   Each authority shall in particular be endowed with:

—   investigative powers, such as powers of access to data forming the subject-matter of processing operations and powers to collect all the information necessary for the performance of its supervisory duties,

—   effective powers of intervention, such as, for example, that of delivering opinions before processing operations are carried out, in accordance with Article 20, and ensuring appropriate publication of such opinions, of ordering the blocking, erasure or destruction of data, of imposing a temporary or definitive ban on processing, of warning or admonishing the controller, or that of referring the matter to national parliaments or other political institutions,

—   the power to engage in legal proceedings where the national provisions adopted pursuant to this Directive have been violated or to bring these violations to the attention of the judicial authorities.

Decisions by the supervisory authority which give rise to complaints may be appealed against through the courts.

4.   Each supervisory authority shall hear claims lodged by any person, or by an association representing that person, concerning the protection of his rights and freedoms in regard to the processing of personal data. The person concerned shall be informed of the outcome of the claim.

Each supervisory authority shall, in particular, hear claims for checks on the lawfulness of data processing lodged by any person when the national provisions adopted pursuant to Article 13 of this Directive apply. The person shall at any rate be informed that a check has taken place.

5.   Each supervisory authority shall draw up a report on its activities at regular intervals. The report shall be made public.

6.   Each supervisory authority is competent, whatever the national law applicable to the processing in question, to exercise, on the territory of its own Member State, the powers conferred on it in accordance with paragraph 3. Each authority may be requested to exercise its powers by an authority of another Member State.

The supervisory authorities shall co-operate with one another to the extent necessary for the performance of their duties, in particular by exchanging all useful information.

7.   Member States shall provide that the members and staff of the supervisory authority, even after their employment has ended, are to

be subject to a duty of professional secrecy with regard to confidential information to which they have access.

Article 29

Working Party on the Protection of Individuals with regard to the Processing of Personal Data

1.   A Working Party on the Protection of Individuals with regard to the Processing of Personal Data, hereinafter referred to as 'the Working party', is hereby set up.

It shall have advisory status and act independently.

2.   The Working Party shall be composed of a representative of the supervisory authority or authorities designated by each Member State and of a representative of the authority or authorities established for the Community institutions and bodies, and of a representative of the Commission.

Each member of the Working Party shall be designated by the institution, authority or authorities which he represents. Where a Member State has designated more than one supervisory authority, they shall nominate a joint representative. The same shall apply to the authorities established for Community institutions and bodies.

3.   The Working Party shall take decisions by a simple majority of the representatives of the supervisory authorities.

4.   The Working Party shall elect its chairman. The chairman's term of office shall be two years. His appointment shall be renewable.

5.   The Working Party's secretariat shall be provided by the Commission.

6.   The Working Party shall adopt its own rules of procedure.

7.   The Working Party shall consider items placed on its agenda by its chairman, either on his own initiative or at the request of a representative of the supervisory authorities or at the Commission's request.

Article 30

1.   The Working Party shall:

(a)   examine any question covering the application of the national measures adopted under this Directive in order to contribute to the uniform application of such measures;

(b)   give the Commission an opinion on the level of protection in the Community and in third countries;

(c)   advise the Commission on any proposed amendment of this Directive, on any additional or specific measures to safeguard the rights and freedoms of natural persons with regard to the processing of personal data and on any other proposed Community measures affecting such rights and freedoms;

(d)   give an opinion on codes of conduct drawn up at Community level.

2.   If the Working Party finds that divergences likely to affect the equivalence of protection for persons with regard to the processing of personal data in the Community are arising between the laws or practices of Member States, it shall inform the Commission accordingly.

3.   The Working Party may, on its own initiative, make recommendations on all matters relating to the protection of persons with regard to the processing of personal data in the Community.

4.   The Working Party's opinions and recommendations shall be forwarded to the Commission and to the committee referred to in Article 31.

5.   The Commission shall inform the Working Party of the action it has taken in response to its opinions and recommendations. It shall do so in a report which shall also be forwarded to the European Parliament and the Council. The report shall be made public.

6.   The Working Party shall draw up an annual report on the situation regarding the protection of natural persons with regard to the processing of personal data in the Community and in third countries, which it shall transmit to the Commission, the European Parliament and the Council. The report shall be made public.

CHAPTER VII

COMMUNITY IMPLEMENTING MEASURES

Article 31

The Committee

1.   The Commission shall be assisted by a committee composed of the representatives of the Member States and chaired by the representative of the Commission.

2.   The representative of the Commission shall submit to the committee a draft of the measures to be taken. The committee shall deliver its opinion on the draft within a time limit which the chairman may lay down according to the urgency of the matter.

The opinion shall be delivered by the majority laid down in Article 148 (2) of the Treaty. The votes of the representatives of the Member States within the committee shall be weighted in the manner set out in that Article. The chairman shall not vote.

The Commission shall adopt measures which shall apply immediately. However, if these measures are not in accordance with the opinion of the committee, they shall be communicated by the Commission to the Council forthwith. It that event:

—   the Commission shall defer application of the measures which it has decided for a period of three months from the date of communication,

—   the Council, acting by a qualified majority, may take a different decision within the time limit referred to in the first indent.

FINAL PROVISIONS

Article 32

1.   Member States shall bring into force the laws, regulations and administrative provisions necessary to comply with this Directive at the latest at the end of a period of three years from the date of its adoption.

When Member States adopt these measures, they shall contain a reference to this Directive or be accompanied by such reference on the occasion of their official publication. The methods of making such reference shall be laid down by the Member States.

2. Member States shall ensure that processing already under way on the date the national provisions adopted pursuant to this Directive enter into force, is brought into conformity with these provisions within three years of this date.

By way of derogation from the preceding subparagraph, Member States may provide that the processing of data already held in manual filing systems on the date of entry into force of the national provisions adopted in implementation of this Directive shall be brought into conformity with Articles 6, 7 and 8 of this Directive within 12 years of the date on which it is adopted. Member States shall, however, grant the data subject the right to obtain, at his request and in particular at the time of exercising his right of access, the rectification, erasure or blocking of data which are incomplete, inaccurate or stored in a way incompatible with the legitimate purposes pursued by the controller.

3. By way of derogation from paragraph 2, Member States may provide, subject to suitable safeguards, that data kept for the sole purpose of historical research need not be brought into conformity with Articles 6, 7 and 8 of this Directive.

4. Member States shall communicate to the Commission the text of the provisions of domestic law which they adopt in the field covered by this Directive.

Article 33

The Commission shall report to the Council and the European Parliament at regular intervals, starting not later than three years after the date referred to in Article 32 (1), on the implementation of this Directive, attaching to its report, if necessary, suitable proposals for amendments. The report shall be made public.

The Commission shall examine, in particular, the application of this Directive to the data processing of sound and image data relating to natural persons and shall submit any appropriate proposals which prove to be necessary, taking account of developments in information technology and in the light of the state of progress in the information society.

Article 34

This Directive is addressed to the Member States.

Done at Luxembourg, 24 October 1995.

For the European Parliament   For the Council

The President   The President

K. HÄNSCH   L.ATIENZA SERNA

INDEX

NB: alphabetic arrangement: a group of letters is followed by a space is filed before the same group of letters followed by a letter. For example, "data haven" appears before "database".